FROM WILDERNESS TO METROPOLIS

THE HISTORY AND ARCHITECTURE OF DADE COUNTY (1825-1940)

SECOND EDITION

Published By
Metropolitan Dade County
Office of Community Development
Historic Preservation Division

The preparation and publication of this book
was supported with grants from:
The National Endowment for the Arts,
a Federal Agency, Washington D.C.
The Metro-Dade Office of Community Development,
Under the Community Development Block Grant Program,
U.S. Department of Housing and Urban Development.
The National Park Service,
Under the U.S. Department of the Interior,
Administered by the State of Florida, Division of Historical Resources.

ISBN 0-9618373-1-4

"Library of Congress Catalog Card Number:"
92-61484

CREDITS

Ivan A. Rodriguez: Author, architecture
Margot Ammidown: Author, history
Emily Perry Dieterich: Second edition revisions, history
Bogue Wallin: Introduction

Photographic Research, first edition: Margot Ammidown
                        second edition: Emily Perry Dieterich

Editorial Committee, first edition: Ivan A. Rodriguez
                                     Margot Ammidown
                                     Bogue Wallin
                                     Joyce Meyers
                                     Sarah Eaton

              second edition: Ivan A. Rodriguez

Production Manager: Bogue Wallin, first edition
                   Teresa Lenox
                   Keith Root, second edition

Design and Art Work: First Edition:
                Graphics Modern:
                Woody Vondracek
                Christina Hayes, artwork
                Birmy Graphics, typesetting

                Second Edition:
                Metro-Dade Department of Communications
                Waldo Velazquez, artwork
                Gregory Rexach, typesetting

Line Editor: Kathy Welsch, first edition

Word Processing: Maria Temkin, first edition
                  Irelene T. King, second edition

Former staff whose work contributed to this publication:
Nancy Hoffman (Assistant Director, 1977-1979),
Joseph Daigle, Karen Degannes, Timothy Dyer,
Dan Elswick, Judy Fagin, Jill Fain, Paul George,
Ralph Gonzalez, Tony Gonzalez, Ewart Hartley,
Johnny Hunter, Barry Klein, Victor Manos,
Don McKenzie, Barbara Rey, Mary Jane Tucker.

Printed by: Bayshore Graphics, Inc.

Special Thanks To:

Carol Alper
Sam Boldrick, Miami-Dade Public Library, Florida Collection
Michael Carlebach, University of Miami
Barbara Capitman, Miami Design Preservation League
Robert Carr
Charles Chase
Ken De Garmo
Margaret Doyle
Dorothy Fields, Black Archives, History and Research Foundation
Norman Gillespie, Miami-Dade Public library, Florida Collection
Sallye Jude
Katherine Lee
Susie Littlefield
Dolly MacIntyre
Aristides Millas, University of Miami
Gary Monroe
Arva Moore Parks
Thelma Peters
F. Blair Reeves, University of Florida
Keith Root
Vivian Rodriguez
Becky Smith, Dawn Hugh, Historical Association of Southern Florida
Jean Taylor
Richard Tobin
Terry Vanden-Bosch
Ann Weaver
Woody Wilkins
George Wrentz, Ferendino, Grafton, Spillis & Candela

The many volunteers who participated in the Dade County Historic Survey

The second edition of **FROM WILDERNESS TO METROPOLIS** was at the press on August 24, 1992. On that date, Hurricane Andrew swept across the southern portion of Dade County leaving a trail of destruction that effected many historic sites. Many of the historic sites in South Dade were severely damaged. A few were totally demolished. One of our greatest losses was the Redland Community Methodist Church, located in the Redland Historic District. The small wood-frame church has been a focal point of the community since its construction in 1914. The Redland Fruit and Spice Park situated directly across the street from the church also suffered extensive damage. Anderson's Corner, a National Register site that housed a popular restaurant, sustained structural damage. The Charles Deering Estate, one of the historic gems of South Florida, was hard hit from the storm which caused extensive landscape damage, particularly to the Royal Palm grove, and the complete destruction of the front of the Richmond Inn. These are just a few examples of the damage incurred by Hurricane Andrew in South Dade. However, all is not lost. Currently, the Metro-Dade Historic Preservation Division, the State Bureau of Historic Preservation and the National Trust for Historic Preservation are working together to locate funding sources to help owners of historic properties affected by Hurricane Andrew. We are also trying to salvage materials and plan for the recovery and restoration of the unique historic homes, public buildings and landscapes of South Dade County. If you can provide any information or assistance in this endeavor please contact the Metro-Dade Historic Preservation Division at (305) 545-4228.

It has been seven years since From Wilderness to Metropolis was first published. The publication was so well received that it sold out much sooner than expected. Many copies went to schools, libraries, historical organizations and government agencies. The rest rapidly vanished at specialty bookstores and street art festivals.

By 1986, it was obvious that a reprint would be needed immediately. But in the three years since the book's publication, our physical environment had changed so much and so rapidly that the first edition already was outdated. Our decision was to take the extra time and do a revised edition.

We embarked upon this task, thinking that within several months the second edition would be out, before the first was totally exhausted. Much to our surprise, the project has taken three years, and the first edition has long been out of print. Updating the first edition was done within the limitations of our existing operation, without additional staff or funds. As a result, there was always a more pressing issue on the office's agenda to force the revision back up on the shelf, in search of "spare time".

In the course of the project there were so many updates and revisions to already revised copy that it was hard to keep up with the changes. Some were positive and gratifying, resulting in the restoration of many of our fine landmarks. Others were serious blows to the historic preservation effort. Much of the material had to be updated to reflect these changes.

Among the changes the reader will notice in this new edition are 20 new pages of printed information and photographs. New photos enrich existing and added portions of the text. There are expanded photo sections on South Dade's residences, Brickell Avenue's high rise transformation and Northeast Dade's residential neighborhoods. A photo index was added for easier reference. New sections were added about major sites that have come to the public spotlight since the time of the original publication. These include the Charles Deering Estate in South Dade and Vanderbilt Estate on Fisher Island.

The next addition is of more sobering nature. Trying to update the appendix on "Selected List of Significant Sites" showed how many of the structures originally listed had been demolished in such a short time. We decided to add a "List of Demolished Sites" appendix to point out this grave fact. This list calls attention to the crisis situation that local historic sites continue to face, in spite of the great accomplishments of the historic preservation effort.

We wish to thank our readers for their patience in waiting for this publication. Phone and mail requests have not stopped coming in since the first edition went out of print.

Now, enjoy the second edition of From Wilderness to Metropolis!

TABLE OF CONTENTS

INTRODUCTION

Historic preservation in South Florida is a relatively new phenomenom. Only in the last ten years have South Floridians begun to recognize that there is a history here, albeit brief in comparison to New England or Europe, but nonetheless rich, and old buildings need not have been the resting place of George Washington to be worthy of preservation. Because a small but determined preservation community has brought national attention to South Florida's historic architecture and begun to develop awareness for historic older buildings, South Floridians are now more actively participating in preserving their community.

Prior to 1972 preservation in South Florida was limited and involved a building by building approach. It began in 1925 with the moving and reconstruction of what were believed to be the Fort Dallas Barracks by the Daughters of the American Revolution (DAR). In 1940, the Historical Association of Southern Florida (HASF) was founded to record and collect the history of South Florida. The next significant preservation effort was Dade County's acquisition of Vizcaya in 1953 for restoration as a museum. That was followed with the formation of the Vizcayans in 1957, to support Vizcaya, and the founding of the Villagers in 1966 to avert the demolition of the Douglas Entrance in Coral Gables.

In the last decade, however, preservation and the interest in local history have increased significantly. In 1972 it was recognized by a subcommittee of the Villagers that preservation, to be successful, would require a different approach — more forethought and planning. In response to this need Dade Heritage Trust (DHT) was formed to promote the preservation and reuse of the county's old and historic buildings. While the formation of Dade Heritage Trust is a symbolic turning point for preservation in South Florida, a number of organizations and individuals also have been responsible for many recent successful preservation projects indicated in the accompanying chronology.

The success of preservation in South Florida is a reflection of an increased interest in local history and the important role history has in our everyday life. Through the appreciation of South Florida's history has come an understanding of how South Florida has evolved into what it is today. While that understanding can be easily gleaned from an exhibit at the Historical Museum, research in a library or from the oral histories of South Florida's older residents, it is the visible reminders of history that give South Florida its unique character—its sense of place. The most pervasive visual reminders of South Florida's history and character are its older buildings. Without these buildings, these reminders, we lose an important visual yardstick with which to measure our accomplishments, our failures and the overall change in character of South Florida. As an example, the idea that Miami will be a different place sixty years from now will be reflected in the contrast of buildings recently completed on Brickell Avenue with those yet to come—much as the few remaining Brickell mansions of the 1920s are a reflection of what Miami was seventy years ago.

The realization by a community that its older buildings are historic and a meaningful part of its existence is a reflection of a community's change in how it perceives itself. With the recognition that older buildings may be worthy of preservation, a community is tacitly admitting that it has a history significant to its future. The current trend regarding preservation in South Florida seems to suggest that such a change of attitude is taking place. If this is the case it would be a very similar realization to that of the nation as a whole at the turn of the century when the conscience of the country was piqued by the widespread belief that the American frontier had been closed. The effect of such a realization helped to spur a change in how the American public not only viewed itself but its surroundings as well.

In 1893, Frederic Jackson Turner, a recognized historian of the period, declared the American frontier closed. Turner's thesis was that the West had been explored and settlement was pervasive—"Pioneering was dead." Ironically, Miami's pioneer era had a little less than a decade left, but however premature or inaccurate Turner's thesis, it was popularly accepted as evidenced by Frank Norris' 1902 article "The Frontier Gone at Last," which stated, "so lament it though we may, the frontier is gone, an idiosyncrasy that has been with us for thousands of years, the one peculiar picturesqueness of our life is no more."

The popular acceptance of Turner's "lamentable" thesis had a profound impact on the American people. Closely associated with the American frontier was the uniquely American lifestyle of the self-sufficient pioneer from which many American values evolved. Teddy Roosevelt called it "the strenuous life," and in an article by the same name he describes it as "the life of toil and effort, of labor and strife" which "is the highest form of success" that came "to the man who does not shrink from danger, from hardship, or from bitter toil." Even popular fiction of the period, such as Owen Wister's *The Virginian* and Jack London's *Call of the Wild,* extolled the belief that traditional American values like bravery, honesty, ingenuity and leadership, were derived from the American frontier. With the frontier closed, the American public, for the most part, believed that the country had come to a turning point in its history—"American civilization was no longer becoming, it had become."

Although this frightening realization was tempered—Norris viewed the frontier as ever-expanding to eventually include "Marines on the Asian shore," while Roosevelt believed the strenuous life could become the moral basis of American everyday life—the American public became infatuated with what was perceived as the end of an era. The possibility that the American way of life would die with the frontier helped to spur a change in perception regarding the American frontier. Suddenly the frontier began to be perceived as a dwindling resource rather than the cornucopia of raw materials and land as it had traditionally been viewed. When

—1972— Dade Heritage Trust (DHT) is formed as the first organization in Dade County charged with the responsibility of preserving historic architecture countywide.

—1973— The city of Coral Gables adopts the first Historic Preservation Ordinance in Dade County which followed in the long tradition of such ordinances initiated by Charleston, South Carolina in 1935.

—1973— An aggressive effort is made to list Dade County's most recognized buildings in the National Register of Historic Places.

—1976— The Miami Design Preservation League is founded to promote the awareness and preservation of the Art Deco architectural style countywide and specifically in the city of Miami Beach.

—1976— Anderson's Corner is slated for demolition by the Unsafe Structures Board, but an eleventh hour effort of The Villagers staves off demolition.

—1977— The State of Florida initiates the restoration of the Barnacle and turns the Cape Florida Lighthouse into an historical attraction.

—1977— The comprehensive Dade County Historic Survey is initiated by the Metro Dade Office of Community and Economic Development and the Metro Department of Parks and Recreation.

—1977— Black Archives History and Research Foundation of South Florida is founded to collect and preserve the history of Miami's black community and promote its preservation.

—1977— The National and Tropical Audubon Society begins the restoration of the Doctor Arden Hayes Thomas House as its South Florida headquarters.

—1978— The restoration of Doctor Jackson's Office and Surgery, for whom Jackson Memorial Hospital was named, is initiated by DHT.

—1978— The Wagner House, the oldest known residence in Dade County is moved to Lummus Park in downtown Miami for restoration by DHT.

—1979— One of the nation's largest and youngest historic districts is declared on Miami Beach by the National Register of Historic Places recognizing the historical and architectural significance of over eight hundred Art Deco style buildings.

—1979— Art Deco Development Corporation is formed and the first efforts at acquisition and rehabilitation along Miami Beach's Ocean Drive begin.

—1979— Restoration of the Alamo, the first hospital of the Jackson Hospital complex, is initiated by the Public Health Trust.

—1979— The Butler Building, the last remaining worker's residence built by Henry Flagler in the late 1890's, is relocated and scheduled for preservation in the proposed Fort Dallas Park.

—1980— The Coral Gables House, Merrick Manor, the home of Coral Gables founder, George Merrick, is restored by the City of Coral Gables in conjunction with the Junior League of Miami.

—1980— The Dade County Historic Survey is completed identifying almost 6,000 sites of some historical, architectural or archeological significance.

—1981— The architectural firm of Anderson, Notter, and Finegold publishes the Preservation and Development Plan of the National Register Art Deco District on Miami Beach.

—1981— The Metro Dade County Commission adopts a countywide historic preservation or-this attitude was coupled with a fledgling conservation movement, the result was the formation of a National Park System in 1906, signed into law by Teddy Roosevelt to protect and preserve the "frontier" for the use and benefit of the American people. Through the establishment of the National Park System a piece of the frontier was preserved and because of the lifestyle associated with the frontier, traditional American values, at least in concept, were preserved as well.

dinance giving municipalities until July 1, 1982 to adopt similar ordinances.

—1981— The newly formed Metro Historic Preservation Board begins the designation of historic buildings and archeological sites under authority of the new ordinance.

—1982— The municipalities of Miami, Miami Beach, Miami Shores, Miami Springs, Hialeah, Opa-locka, Homestead, and South Miami adopt historic preservation ordinances to meet the deadline established in the county ordinance.

Although the growth of the conservation movement is a reflection of a change in values of the American people, it did not go unchallenged. When the growing concern for conservation seemed to be in the way of "progress and prosperity" the debate was often heated and, not surprisingly, the arguments differed little from those heard today. The first real debate of this kind in Congress concerned Hetch Hetchy Valley.

On December 6, 1912, the United States Senate voted to allow the damming of the Hetch Hetchy Valley in Yosemite National Park to provide water for the city of San Francisco. John Muir, President of the Sierra Club, appeared before several committees of Congress for more than five years trying to persuade legislators that the badly needed water for San Francisco should not be gotten at the expense of destroying nature's "temple," the Hetch Hetchy Valley. In perhaps his most impassioned plea Muir wrote, "these temple destroyers, devotees of ravaging commercialism, seem to have a perfect contempt for nature, and, instead of lifting their eyes to the god of the mountains, lift them to the almighty dollar."

Muir and his group of conservationists lost. The senate voted forty-three to twenty-five passing the bill to dam Hetch Hetchy; yet, twenty-nine senators decided not to decide, given the divisiveness of the issue, and abstained or were conspicuously absent from the vote. Finley Gray of Indiana echoed the popular sentiment of the majority vote when he said, " . . . much as I admire the beauties of nature and deplore the desecration of God's creation, yet when these two considerations come in conflict, the conservation of nature should yield to the conservation of human welfare."

Although this first collusion in the political arena of conservation ideology and "ravaging commercialism" was decided in favor of damming the Hetch Hetchy Valley, it clearly exemplifies the growing change in American attitudes with regard to the natural environment. As Roderick Nash summarized in his recent book, *The Call of the Wild*, "the most significant aspect of the Hetch Hetchy Controversy was that it occurred at all. One hundred or even fifty years earlier a similar proposal to dam a wild river would not have occasioned the slightest ripple of American protest. Traditional assumptions about the use of undeveloped country did not include reserving it in national parks. The emphasis was all the other way—on developing it in the name of progress and prosperity."

The parallels between the country at the turn of the century and South Florida today are strong. Like the end of the frontier, South Florida, too, seems to be at the end of a period in its history. Dade County in the last twenty-five years has changed dramatically: from a population of nearly 1.25 million to almost 2 million; from a local economy dependent on tourism and its ripple effects of development and commercial-retail to become the financial and trade center of the Caribbean basin; from a predominantly North American city to a multi-cultured cosmopolitan city—the home of Caribbean refugees and recent imigrants; and from a vacation mecca to a Grand Central Station of tourism. Never before has South florida been so populated, so culturally diverse or so dependent on foreign trade and commerce.

Like the growth of the conservation movement at the turn of the century preservation in South Florida is rooted in a desire to retain a real and tangible link to the character and values of a former time rather than a bookish understanding of our history. While the conservation of our wilderness gives us an insight into the rigors of frontier life, so, too, does the preservation of the Art

Deco National Register District give us an understanding of a turbulent period in our nation's cultural history.

Finally, the similarities between the Hetch Hetchy controversy and the perception of preservation as a deterrent to progress demonstrate how new an idea preservation is in South Florida. The recognition of older buildings as a viable, reusable resource is almost virtually untapped.

From Wilderness to Metropolis was written with South Florida's rapidly changing character as a community in mind. With almost daily alterations in our streetscapes a readily accessible publication is needed that will explain which old buildings are worthy of preservation. This book is also intended to increase an awareness of South Florida's historic architecture among South Floridians. Through a more widespread appreciation for our rich and unique history more informed decisions can be made regarding the preservation and maintenance of our historic architecture.

Although *From Wilderness to Metropolis* is intended to help create an awareness of Dade County's historic buildings it also illustrates how much and how rapidly South Florida has changed. The period covered by the book is from 1825, when the earliest remaining building in Dade County was built, the Cape Florida Lighthouse, to 1945, when the last significant buildings of the Miami Beach National Register Architectural District were completed. Perhaps through an understanding or an awareness of the meteoric changes in South Florida's recent history, like the popular acceptance of the closing of the Frontier at the turn of the century, a change of values will occur among South Floridians. Rather than view old buildings as an obstacle to progress, an informed community can view them as a finite and dwindling economic and cultural resource. Should this change of perception occur the future of our past, as reflected in old buildings, would be a secure one.

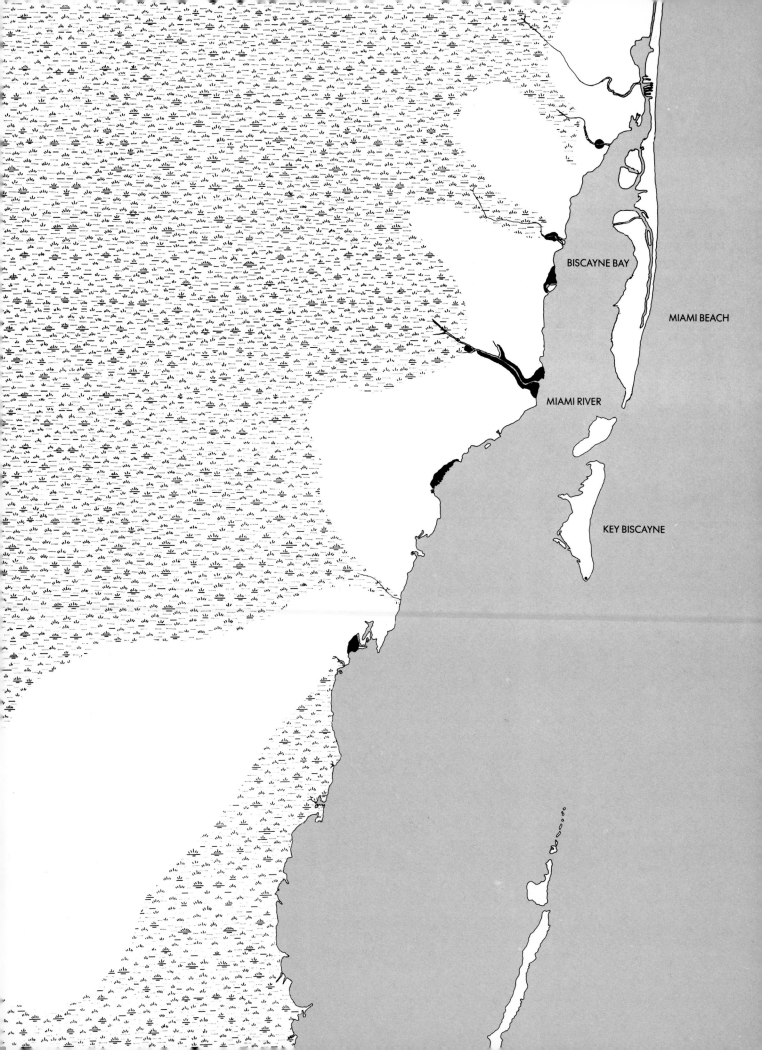

BISCAYNE BAY

MIAMI BEACH

MIAMI RIVER

KEY BISCAYNE

SEMINOLE INDIANS, LATE 1890'S (THE HISTORICAL ASSOCIATION OF SOUTHERN FLORIDA)

THE PIONEER ERA

About the same time American journalist Horace Greeley allegedly exclaimed, "Go west young man, go west," some hearty souls instead turned in a southerly direction. The mid-nineteenth century marked the beginning of the continous settlement of Dade County. Previous attempts had been thwarted by geographic, political and practical circumstances, and although there were several efforts made by the Spanish to populate the southeast coast of the East Florida Territory, Dade County's first stable pioneer community was established around the time Florida became a state in 1845.

In some ways, the settlement of South Florida paralleled pioneer efforts in the American West: the West as well as South Florida, was settled by significant numbers of people who were first or second generation immigrants. The 1850 census for Dade County shows that of ninety-six residents, fifty-eight were born outside the United States.[1] Also among Florida and Western pioneers alike were disproportionate numbers of young,

single men for whom the most persistent obstacles were hostile Indians and isolation.

Geographically, however, southeast Florida differed considerably from other frontiers of the era. The habitable portion of the southeast coast was formed by a narrow limestone ridge approximately five miles across at its widest point. It was cut in several places by rivers originating in the Everglades. Along these freshwater rivers were dense hammocks of hardwood trees such as oak, mahogany, and ironwood. Most of the ridge itself was flat sandy pineland from which the underlying rock frequently protruded. The Everglades was a much larger body of water than it is today,[2] and extended eastward to Biscayne Bay or the Atlantic Ocean at points making the construction of a road from settlements in the northern part of the state difficult. However, Key West, which was established in 1821, and subsequently grew into a significant seaport, provided reasonable access to civilization.

Spain made several attempts to settle the southeast coast beginning with a short-lived Jesuit mission on the Miami River in 1567.[3] Prior to the U.S. acquisition of the East Florida Territory in 1821, Spain offered significant land donations in Florida to anyone loyal to the Spanish government who would live on and defend his property. This was the Crown's final attempt to secure the remote regions of its territory. There were five grants verified in the current Dade County area by the U.S. Commission established in 1821 to confirm Spanish land donations.[4] There were also several unsuccessful claimants as well as a few transients living in Southeast Florida.

These settlers lived an extremely isolated existence and primarily made their living by "wrecking," or salvaging lost merchant ships. As the population grew so did the wrecking profession. Many wreckers were reputable, licensed traders.[5] Others were no less than pirates who were frequently accused of "salvaging" ships that were not aground. In an effort to protect vessels from the more nefarious practitioners of the trade, as well as from storms and reefs, the United States government erected a series of lighthouses along the Florida coast. One of these was the Cape Florida Lighthouse built in 1825.[6] It was the first U.S. government structure in the Dade County area.

The United States took possession of Florida in 1821 under the terms of the Treaty of Paris. Spain willingly signed over the territory after years of problems stemming from border disputes between the Florida Indians and U.S. citizens. The Seminole Indians, made up mostly of splinter groups from the Creek Confederation, were frequently accused of harboring or aiding runaway slaves and of constantly harassing white border dwellers.[7] Neither were the Indians friends to the Spanish government. They were, however, on good terms with the British who were suspected of using them to agitate the already unstable situation. The U.S. suffered some compunctions about invading a foreign territory to chastise the Indians, but did so anyway under the command of Andrew Jackson in 1818,

beginning the First Seminole Indian War.

The Second Seminole War was a variation of the same irresolvable theme: the inability of Indians and white Americans to co-exist in peaceful proximity. The second of the Florida Indian wars began in 1835 in the historical period known as the "Age of Jackson" (1828-1848).[8] Most characteristic of this era was a new sense of nationalism that demanded the expansion of the United States under the belief that any organized foreign elements in the continent, including the American Indians, were an obstacle to what later romantically came to be called our "Manifest Destiny." In an effort to clear the way, the United States devised the plan to remove all of the eastern tribes west of the Mississippi River. The objective of transferring these tribes to less valuable land in the West was formalized as a national policy under the Jackson presidency with the passage of the Indian Removal Act on May 28, 1830. In the process of its implementation in Florida, the Indian Removal Act served to force hundreds of Indians who were resisting relocation, farther southward in the state and eventually into the expansive and seemingly inhospitable wetlands of the Everglades. Although roving bands of Creeks were in South Florida during the Spanish era, the Seminoles had made the deepest Everglades their home by the early 1830's.[9]

By the mid-1830s in what is now Dade County there were a few settlers scattered widely along the coastal ridge. In their midst, extending on both sides of the Miami River, was the large slave operated plantation of Richard Fitzpatrick. Fitzpatrick began buying up the Spanish land grants in 1830,[10] and within a few years had what former U.S. Senator from Florida, Steven Mallory said, "…would have been the most beautiful and productive plantation in the South."[11] It did not fulfill that expectation because in 1836 the homesite was completely destroyed by Seminoles.

Richard Fitzpatrick was instrumental in the founding of Dade County. He was a member of the Florida Legislative Council in

1836 when that body voted to create Dade County, separating it from the larger Monroe County.[13] The name was chosen to honor Major Francis Langhorn Dade who shortly before was killed in a Seminole attack which marked the beginning of the Second Seminole War.

Had it not been for the Seminole Wars, Dade County might have developed as a very different place. Fitzpatrick was using his considerable financial and political influence to establish the county in the tradition of the Southern plantation system. He hoped to attract other aristocratic planters to South Florida which he thought excellently adapted to the production of sugar, tobacco and cotton.[14] Before he was able to realize his somewhat self-interested plan, the Seminole War came to Dade County. Upon word of the murder of a family of settlers at the New River, in January of 1836, the Fitzpatrick plantation was abandoned.[15] Later in the year, the Cape Florida Lighthouse was attacked, partially burned, and one of the keepers killed.[16]

During the Second Seminole War, which lasted from 1835 to 1842, the military attempted to insure the safety of Biscayne Bay by establishing an encampment on Key Biscayne in 1836. Some time later the stronghold was moved to land leased from Fitzpatrick on the north bank of the Miami River.[17] The mouth of the Miami River was a more strategic location because it provided the best access to the Everglades. Construction of buildings began in 1838 and the installation was named Fort Dallas. The fort complex was expanded several times during subsequent occupations.

Although there was not an official end to the Second Seminole War, in 1842 hostilities subsided to the point that settlers felt safe in returning to the area. Richard Fitzpatrick sold his ruined plantation to his nephew, William English, who set about rebuilding the operation on the abandoned Fort Dallas site. On the south bank of the river he platted the "Town of Miami" in 1842.[18] A few lots were sold in English's "town," but it was by no means a venture that reached fruition. There was probably limited interest in buying one of English's relatively small "town" tracts when up to 160 acres could be claimed for free

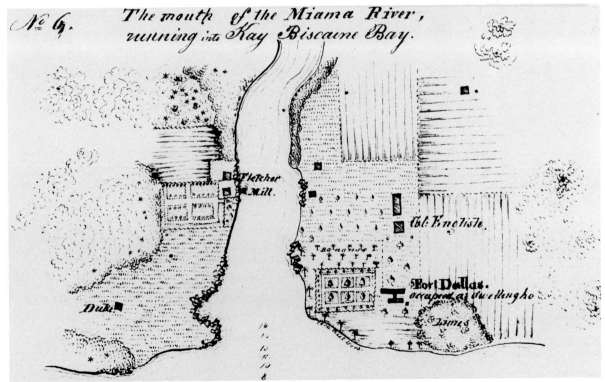

THIS COAST SURVEY MAP OF 1849 IS ONE OF THE EARLIEST DETAILED MAPS OF THE PIONEER SETTLEMENT AT THE MOUTH OF THE MIAMI RIVER. (ARVA MOORE PARKS COLLECTION)

under the Armed Occupation Act of 1842. This federal legislation was designed to encourage people to populate areas threatened by hostile Indians by offering land to any man or head of a family who would improve and defend the said property for five years after which time he would receive title. There were many applicants for land in the Dade County area under this act, but by 1850 only one is known to have been still living on his claim.[19]

William English left South Florida in 1849 to try his luck in the California Gold Rush hoping to gain enough capital to develop the town of Miami as he envisioned it. He never returned, though. English died in California, the victim of an accidental gunshot wound.[20]

Enough people remained in the vicinity of the Miami River to form a small pioneer community. The county seat had been moved from Indian Key to Miami in 1844 making it the political center of the county.[21] Most people living in the area at that time were involved in the production of coontie starch. Several pioneers had rather substantial mills which processed the root of the indigenous coontie plant. Coontie starch, which was similar to arrowroot, was a popular commodity in the Key West markets. In the next few decades starch making became a major pioneer industry.

The Third Seminole War, which lasted roughly for the decade of the 1850s, was fought mostly in Central Florida, but nonetheless Fort Dallas was reopened in 1855.[22] This time, instead of its inhabitants composing the entire population of the county, the fort became the lively nucleus of the community that already existed on the river banks. Due largely to the presence of the fort and the mill of George Ferguson which employed over twenty men, a number of people were attracted to the land surrounding the Miami River above some other equally scenic and productive property.

The fort served its purpose well by helping to make pioneers feel secure in their new home. There was also, at last, friendly contact between some residents and Indians during this time. After many attempts the settlement seemed established on firm ground in 1858 when Fort Dallas closed for the final time. For a couple of years settlers existed peacefully on the river, but in 1861 the stable growth of the emerging bay side community was deferred once again when the Civil War extended a disruptive tentacle to South Florida.

Trade ships had long sailed the waters off the Florida coast. When the Civil War erupted, it became crucial for the North to halt the flow of goods from foreign vessels into the ports of the non-industrialized Southern states. The federal naval depot in Key West was the home base of the Union blockade efforts in the Florida Straits. Despite the fact that Florida seceded from the United States in 1861, Key West remained firmly under the control of the North.

THE COONTIE MILL OF CHARLES PEACOCK IN COCONUT GROVE, WITH ITS PALMETTO ROOF AND UNENCLOSED WALLS WAS TYPICAL OF MANY OF THE EARLY MILLS. (MUNROE COLLECTION, THE HISTORICAL ASSOCIATION OF SOUTHERN FLORIDA)

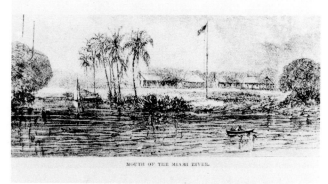

SKETCH OF OLD FORT DALLAS FROM "ALONG THE FLORIDA REEF," *HARPER'S NEW MONTHLY MAGAZINE*, 1871. (THE HISTORICAL ASSOCIATION OF SOUTHERN FLORIDA)

The inhabitants of Miami, who were not ideologically united were occasionally subject to search parties from either army looking for traitors.[23] Some Dade Countians were active blockade runners, while others served as pilots on Northern patrol boats.[24] Not only could residents not trust strangers or soldiers, but their closest neighbors were suspect as well.

The wartime conditions did nothing to further the growth of Dade County. Although more people came to the area than ever before, the influx was composed primarily of transients, a large number of whom were renegades, draft evaders, or spies. Most had no intention of settling in the region, but even if they had, during the war there were no means by which one could gain title to government owned land. The Federal Homestead Act was passed in 1862, but was invalid in states that seceded from the Union.

In 1865, when the war ended, settlement quickly resumed. A great deal of land in Dade County became available under the Homestead Act. Newcomers filed claims, and so did a number of other people who had been here for some time but were previously unable to acquire land. An early, but typical homesteader was William Wagner who settled a piece of land north of the Miami River in 1855.[25] A discharged Mexican War veteran, Wagner followed his former company from Charleston, South Carolina when they came to reopen Fort Dallas. He opened a sutler's store near the fort and farther up river Wagner built a coontie mill and a home for his family who joined him in 1858.[26] Wagner was well established on his land long before his homestead claim was finally confirmed in 1876.[27]

After the war, Dade County government was dominated for more than a decade by a notorious carpetbag regime, which in addition to its many misdeeds, publicized the area and attracted visitors.[28] Wealthier settlers were also encouraged to try their hand at the subtropical frontier. Among these were E. T. Sturtevant of Cleveland, Ohio, and William Brickell who, in 1870, bought the English property from his heirs and immediately assumed a role in the forefront of the settlement.

In the mid-1870s, the Fort Dallas tract was sold to the Biscayne Bay Company, based in Augusta, Georgia.[29] A series of resident managers stayed on the property, and although some hammock land was cleared, no major work appears to have been done at this time. J. W. Ewan began managing the Biscayne Bay Company tract in 1877.[30] Ewan, who became known as the "Duke of Dade," was a popular character on the bayfront. When he took over the property, he fenced in a few acres, built a dock, and added several outbuildings. In one of the old buildings erected by William English, Ewan opened a trading store which competed with William Brickell's on the south bank of the Miami River.

In the last decades of the nineteenth century, as one homestead after another was claimed, the vacant map of Dade County began to fill in. In areas where there were clusters of settlers, as previously happened around the Miami River, communities began to form and small centers evolved amidst the homes and family businesses. The most significant of these at the time were Coconut Grove, Lemon City and Cutler.

COCONUT GROVE

Long before the homestead era, settlers were attracted to the area a few miles south of the Miami River where the land rose up to cover a scenic limestone bluff. Temple Pent, a seaman from Key West, is rumored to have lived in Coconut Grove.[31] Although he filed a claim for land in 1821 in the area of today's South Bayshore Drive, it was not approved. The Frow family is also among Coconut Grove's earliest residents, but Edmund D. Beasley was the first U.S. citizen to go down in the record books as a landowner there when he applied for a homestead on November 14, 1868.[32] Even though he did not file a claim until 1868, Beasley is believed to have been living in what became Coconut Grove as early as the 1830s. Sons of both Temple Pent and Simeon Frow later claimed homesteads in Coconut Grove as well.

Coconut Grove was named by Dr. Horace Philo Porter, a Yale Medical School graduate and Civil War veteran who applied for, and received permission to open the first "Cocoanut Grove" post office in 1873,[33] but Porter did not remain in Coconut Grove very long and was both preceded and followed by others who left a greater mark. In fact, if ever a community took on a character of one man, Coconut Grove assumed that of a later arrival, Ralph Middleton Munroe.

Ralph Munroe's fascination with the sea and the stories he heard about the Florida frontier first brought him to the Biscayne Bay area in 1877. When his wife became ill with tuberculosis in 1882, he brought her to the warm climate and natural beauty he had visited five years earlier. Mrs. Munroe died at their camp near the Miami River, and when her husband returned north he found that their young daughter too had passed away.[34]

COMMODORE RALPH M. MUNROE IN 1931. (ROMER COLLECTION, MIAMI-DADE PUBLIC LIBRARY)

Munroe, then a widower with few family ties, turned his attention more to South Florida. He wrote to Charles and Isabella Peacock whom he met during his stay in Miami, and convinced them to start a hotel. The Peacocks purchased part of the former Beasley homestead from the Frows and the Bayview House opened late in 1882.[35] A few years later, the Peacocks opened an expanded version of the hostelry, the Peacock Inn.

Munroe became a regular visitor to the early inn and also encouraged many friends and relatives to come. He decided to move to Coconut Grove permanently in 1888.[36] Others soon followed. The people Ralph Munroe attracted to the small community were a combination of sailing enthusiasts, writers, naturalists, and intellectuals. To him the settlement must have been reminiscent of the childhood summers he spent in Concord, Massachusetts. There Henry Thoreau had

THE PEACOCK INN, OPENED IN 1882, WAS THE FIRST HOTEL IN THE MIAMI AREA. PEACOCK PARK IN COCONUT GROVE, PRESENTLY OCCUPIES THE ORIGINAL SITE OF THE INN. (MUNROE COLLECTION, THE HISTORICAL ASSOCIATION OF SOUTHERN FLORIDA)

worked for his grandfather. Munroe learned to play croquet with Ralph Waldo Emerson's daughter and became acquainted with the ideals of the Transcendentalist Movement.[37]

While living in Coconut Grove, Munroe enhanced his reputation as a boat designer. The first boat he designed specifically for sailing in Biscayne Bay was a sleek, shallow draft sharpie named *Kingfish*. So admired was his design that, when Munroe wanted to buy some land from John Frow, Frow would not sell unless the *Kingfish* was part of the deal.[38]

Commodore Munroe also became keenly interested in botany. His fascination with the subtropical flora of South Florida, combined with his knowledge of photography, provided the scientific community with the first visual documentation of many of the unusual plant species that flourished around the fertile shores of Biscayne Bay. Munroe's photographs are also among the earliest records of the unique bit of humanity that dwelled amidst the horticultural wonders on the Florida frontier. Commodore Munroe lived in Coconut Grove until his death in 1933.[40] Throughout his life he remained an

activist who promoted concern for the environment and opposed reckless development.

Side by side with Commodore Munroe's significant contributions to the development of the unique character of Coconut Grove, were the efforts of the Peacocks. The Peacock Inn became the center of the community and the warm and friendly Peacocks were almost parental figures. Charles Peacock became the new postmaster, operating the post office from a room at the inn. Isabella Peacock took up a collection for a Sunday school which evolved into the first Coconut Grove schoolhouse.

As business at the Peacock Inn grew, so did the number and variety of patrons, and more employees were needed. Several black families, mostly from the Bahamas, moved to Coconut Grove. One of the earliest black settlers in Coconut Grove was Mariah Brown, who came with the opening of the inn. Originally the employees lived on the premises, but as more families arrived, a settlement was founded on a portion of the Joseph Frow homestead.[41] A back road was cut through the Peacock, Frow, and Munroe properties, link-

GROUP OF BLACK PIONEERS, MOSTLY BAHAMIANS WORKING AT THE PEACOCK INN, ARE PHOTOGRAPHED IN FRONT OF COMMODORE MUNROE'S BOATHOUSE. (MUNROE COLLECTION, THE HISTORICAL ASSOCIATION OF SOUTHERN FLORIDA)

E.W.F. STIRRUP BUILT HIS HOUSE IN 1897 OUT OF PINE CUT FROM THE SITE AND MILLED AT THE MUNROE SAWMILL. THE ORIGINAL BAHAMIAN STYLE PORCH ACROSS THE FRONT WAS REMOVED AND AN L-SHAPED WING WAS ADDED IN 1912.

ing Coconut Grove with the Cutler settlement farther south. On the west side of the road to Cutler, the first black settlement was established. The force that pulled the black community together was Ebenezer Woodberry Frank Stirrup. An immigrant from the Bahamas, E.W.F. Stirrup moved to Key West in 1888, and soon travelled to Cutler, where he worked in a pineapple plantation. With the money he earned he bought land in what soon became the Charles Avenue settlement. Eventually Stirrup built over one hundred houses in Coconut Grove, including his own home.

Coconut Grove was by no means an elitist settlement. Munroe's intellectual friends blended well with the slightly eccentric pioneer settlement. Coconut Grove emerged

THE CHARLES AVENUE SETTLEMENT WAS THE FIRST BLACK COMMUNITY ESTABLISHED IN DADE COUNTY. MR. STIRRUP BUILT HOUSES TO ACCOMMODATE THE NEWLY ARRIVED WORK FORCE FROM THE BAHAMAS. THE HISTORIC CHARLES AVENUE CEMETERY IS IN THE FOREGROUND.

as a unique village, a small settlement where rich, poor, white, black, intellectual and uneducated lived and worked together without the usual geographic and social divisions that marred other communities.

LEMON CITY

For a time the area known as Lemon City was just as important as Coconut Grove. But Lemon City met an earlier demise with the northward expansion of the city of Miami in the early decades of the twentieth century. Lemon City evolved on what was the homestead of John Saunders, in the vincity of N.E. 61st Street, on Biscayne Bay. Saunders came to Dade County in 1876 and became a squatter on the land he later officially claimed. When he made his final proof in in 1889, his witnesses and closest neighbors were Edward Pent and William Mettair.[43] Even before his final patent came through, Saunders began selling portions of his 148 acres. One tract was sold to Eugene C. Harrington who then subdivided it into 81 very small lots around 1889. He named the subdivision "Lemon City."

Saunders continued selling off parcels of his land and before long there were a number of people living in the pioneer community. The main activity at Lemon City came to center around a small commercial dock at the end of Lemon Avenue (today's N.E. 61st Street). Within a few years, Lemon City had a post office, a dry goods store, and an attractive two-story hotel, the Lemon City Hotel built by Mrs. Cornelia Keyes, Eugene Harrington's mother.[44] Besides the commercial businesses, a visitor in 1891 estimated that there were about eighty residences in the surrounding area.[45]

A few scattered remnants of the early Lemon City survived until modern times, but within the last few years, tangible evidence of the pioneer settlement has almost completely disappeared. The original subdivisions have been replatted, and the old places torn down in favor of the new. Despite that fact, Lemon City retains a prominent place in Dade County's history as one of the first organized communities.

AN EARLY LEMON CITY HOME PHOTOGRAPHED CIRCA 1900. (THE HISTORICAL ASSOCIATION OF SOUTHERN FLORIDA)

CUTLER

Cutler was a much smaller and less established settlement than were either Coconut Grove or Lemon City. This was a result of the fact that most of the land was owned by the family of Dr. Henry Perrine. On July 2, 1838, a special congressional act was passed granting 24,000 acres to Dr. Perrine on which he was to conduct horticultural experiments. Perrine, however, was killed by Indians in a raid which took place on Indian Key in 1840.[46] His wife and son were among the survivors. The huge grant reverted to Perrine's heirs, but

THE RICHMOND HOUSE SHORTLY AFTER ITS CONSTRUCTION, CIRCA 1986. IN 1900 IT WAS ENLARGED BY THE ADDITION OF ANOTHER STRUCTURE WHEN IT BECAME THE RICHMOND INN. BETWEEN 1916 AND 1922 THE PROPERTY WAS FURTHER IMPROVED BY CHARLES DEERING. (THE HISTORICAL ASSOCIATION OF FLORIDA)

BROWN AND MOODY'S STORE WAS ONE OF THE EARLY COMMERCIAL STRUCTURES IN THE SETTLEMENT OF CUTLER.

they did not have the capabilities to develop the property. In their absence, squatters settled on some of the more desirable stretches on the bay.

John Addison came to the South Dade area after the Civil War and eventually was deeded a tract by the Perrine family.[47] The Addisons served as hosts to many people who visited the region south of Biscayne Bay which prior to the 1880s was known by the Indian name for the area, the Hunting Grounds. In 1872, Charles Seibold from Brooklyn, New York, was a guest of the Addisons. He ended up staying in Cutler for the remainder of his life. Seibold eventually built a home on, as it was then called "Cutler Road," and in 1899 married Maude Richards, granddaughter of Miami River homesteader, William Wagner.

Cutler got its name from Dr. William C. Cutler of Chelsea, Massachusetts, who attempted to found a settlement in the early 1880s on a tract of land he had purchased just north of the Perrine Grant.[48] Dr. Cutler did not remain in the area for long, but one of his followers, William Fuzzard did. Fuzzard built a home north of the Addison's and applied for permission to open a post office which he named for his mentor.[49]

Charles Deering, brother of the man who built Vizcaya, began buying up tracts in South Dade in the early 1900s until he owned most of the village of Cutler. The only known structure from the early days of Cutler still extant on the Deering property is the Richmond Inn built in 1896 by S. H. Richmond, who was appointed resident manager of the property when Henry Flagler's East Coast Railway gained an interest in the property. The Richmond Inn was operated as a rustic hunting lodge catering to local residents and railroad executives who were then coming to Dade County in connection with the extension of the Florida East Coast Railway to Miami.

THE ARCHITECTURAL VERNACULAR OF SOUTH FLORIDA

Few structures remain from the pioneer days of South Florida. Buildings from this period were simple and unpretentious, sometimes crude, and most of them have not survived the passage of time. Architecture, by the learned, classical definition of the trained profession, did not exist in this remote, Southern frontier. The men and women who populated the shores of Biscayne Bay during the nineteenth century carved their way through mangroves and mosquitoes, faced transportation obstacles of perilous navigational channels and fought hostile Indians and violent tropical storms. When it came to building, these people had immediate needs for shelter and defense to resolve, and no time or resources to worry about academic rules of taste or technology. The products of this intuitive approach to building construction were the first manifestations of the architectural vernacular of Dade County.

Vernacular architecture is a spontaneous, often instinctive response to specific needs and local environmental factors, expressed through available resources and based on the builders' previous experience. Thus the knowledge is usually acquired firsthand in the actual building process, or through observation of existing, familiar models. The built environment, in effect, replaces the classroom as training ground. The term vernacular is defined as a common, local vocabulary. Vernacular architecture is generally expressed in functional straightforward forms, through materials and details indigenous to the locale. This honesty and efficiency, however, are not always the rule. Design and construction by inexperienced hands is often based on a painful trial-and-error process. The same holds true for ornament and detail which, when derived from other areas, may not always seem appropriate or pertinent to new, local conditions. Decoration may be copied from memory, thus lacking the proper interpretation and execution. The original meaning of the building forms may be lost and a new function attached to the same element. High pitched gable roofs, for instance, intended to drive-off snow loads in northern climates, become tools to allow for the upward circulation of warm air in subtropical area houses.

The improvised adaptation of previous models to new local conditions and materials, the naive approach to design and the flaws of uninhibited experimentation, all become key components of the architectural vernacular of a region. There should be no question as to the ability of builders of vernacular ar-

chitecture to produce high quality buildings in design and construction. In every city and countryside some of the finest, most representative examples of local architecture are of the vernacular type.

The architectural vernacular of South Florida has acquired distinct, identifiable traits through the years. The hardy wood of local pine, virtually impenetrable by nails, moisture or termites, provided most of the lumber used in early construction. The earth provided the oolitic limestone, usually quarried right from the site and widely used in early construction. The soil was also the source for sand and lime used in later concrete and stucco buildings. The severe winds and tidal action of tropical storms dictated structural reinforcements such as thick, tapering masonry walls and buildings elevated off the ground. Roof overhangs and porches offered relief from the intense heat of the sun and the heavy summer rains. Large openings arranged in cross-ventilation patterns and open spaces such as balconies, courtyards and terraces were all used as abatements to sun, heat and rain, while they maximized the buildings' exposure to cooling breezes.

Many external forces also played important roles in the formation of the South Florida architectural vernacular. The early settlers' varied backgrounds included plantations of the deep South, the urban Northeast, the tropical shores of the Bahamas and Key West, and the recent arrivals from Europe. They used their acquired knowledge and experiences when building their new homes. Materials were not always indigenous. The earliest imports used in construction, furnishing the homes, filling the pantries and clothing the pioneers, were the spoils from the thriving wrecking industry. Other home and building supplies were brought in by boat from North Florida or from out of the state.

This variety of influences and materials that contributed to the architectural vernacular of South Florida is still present. Many of the features and materials that make up the current building vocabulary of the area were introduced back in the pioneer settlement days.

11

GOVERNMENT INSTALLATIONS IN THE SOUTHERN FRONTIER

The Cape Florida Lighthouse, originally built in 1825 and rebuilt in 1846 after being nearly destroyed during an Indian raid, is the oldest standing structure built in Dade County. The United States government erected a series of lighthouses along the Florida east coast to aid the increasing number of sailing vessels engaged in trade with Key West through the reefs and violent storms of the Florida Straits.

The design for the lighthouse was not spontaneous nor was it local; therefore, it does not quite qualify as a true example of early South Florida vernacular architecture. It was based on the standard lighthouse design repeatedly employed by the government across the country.[50] The material was red brick, foreign to the limestone-based South Florida subsoil. The structure, however, did respond to local needs, as it was believed to be built strong enough to withstand the punishment of violent hurricanes. The tower, orig-inally sixty-five feet tall, was built by Bostonian, Samuel Lincoln,[51] with solid brick walls five feet thick at the bottom, tapering to a thickness of two feet at the top. The thickness of the solid masonry walls and the tapering effect, both added strength and stability to the tall, slender tower. No one anticipated that a fraudulent contractor would use inferior quality hollow bricks in order to pocket the extra cash,[52] nor the Indian attack that left the lighthouse in ruins only ten years after its construction. In July, 1836, John Thompson, assistant keeper of the lighthouse and Aaron Carter,[58] a black assistant, were victims of a siege by Seminole Indians from the mainland. The two men ran for cover to the lighthouse, amidst a shower of bullets. The Indians set fire to the base of the lighthouse, and the inferno quickly spread through wooden doors and windows and up the wooden stairs, fueled by the oil used for the lantern. The interior was gutted. Carter was killed, while Thompson lying wounded out on the lantern, his feet burning from the roaring blaze, threw a keg of gunpowder down the shaft of the tower to end it all. The explosion extinguished the fire

CAPE FLORIDA LIGHTHOUSE AND THE CARETAKER'S HOUSE PHOTOGRAPHED AFTER THE TURN OF THE CENTURY. ABANDONED AFTER THE CONSTRUCTION OF THE FOWERY ROCK LIGHT IN 1878, THE LIGHTHOUSE STOOD IDLE THROUGH A CHAIN OF OWNERSHIP UNTIL 1967, WHEN IT WAS PURCHASED BY THE STATE OF FLORIDA AND RESTORED WITHIN THE CAPE FLORIDA STATE PARK, LATER RENAMED BILL BAGGS STATE PARK. (MUNROE COLLECTION, THE HISTORICAL ASSOCIATION OF SOUTHERN FLORIDA)

and the Indians began to retreat, leaving both men for dead. A navy schooner twelve miles out heard the blast and headed for shore,[54] rescuing John Thompson who lived to write a detailed account of his harrowing experience.

What is believed to be Dade County's only other nineteenth century example of U.S. government architecture was actually not built by federal employees at all. Although the limestone structure that currently stands in Lummus Park is commonly referred to as the Fort Dallas barracks, local historians now believe that the building was originally con-

ground.[56] If whole or split logs were used in the construction, some may have been felled from the area, but all milled lumber was brought in by schooner. The quartermaster in charge of material for the 1838 construction wrote that he needed "a thousand feet of board, sheathing, and shingles because no trees in the area are large enough to make clapboard."

The fort was very actively used between 1839 and 1842, but a visitor in 1849 noted only the log buildings.[58] Later that year, however, William English who had purchased

THE FORMER WILLIAM ENGLISH SLAVE QUARTERS, BUILT IN 1849 AND LATER USED BY THE MILITARY AT FORT DALLAS, WAS RELOCATED TO LUMMUS PARK IN 1925. IN WHAT WAS PERHAPS THE FIRST CONSCIOUS HISTORIC PRESERVATION EFFORT IN DADE COUNTY, THE BUILDING WAS TAKEN APART, STONE BY STONE, AND RE-ASSEMBLED IN ITS NEW RIVERFRONT LOCATION FURTHER UPSTREAM. THE DAUGHTERS OF THE AMERICAN REVOLUTION HAVE OCCUPIED THE BARRACKS SINCE 1929.

structed in 1849 as slave quarters for the William English plantation. The original Fort Dallas buildings erected on the north bank of the Miami River in 1838 were probably the two log buildings noted in an 1838 letter from Lieutenant Webster to General Jesup who was in command of the Florida troops.[55] No physical description of the fort has been found, but if it was typical of others in Florida of the period, the buildings may have been surrounded by a wall of long, split logs fastened with timbers, and with firing loop holes cut in the enclosure about eight feet off the

the property during a lull in the war-time activities, built two limestone buildings, among other structures, from rock quarried nearby. When the military returned they found the stone buildings extant minus all wood. In fact, milled lumber was such a rare commodity among Dade's pioneers that every time a wooden structure was briefly abandoned, it was dismantled, and the lumber reused elsewhere.

In 1855, when Fort Dallas was reopened, the military went about repairing and adapting English's stone structures. One

THE BISCAYNE HOUSE OF REFUGE WAS ERECTED IN 1875 BY THE U.S. COAST GUARD TO ASSIST SHIPWRECK VICTIMS. THE RAISED FOUNDATION AND THE WRAP-AROUND PORCH ARE FEATURES THAT BECAME TYPICAL OF PIONEER BUILDINGS IN THE SOUTH FLORIDA AREA. IT WAS FORMERLY LOCATED ON MIAMI BEACH. NEAR INDIAN CREEK. (ROMER COLLECTION, MIAMI-DADE PUBLIC LIBRARY)

of the stone buildings was two stories, 42 x 20 feet to which rough flooring and a roof were added as well as a ten foot wide piazza on the front. The other stone building, the one that is now in Lummus Park, was one story, 95 x 17 feet to which a wooden second story was added. The first floor was used as storage and the second as additional housing for the troops.[59]

During this occupation, the fort became a substantial complex and quite a few additional buildings were constructed. Most of the military built structures were wood frame construction with vertical board and batten siding and ranged in size from 30 x 19 feet to 12 x 12 feet. Wide piazzas were constructed on the front of the larger buildings. Wood used for the framing was cut from a site near the post, but milled lumber was still shipped in from New York, Savannah, and Key West.[60] Other smaller outbuildings, some with thatched palmetto roofs, were also added.

The new fort, with its finished buildings, Bermuda grass, coconut trees, flower and vegetable gardens, all neatly laid out under a high-flying American flag created the impression of a well established community on the Miami River. That was not really the case outside of the military personnel and base. Fort Dallas closed again in 1858. By 1874 not one of the wood structures is known to have been standing.[61]

William English's stone buildings, however, did make it into the twentieth century, but only the one story former slave quarters and military storehouse lasts today. Although the durability of stone construction was proven many times over, it was the wood frame architecture of the type at Fort Dallas that seems to have been favored by area pioneers. Stone construction did not proliferate, but the wood frame, vertical board and batten type did. Despite the difficulty of acquiring adequate lumber, it must have been preferable to quarrying large amounts of rock by chipping it away with an axe. William English, after all, did have a large contingent of slaves to do his work for him. Even though limestone construction was a rarity in Miami's early built environment, the building now standing in Lummus Park represents one of the earliest expressions of the formation of South Florida's architectural vernacular.

TYPICAL HOMESTEAD IN SOUTH FLORIDA, SHOWING THE MAIN HOUSE AND A NUMBER OF OUTBUILDINGS. (THELMA PETERS, PRIVATE COLLECTION)

THE WAGNER HOUSE

Pioneer William Wagner came to the Miami area in 1855.[62] The evolution of the Wagner residence, from pioneer homestead to museum-in-the-park, also typifies the broad spectrum of internal and external forces that have contributed to the architectural vernacular of South Florida. Built before 1858,[63] it is the oldest known house still standing in Dade County, and along with the William English slave quarter/barracks, one of the two surviving buildings of the early days of settlement along the Miami River. Its construction is evidence of the resources available to the builder during the different phases of development in South Florida.

The Wagner residence is similar in layout and proportions to the wood frame early Victorian cottages that dotted the American countryside during the 1850's. But in South Florida, the technology and embellishments of the "Carpenter Gothic" influence could not reach full expression. Balloon frame construction and stock lumber such as vertical board and batten siding and applied "gingerbread" ornament, staple for buildings of that time, were not available in South Florida. Balloon frame construction, which spread through the United States in the 1840s, allowed for a lighter, easier to build system, using smaller, standard sized lumber, nailed upright.[64] The structural frame of the Wagner house employs the earlier method of hand-hewn heavier timbers, joined by mortise and tenon connections and pegs. Milled lumber can also be found in the house, with visible circular saw marks as evidence of later construction techniques. Later yet, hand-sewn, balloon-frame 2" x 4" studs were added. The original siding for the Wagner house was made of wide vertical boards butting together. This siding was gradually replaced or covered by vertical board and batten, horizontal weatherboard and drop siding, as more stock lumber supplies became available to South Florida builders.

The Wagner family, in subsequent alterations, added a rear porch to the original building. When the Cassell family bought the house in 1909, the character of the house, just as that of the entire area, began to change. The pioneer homestead became an early suburban subdivision of the city of Miami. The Highland Park Subdivision was the new set-

THE WAGNER HOUSE AS IT WAS DISCOVERED IN 1978.

THE WAGNER RESIDENCE, ORIGINALLY BUILT CIRCA 1858, RELOCATED TO LUMMUS PARK AND RESTORED BY DADE HERITAGE TRUST AND THE CITY OF MIAMI.

THE MAUDE SEYBOLD BLACK HOUSE, BUILT CIRCA 1899 NEAR THE SETTLEMENT OF CUTLER, IS ONE OF THE REMAINING HOUSES FROM THE PIONEER PERIOD IN DADE COUNTY.

Maude and her husband Charles Seibold settled in South Dade and built this house around 1898.[69] The structure is balloon-frame, with additional cross bracing members used for structural reinforcement. Although the house has been enlarged and altered through the years, its true pioneer character is still very much in evidence.

THE BARNACLE

ting for the old house. Decorative fishscale shingles on the front gable end[65] and a Mission-influenced porch,[66] built of oolitic limestone with a stuccoed parapet, were added in the 1920s, giving the aging house a street orientation and a new look. This porch was later enclosed and additions eventually engulfed the entire original structure. The relic was well hidden out of the sight and out of the memory of most people in Miami. In the 1970s, the impending threat of development from a proposed Rapid Transit Station site prompted the property owner[67] to donate the house to the Dade Heritage Trust. This private preservation group became guardian to the ragged, old gem and undertook its relocation to Lummus Park and subsequent restoration.[68]

Few pioneer residential buildings still stand. The Maude Seibold Black house, just north of the Cutler settlement, is one such structure. Granddaughter of William Wagner,

Commodore Ralph Munroe's residence, The Barnacle, is without a doubt, the most ingenious and sophisticated work of vernacular architecture remaining from the pioneer days of South Florida. Built in 1891, the design reflects Munroe's knowledge of boat building and naval architecture. The building is oriented with the main entrance facing southeast, thus opening the house to the cooler summer breezes and the winter sun. A wide veranda on the entrance facade opens on three sides of the house, addressing the outdoors life style of the Commodore, while keeping the hotter, west side more enclosed. Inside the house, four corner rooms open to the central octagonal dining room, the focal point of the interior space. The second story skylight above this space is operated through ropes and pulleys to allow the opening of diamond shaped windows oriented to continually funnel the bay breezes

THE BARNACLE, BUILT BY COMMODORE MUNROE IN 1891 AS A ONE STORY HOUSE. (MUNROE COLLECTION, THE HISTORICAL ASSOCIATION OF SOUTHERN FLORIDA)

THE BARNACLE BEING RAISED IN 1908 TO ACCOMMODATE A SECOND STORY BELOW. (MUNROE COLLECTION, THE HISTORICAL ASSOCIATION OF SOUTHERN FLORIDA)

THE BARNACLE AS A TWO STORY RESIDENCE. THE FIRST STORY IS DONE IN RUSTICATED CONCRETE BLOCKS, POPULAR BUILDING MATERIAL IN THE EARLY 1900S, WHILE THE SECOND STORY SHOWS THE ORIGINAL WOOD FRAME CONSTRUCTION. (MUNROE COLLECTION, THE HISTORICAL ASSOCIATION OF SOUTHERN FLORIDA)

into the house. Outside, this skylight caps off the flared hip roof.

Munroe built a structure to withstand the tropical storms of South Florida. The frame, built from wreck timber cut to size in his own sawmill, was bolted down to the foundation.[70] The foundation consisted of pine posts set deep into the ground and treated with crude oil to deter the devastating bite of the termites. The rest of the timber used for flooring, siding, roof shingle and millwork was brought from Pensacola. The house was approximately eight steps off the ground,[71] as a consideration to possible floods in such close proximity to the bay.

When the Commodore remarried and started a new family, the need for space began to increase and the Barnacle was enlarged in 1908. Pleased with his original concept, the house was lifted to a second story level and a first story was built underneath the original structure.[72] The wooden foundation piers were replaced with concrete piers for more strength. In subsequent years the roof shingles were changed to Ludovici tiles,[73] the exterior was stuccoed over, an indoor bathroom and a new kitchen were installed and several outbuildings added.[74]

The Barnacle remains as one of the finest examples of vernacular architecture in Dade County. Although it is a more self-conscious design effort than generally expected from vernacular architecture, it is an excellent response to the local environment, it uses local materials, and it is inspired by the experiences of its builder, in this case a ship designer. Commodore Munroe had made the greatest single contribution so far to the formation of a building vocabulary typical of South Florida.

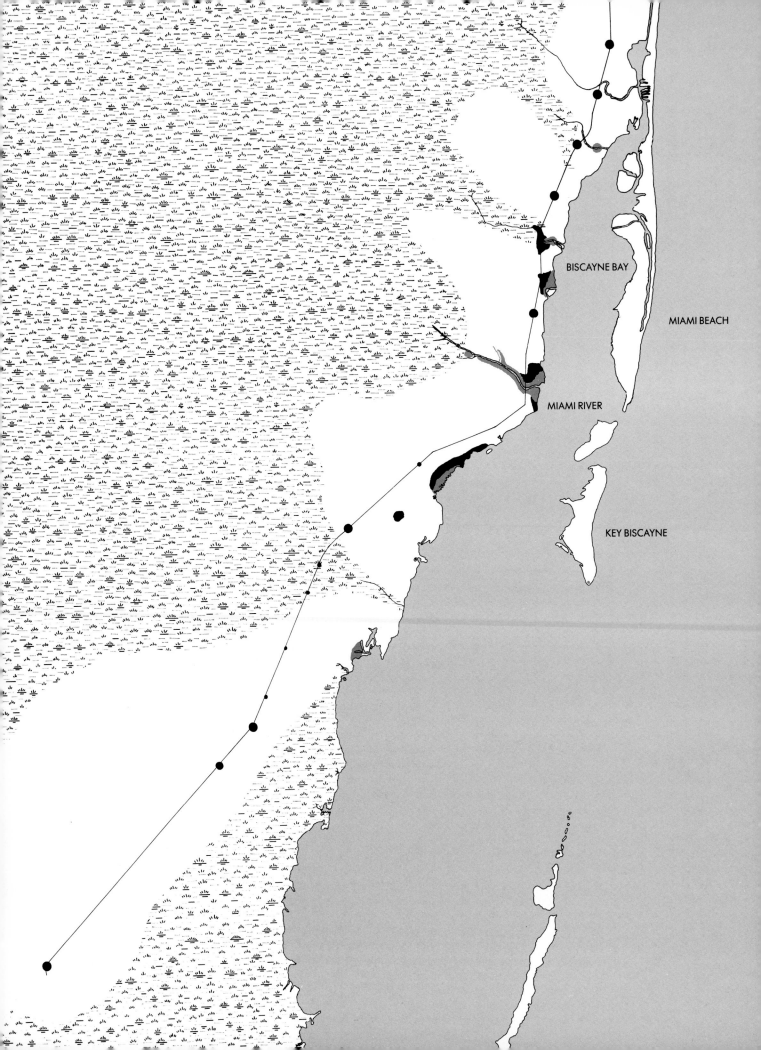

BISCAYNE BAY

MIAMI BEACH

MIAMI RIVER

KEY BISCAYNE

THE MIAMI RIVER MOUTH CIRCA 1895. PICTURED ARE THE BRICKELL STORE ON THE SOUTH BANK AND PORTIONS OF FORT DALLAS AND JULIA TUTTLE'S HOMESITE ON THE NORTH SIDE. (ROMER COLLECTION, MIAMI-DADE PUBLIC LIBRARY)

FORMATIVE YEARS

While settlement in Dade County extended over a much greater radius by the late 1800s, the Miami River settlement, although somewhat reduced in prominence from the days of Fort Dallas, remained at least at the geographical heart of the activity. What might loosely be termed a business center was constituted by the rustic trading posts of William Brickell and J. W. Ewan at the mouth of the river. They did the bulk of their business with Seminole Indians. As the Indians poled their cypress canoes to and from the riverfront docks of the traders, they glided past the hardwood hammocks and small unpainted wood frame houses, vegetable gardens and fruit groves of the homesteads that lined the length of the river. Although it must not have seemed it at the time, this still remote tropical settlement was on the verge of transition. In November of 1891, when a young widow, Julia Sturtevant Tuttle, purchased the six hundred and forty acre Biscayne Bay Company tract, she did so with a vision of what she wanted Miami to be.

It was a mere four years before Julia Tuttle convinced Henry Flagler of the impending rewards of extending his railroad to Miami. The event that caused Flagler to take serious interest in Miami was the freeze of 1894-1895 which devastated the North Florida grove industry. Although legend has it that Mrs. Tuttle promptly sent Flagler some fresh orange blossoms to demonstrate that South Florida was untouched, James Ingraham, an associate of Flagler's who was in Miami at the time, claimed that it was he who "gathered a bouquet of blossoms from various citrus trees, wrapped them in a damp rag, and after an interview with Mrs. Tuttle and Mr. and Mrs. Brickell of Miami, hurried to St. Augustine..." where he presented the fresh and fragrant flowers to a chilly Mr. Flagler.[2]

In addition to the climate, offers of free land from both Mrs. Tuttle and the Brickells finally won Flagler over. When he did acquiesce, it was not only a railroad that Flagler agreed to build. Mrs. Tuttle had also proposed that he construct a hotel of the Fort Dallas property, half of which she would give him in return.[3] On the remainder of the Fort Dallas tract, less Mrs. Tuttle's homesite of about ten acres, Flagler agreed to lay out a town, at his own expense "as may mutually be thought desirable," but he reminded Mrs. Tuttle of his hesitations writing "...even with [the land donations], I shrink from the expenditure, for I feel satisfied that it will be years before the Road can earn anything, and that I am incurring a great risk, with comparatively little inducement."[4]

On Tuesday, March 3, 1986, John Sewell, a Flagler employee, left Palm Beach for Miami Bringing with him his brother E.G. Sewell and a labor force of twelve black men led by A.W. Brown to begin construction on the Royal Palm Hotel.[5] When Sewell and his crew arrived, they found that Julia Tuttle had begun work on several buildings. A street, Miami Avenue, then Avenue D, was laid out according to the plat for "Miami" drawn up by surveyor A. L. Knowlton at the behest of the Fort Dallas land Company whose principal officers were William and Mary Brickell, Julia Tuttle and Henry M. Flagler.[6] The extension of the F.E.C. line to Miami was completed shortly thereafter, and on April 15, 1896, the first train steamed into Miami.

On July 28, that same year, the city of Miami was incorporated. John B. Reilly, formerly a bookkeeper for the Florida East Coast Railroad, was elected as the first mayor. By the date of incorporation, John Sewell claims to have counted 3,000 citizens in Miami.[7] That figure represented a drastic jump in the population, considering that the 1885 Florida State Census only counted 332 people in the entire county.

All the activity that spring and summer of 1896 was only the beginning of the changes Henry Flagler would bring to Dade County. His omnipotent sweep into South Florida was not an unprecedented occurrence from a national perspective. During the latter half of the nineteenth century the railroads became one of the most significant factors in America's economic growth, and railroad executives among the most influential people.

Henry Flagler made his fortune as a

JULIA TUTTLE, 1895. (HISTORICAL ASSOCIATION OF SOUTHERN FLORIDA)

WORK CREW AT THE ROYAL PALM SITE IN 1876. (HISTORICAL ASSOCIATION OF SOUTHERN FLORIDA)

HENRY FLAGLER. (HENRY FLAGLER MUSEUM)

partner and founder, with John D. Rockefeller, of the Standard Oil Company. Later in life he became a true railroad tycoon. As president of the Jacksonville, St. Augustine and Indian River Railway, renamed the Florida East Coast Railway, he bought and consolidated several railroads in the North Florida area, rapidly extending his empire south from St. Augustine to West Palm Beach by 1894.[8]

With the arrival of the extension of Flagler's railroad to Miami in April 1896, life changed dramatically, not just in Miami where building supplies and new residents were disembarking in startling repetition, but

THE NATURAL ROCK BRIDGE AT ARCH CREEK WAS AN EARLY OUTDOOR ATTRACTION FOR TOURISTS AND HOME-STEADERS ALIKE, AS SEEN IN THIS 1908 VIEW OF A GROUP OF PICNICKERS. THE EROSION OF THE CREEK ON THE POROUS LIMESTONE CREATED THE BRIDGE OVER THOUSANDS OF YEARS. IN 1974, ONE DAY AFTER THE STATE OF FLORIDA PURCHASED THE SITE FOR PRESERVATION, THE BRIDGE COLLAPSED. IN 1982, THE ARCH CREEK PARK OPENED AND A REPLICA OF THE BRIDGE HAS BEEN BUILT ON THE ORIGINAL SITE. (HISTORICAL ASSOCIATION OF SOUTHERN FLORIDA)

21

all along the F.E.C. line where stations were built to accommodate farmers who needed a quicker means of getting their produce to market. Beginning in the northernmost end of Dade County was the Ojus station, and less than a mile to the south was the Fulford station. Next in line was the Arch Creek station, the Biscayne station, then Little River, Lemon City and Buena Vista.

A number of these places existed to some degree before the railroad. Much of north Dade County was taken up in homesteads prior to the turn of the century. The railroad had a profound effect on their development though. It formed centers, encouraged expanded agricultural production and brought new residents. Lemon City, although it was previously well-established, was also altered. Its commercial docks could not compete with the efficiency of railroad shipping, causing its business center to move from the bayfront, westward, nearer the tracks.

With a chain of permanent settlements well established, Miami's next step toward civilization was the completion of the Royal Palm Hotel. The official opening of the hotel occurred on January 16, 1897, when an informal party was held.[9] Besides its natural resources, Miami now had the means of importing tourists and the luxury and ambience of a Flagler hotel to attract them.

ARCHITECTURAL VERNACULAR IN THE RAILROAD ERA OF MIAMI

The arrival of the railroad to Miami had a profound influence on the formation of an architectural vocabulary in South Florida. Several factors contribute to the transformation from the simple, many times crude buildings of pioneer days to the architecture of the railroad era. The most direct effect of the railroad extension was the significant boost to the population and economy of the area. It also facilitated the import of building materials and influences, as outside sources became more accessible. One result was larger scale buildings than those from the frontier days, still simple in construction and detailing, but relying more heavily on manufactured products.

THIS ARCH CREEK RESIDENCE WAS THE HOME OF THE PIONEER BURR FAMILY. IT WAS BUILT IN 1907 AND STILL STANDS ON EAST DIXIE HIGHWAY. (THELMA PETERS COLLECTION)

THE HOME OF CAPTAIN WILLIAM FULFORD IN NORTH DADE. BUILT AROUND THE TURN OF THE CENTURY, IT REFLECTED FULFORD'S KNOWLEDGE OF SHIP BUILDING. THE HOUSE BURNED DOWN IN THE 1950S. (THELMA PETERS COLLECTION)

DR. DUPUIS OFFICE AND DRUGSTORE, BUILT IN 1902, IS THE FIRST KNOWN CONCRETE STRUCTURE NORTH OF MIAMI. DR. DUPUIS CAME TO LEMON CITY IN 1898 WHERE HE SET UP HIS MEDICAL PRACTICE. A STRONG BELIEVER IN THE HEALTHFUL VIRTUES OF MILK, DR. DUPUIS STARTED THE WHITE BELT DAIRY, AT ONE TIME, ONE OF THE LARGEST DAIRIES IN MIAMI.

THE FIRST F.E.C. RAILROAD DEPOT OF ANY SUBSTANCE IN MIAMI WAS BUILT NEAR N.E. 6TH STREET AND 2ND AVENUE, AROUND THE TURN OF THE CENTURY. IT WAS A SMALL RECTANGULAR BUILDING MOVED FROM ST. AUGUSTINE (RIGHT). A SERIES OF BREEZEWAYS SERVED AS LOADING PLATFORMS AND ENTRANCE PAVILLION TO THE DEPOT. (HISTORICAL ASSOCIATION OF SOUTHERN FLORIDA).

The early buildings associated with the Florida East Coast Railroad were designed and built by a work force from outside of Miami and patterned after established national models. They did employ, at least partially, local materials, and their building forms were adapted to local conditions and needs. Still, the architecture was a far cry from indigenous.

Structures erected by the F.E.C. were utilitarian, solid and handsomely built, combining local lumber with finished wood and millwork which the railroad now made available. Building functions ranged from depots to station houses for railroad workmen to warehouse sidings to accommodate the produce waiting to be loaded on the trains. There was a great similarity in design in all these buildings—massing, roof configuration, materials, details and even paint color were evidence of the consistent quality of construction of the work team that Flagler brought to Miami.

The first Miami depot was a small wood frame structure located near the present site of the Dade County Courthouse. Within the next two years, the Miami depot was relocated near the present area of N.E. 2nd Avenue between 6th and 7th Streets, the site now occupied by the Freedom Tower. The structure, however, was not even locally built, but rather, it was the old depot from St. Augustine, relocated to Miami aboard a railroad flatbed.[10] The structure was altered and enlarged to accommodate the needs of the growing city.

A new depot was built in 1912, on the site immediately west of the Dade County Courthouse. The elevated loading platform, the broad roof and generous overhang, the long, narrow plan, were all typical of railroad depots across the country. The unadorned building is expressive of its utilitarian nature and of the struggling days of the fledgling town. The hip roof with broad eaves for weather considerations and the dormers identifying the presence of an attic are some of the more salient features, simple as they may be. Construction was utilitarian, hence its major asset. The shape of the brackets supporting the roof overhang, for instance, was an honest expression of the stresses being transmitted from the roof to the vertical supports. They widened at the ends and ta-

THE MIAMI DEPOT WAS RELOCATED IN 1912 TO A SITE JUST WEST OF THE DADE COUNTY COURTHOUSE. TYPICAL OF THE MODEL REPEATEDLY USED BY THE F.E.C., THE BUILDING HAD A LARGE HIP ROOF AND BROAD OVERHANGS SUPPORTED ON LARGE WOODEN BRACKETS. CONTROVERSIAL SINCE ITS CONSTRUCTION, THE BUILDING WAS DEMOLISHED IN 1963 BECAUSE IT WAS CONSIDERED AN EYESORE AND INCONVENIENTLY LOCATED FOR AUTOMOBILE TRAFFIC. (HISTORICAL ASSOCIATION OF SOUTHERN FLORIDA)

pered at the center, creating the graceful, curved shape of the brackets, devoid of any "Gingerbread" excess. Roof overhangs acquired a different expression in other railroad buildings, like the Perrine Section House, now demolished, and the Homestead Section House (Florida Pioneer Museum). The brackets and posts became supports for a Southern style verandah which appeared to wrap around three sides of the house. Double-hung sash windows and beaded boards used for interior panelling are found repeatedly in these buildings.

The Royal Palm Hotel was the largest, most significant building associated with the Florida East Coast Railroad in Miami. Only nine years earlier the Hotel Ponce de Leon had opened in St. Augustine. Flagler had spared no expense to make the hotel itself a tourist attraction through its elegance and unique architecture. The young New York firm of Carrere and Hastings was commissioned for the job. Carrere and Hastings, both in their twenties, had received their education at L'Ecole des Beaux Arts in Paris, and in the studios of McKim, Mead and White, one of the leading architectural firms in the country at that time. Although the architects' designs

THE PRINCETON STATION, RELOCATED TO KEY BIS-CAYNE IN THE 1960s, HAS BEEN MOVED BACK TO SOUTH DADE AND RESTORED AS PART OF THE GOLD COAST RAILROAD MUSEUM, ADJACENT TO METROZOO.

THE HOMESTEAD SECTION FOREMAN'S HOUSE (FOREGROUND) AND DEPOT (BACKGROUND) WERE MOVED TO FLORIDA CITY IN 1967 AND 1976 RESPEC-TIVELY AND WERE RECENTLY RESTORED AS THE FLORIDA PIONEER MUSEUM.

24

THE ROYAL PALM HOTEL HAD A LARGE FRENCH MANSARD ROOF PIERCED BY DORMERS AND A COLUMNED PORTE COCHERE OF CLASSICAL INFLUENCE AS BREAKS IN THE MONOTONY OF ITS LONG MASS. (ROMER COLLECTION, MIAMI-DADE PUBLIC LIBRARY)

leaned more toward the French classical vocabulary of the Beaux Arts, as later seen in their design for the New York Public Library, their work for Flagler was more evocative of the strong Spanish heritage of St. Augustine.[11] The architecture of the Ponce de Leon eludes precise identification as Spanish Renaissance, Moorish or any other style. It does, however, establish a strong precedent for the reintroduction of the Spanish idiom in later years as a favorite Florida style.

The design for the Royal Palm in Miami was not quite the caliber of its St. Augustine counterpart. Flagler had demanded painstaking quality of design and construction in the Ponce de Leon, when St. Augustine, an already established city, was envisioned as the culmination point for the northern tourists. But as the railroad moved south, opening new vacation frontiers, the finances and the labor force had to be channelled in many directions. In both the West Palm Beach and the Miami terminus, not only a railroad and hotel had to be built, but a city to go with them.

The Royal Palm was built in the haste of less than one year by James A. McGuire and Joseph A. McDonald, building contractors for the F.E.C. Corporation.[12] It was a wood frame vernacular structure rather than the sturdier, coquina-faced construction of the Ponce de Leon. Still grandiose in size, the building was 680 feet long[13] with two wings

perpendicular to the main body, five stories tall, with accommodations for over 500 guests.[14]

The French-inspired design was originally used for the Royal Poinciana in Palm Beach, finished only two years before. At the Royal Palm the major decorative feature was its mansard roof dotted with dormers, which broke the monotony of the large unadorned masses. An entrance portico of classical derivation was centered on the north elevation, five bays wide and two stories in height, culminating the main palm-lined approach through the grounds. The major physical asset for the hotel was its site, as it commanded the best view of Biscayne Bay at the mouth of the Miami River from its north bank. The ample, beautifully landscaped gardens were a popular spot for recreational activities that took full advantage of the virtues that year-round outdoor living had to offer.

What the Royal Palm lacked in architectural finesse it made up for in size and social amenities to still deserve recognition as the most important building in these early days of Miami. Its attractions appealed to a very sophisticated clientele. John Sewell later remarked that "it sometimes looked like a special delegation from Congress around the hotel, so many senators and representatives were there."[15] Also sprinkled among the guests were the likes of John D. Rockefeller, Flagler's former business partner, along with the Goulds, Astors and Vanderbilts.

THE MAGNIFICENT VIEW OF THE MOUTH OF THE MIAMI RIVER AND BISCAYNE BAY WAS ENHANCED BY THE HOTEL. THE WELL LANDSCAPED GARDENS OPENED OVER THE RIVER AND THE BAY, WHILE A BULKHEAD ROAD CREATED AN UNDISTURBED WATERFRONT PROMENADE THAT CITY PLANNERS KEEP FIGHTING TO RECREATE. (HISTORICAL ASSOCIATION OF SOUTHERN FLORIDA)

THE ROYAL PALM COTTAGES WERE THE EARLIEST HOUSING DEVELOPMENT IN MIAMI, BUILT ALONG PRESENT DAY S.E. 2ND STREET BY FLAGLER. IN THE BACKGROUND IS THE ROYAL PALM HOTEL AND THE BAY. (HISTORICAL ASSOCIATION OF SOUTHERN FLORIDA)

The Royal Palm remained the grande dame of Miami hotels until the 1926 hurricane dealt it a death blow. That winter season its doors remained closed. Within a few years, Miami's first grand hotel was demolished.

While the Royal Palm Hotel was under construction, the Florida East Coast Railroad built a series of houses for employees of the various Flagler projects. The houses were balloon frame structures, typical of the modest, straightforward frame vernacular homes that lined residential working class developments across the country at the turn of the century. They were simple but comfortable, two and a

ONLY ONE OF THE RESIDENTIAL COTTAGES SURVIVED. ITS APPEARANCE DRASTICALLY ALTERED, IT WAS USED AS THE BUTLER INSURANCE BUILDING FROM 1951 TO 1978.

THE ROYAL PALM COTTAGE HAS BEEN RELOCATED TO THE NEW FORT DALLAS PARK, WHERE IT NOW SERVES AS A LUNCH TIME RESTAURANT. ITS ORIGINAL SITE IS NOW OCCUPIED BY THE PARKING STRUCTURE FOR CENTRUST TOWER.

half stories, with front porches and shallow setbacks, built mostly from local pine and finished lumber brought in by the railroad.

During a visit to Miami to inspect the construction of the Royal Palm, Henry Flagler noticed that the workers were living in crudely built tents. When he realized they had come here to work after the freeze that killed most of the citrus crop in North and Central Florida, Flagler ordered that housing be built for them. Along with John B. Reilly, Flagler walked toward the bay, searching for a site in which to build employee cottages, but quickly he remarked, "These lots will sell for high prices to wealthy people who will build winter homes."[16] They continued west just past the Royal Palm, and on 13th and 14th Streets (present day S.E. 1st and 2nd Streets) the building site for the cottages was selected.

Over thirty employee houses were built. They rented between $15 and $22 a month, depending on the size and indoor plumbing facilities, or they could be purchased, ranging in price from $1,200.00 to $3,000.00.[17]

DOWNTOWN MIAMI

Henry Flagler was a shrewd businessman. There was little point in building a railroad to Miami if there was no place for people to stay, and no way to operate a hotel without surrounding service industries. As a result, it was much more than the construction of a railroad, or even a hotel, that Flagler embarked upon. After his surveyor laid out the town, the work began, building streets and walkways. Worker housing was erected, and a sewer system, water and electric plants were installed.[18]

A major portion of the new population came to Miami under Flagler's employ or came to start related businesses financed by Flagler interests. Very suddenly Miami was no longer a remote outpost. The first local newspaper, an F.E.C. organ, *The Miami Metropolis*, began publication on May 15, 1896, as a weekly. The professional advertisements in that issue included those of several attorneys,

a dentist, three physicians including Dr. J. M. Jackson, a draftsman, a shoe store, the Bank of Bay Biscayne, a tailor, several small hotels, a pool parlor, a few dry goods stores, a hardware store, a drugstore, an insurance company, and six real estate agents.[19]

DR. JAMES M. JACKSON'S OFFICE AND SURGERY WAS BUILT IN 1905 ON PRESENT-DAY FLAGLER STREET AND N.E. SECOND AVENUE. IN 1917, THE BUILDING WAS MOVED TO SOUTH BAYSHORE DRIVE AND S.E. 12 TERRACE. IT IS NOW OWNED BY THE CITY OF MIAMI, AND SERVES AS HEADQUARTERS FOR THE DADE HERITAGE TRUST. DR. JACKSON, ONE OF THE FIRST DOCTORS IN MIAMI, FOUNDED JACKSON MEMORIAL HOSPITAL.

EDWIN NELSON'S FURNITURE STORE AND HOME, ON 12TH STREET, NOW FLAGLER STREET. HE WAS ALSO ONE OF THE CITY'S EARLIEST UNDERTAKERS. (HISTORICAL ASSOCIATION OF SOUTHERN FLORIDA)

By June of 1896, Flagler's men initiated a move to incorporate Miami. One pioneer recorded in his diary that month, "There is a rumor that either J.A. McDonald or his son-in-law, John B. Reilly, will be the first mayor. The railroad crowd is certainly taking control of politics in this neck of the woods."[20] The author of the comment was quite right. Some citizens opposed to the railroad's political domination organized an opposition, but it was of little effect.[21] Miami was a company town and on July 28, 1896, the F.E.C. ticket, without exception (with John B. Reilly as mayor), was voted into office with the help of a large number of black railroad employees who were hurriedly registered before the election.[22] More than one third of the men who voted for incorporation were black citizens. With the exception of Julia Tuttle, pioneers who were here before the railroad had little say in the doings on the north bank of the Miami River.

While Henry Flagler intended to have his way in the formation of Miami, he was what historian Arva Moore Parks called a "benevolent dictator."[23] Despite the fact that there were many heated and sometimes violent arguments on the subject of local politics,[24] Flagler was respected by friend and foe alike. There was no denying the fact that without Henry Flagler, there would have been no city of Miami at all in 1896. His contributions to the development of Miami, aside from the street and public improvements, included land donations for the City of Miami Cemetery, several churches and a public school.

Even though Miami was officially a city after July, it retained something of the pioneer spirit. One newcomer wrote, "In spite of the climatic and other discomforts, this is really a wonderful town. The people are very sociable. Every fellow tries to entertain every other fellow he meets."[25] This spirit was needed several times over the next couple of years when the new city suffered a series of setbacks. On Christmas morning 1896, most of the town burned down in a fast spreading fire. The disaster was followed by the Spanish-American War in 1898, which brought an unruly number of bored and ruffian soldiers to Miami. In September of 1898, Julia Tuttle, still a young woman, died unexpectedly, leaving many of her ambitions for the city unfulfilled. On the heels of that sad event, came the Yellow Fever Epidemic of 1899. Over 240 people were stricken with the disease and Miami

found itself under a quarantine that lasted from September to December of 1899.[26]

Despite the temporary hiatus imposed by fate, Miami continued to grow at the pace initiated by Henry Flagler. In the crude and hastily erected wood frame structures along Avenue D (now Miami Avenue), enterprising businesses such as the Chaille family's Racket Store, the Correll Livery Stable, and Edwin Nelson's Undertaking and Furniture Establishment, resumed their normal routine, and other establishments opened and prospered.[27]

THE CHAILLE FAMILY WAS AMONG THE EARLY MERCHANTS IN DOWNTOWN MIAMI. THE FAMILY HOME WAS BUILT ABOUT 1904 AND STOOD VIRTUALLY UNALTERED AT 22 N.E. 5TH STREET UNTIL ITS DEMOLITION IN 1988. JOSIAH CHAILLE CAME TO MIAMI IN 1899, WAS ELECTED TO THE CITY COUNCIL IN 1918 AND IN 1921 DEVISED THE NEW STREET PLAN THAT GAVE THE CITY OF MIAMI A NEW NUMBERING SYSTEM. (HISTORICAL ASSOCIATION OF SOUTHERN FLORIDA).

Julia Tuttle's strict deed restrictions forbade the sale of alcohol within the city limits[28] causing a vice district to grow just north of the boundaries, but for entertainment in Miami, bicycle racing, poker and baseball were the popular pastimes. In 1906 the first "movie house" opened. Another soon followed called the Alcazar, of which one patron noted, "...no audience but that composed of moles or ground-hogs could sit out an entire performance without suffering asphyxiation."[29] That situation was remedied by a primitive form of air conditioning, an innovative system installed by elevating the auditorium floor, filling the space beneath with a cartload of ice, and propelling the cool air up through the cracks in the floor by the use of a powerful electric fan. The same battered customer who suffered the stifling air before the addition, gave an insight into what life in an early downtown building was like when he noted that the new system,

> ... by a slow-freezing process of the limbs of the audience succeeded in rendering the victims unconscious of the upper strata of heated air enveloping their heads and bodies. Inasmuch as the crude pictures of that period did not impel undivided attention, the audience passed their time enjoying the pleasing sensation of placing warm hands upon ice-cold limbs.

As more businesses opened, the center of commercial activity shifted from Avenue D to what is now Flagler Street. There the size and quality of building increased and stores opened bearing the names of their proprietors. Some, like Burdine and Seybold, are still familiar in the downtown area.

A few architects were among the new arrivals to bring needed talents to the young city. The demand for their services was high. One of the first professional architects in Miami was Walter C. De Garmo, who arrived in 1904.[30] With their arrival the simple wood frame structures gave way to masonry and grew in size and prominence. As a convenience to shoppers who had to suffer the hot sun and frequent rains, a building type became popular in those early days of downtown Miami. It provided a ground floor open arcade over the sidewalk as shelter from the local weather conditions.

Other hotels, like the Halcyon and the Gralynn were built to compete with the tourism business that the Royal Palm originally attracted. Among these, the Halcyon Hotel stood out for its large size and elegant Victorian style complete with medieval inspired tur-

VIEW OF PRESENT-DAY FLAGLER STREET BEFORE THE TURN OF THE CENTURY. THE THREE STORY BRICK BUILDING IS AT THE INTERSECTION OF WHAT IS NOW MIAMI AVENUE. IN THE FOREGROUND IS JOHN SEWELL'S SHOE STORE. SEWELL, WHO ARRIVED AS ONE OF FLAGLER'S RAILROAD WORK SUPERINTENDENTS, WAS LATER MAYOR OF MIAMI. (HISTORICAL ASSOCIATION OF SOUTHERN FLORIDA)

rets. Traces of this building have long disappeared from Miami.

Many of the early residences in downtown Miami also boasted of a Victorian architectural influence. High pitched roofs, turrets and bay windows were not an uncommon sight in Miami during these turn-of-the-century days. The inspiration came from Northern cities where Victorian architecture, especially Queen Anne influenced, was firmly established during the last decades of the nineteenth century as a national style. The national influence on local buildings was concrete evidence that Miami was no longer an isolated frontier, but rather a rapidly growing new urban center.

STREET SCENES

CURRENTLY FLAGLER STREET, THEN 12TH STREET, LOOKING EAST, CIRCA 1908. THE LARGE BUILDING , THIRD FROM THE LEFT, IS PRESENT DAY J. BYRON'S. (HISTORICAL ASSOCIATION OF SOUTHERN FLORIDA)

EARLY RESIDENTIAL STREET IN MIAMI, CURRENTLY N.E. 2ND STREET LOOKING TOWARD THE BAY. (HISTORICAL ASSOCIATION OF SOUTHERN FLORIDA)

PUBLIC BUILDINGS

MIAMI FIRE STATION AND THE CITY HALL, ON PRESENT DAY FLAGLER STREET, DIRECTLY SOUTH OF THE DADE COUNTY COURTHOUSE. THE FIRE STATION WAS DESIGNED BY WALTER C. DE GARMO, THE FIRST ARCHITECT IN MIAMI, AND RESPONSIBLE FOR MANY OF THE EARLY PUBLIC BUILDINGS IN THE AREA. (HISTORICAL ASSOCIATION OF SOUTHERN FLORIDA)

DADE COUNTY COURTHOUSE, AS IT APPEARED AT THE TIME OF CONSTRUCTION IN 1904. THE PRESENT COURTHOUSE BUILDING WAS ERECTED AROUND THIS EARLIER STRUCTURE. (HISTORICAL ASSOCIATION OF SOUTHERN FLORIDA)

31

COMMERCIAL BUILDINGS

THE EARLY COMMERCIAL BUILDINGS HAD A ONE STORY PORCH ACROSS THE FRONT, BUILT RIGHT OVER THE SIDE-WALK. THIS SIMPLE DEVICE WAS A DIRECT RESPONSE TO THE HOT SUN AND RAINY WEATHER OF SOUTH FLORIDA. (HISTORICAL ASSOCIATION OF SOUTHERN FLORIDA).

THE CHAILLE BLOCK, BUILT IN 1914, STILL STANDS, ON NORTH MIAMI AVENUE AND 5TH STREET, AS AN EXCELLENT EX-AMPLE OF THE EARLY COMMERCIAL BUILDINGS OF DOWNTOWN MIAMI.

THE HALCYON HOTEL WAS ONE OF THE ROYAL PALM'S BIGGEST COMPETITORS FOR EARLY MIAMI TOURISM. IT OPENED FOR BUSINESS THE 1905-1906 WINTER TOURIST SEASON AND WAS DEMOLISHED BETWEEN 1937 AND 1939 TO MAKE WAY FOR THE ALFRED I. DUPONT BUILDING, ON EAST FLAGLER STREET AND 2ND AVENUE. ACCORDING TO A *MIAMI HERALD* ARTICLE IN 1937 ARCHITECT STANFORD WHITE DID THE ORIGINAL SKETCH FOR THE BUILDING, FROM WHICH A LOCAL DRAFTSMAN PREPARED THE WORKING DRAWINGS. (HISTORICAL ASSOCIATION OF SOUTHERN FLORIDA)

THE GRALYNN HOTEL, ANOTHER OF THE EARLY HOSTELRIES IN MIAMI, WAS ORIGINALLY BUILT ABOUT 1900 AS A PRIVATE RESIDENCE, NEAR N.E. 6TH STREET AND THE BAY. IN 1908 THE STRUCTURE WAS RELOCATED TO 134 S.E. 1ST AVENUE WHERE IT OPENED AS A HOTEL. YEARS LATER THE GRACEFULLY DETAILED VERANDAS WERE ENCLOSED IN MASONRY. THE BUILDING WAS DEMOLISHED IN 1969. (HISTORICAL ASSOCIATION OF SOUTHERN FLORIDA)

RESIDENTIAL ARCHITECTURE

EARLY RESIDENCES IN MIAMI SHOW THE VICTORIAN INFLUENCE, PARTICULARLY OF THE QUEEN ANNE STYLE, POPULAR AROUND THE TURN OF THE CENTURY. TURRETS, WOOD SHINGLES AND COMBINATION OF MATERIALS ARE AMONG THE SALIENT FEATURES OF THE STYLE, ALL BUT VANISHED FROM TODAY'S DOWNTOWN MIAMI. (HISTORICAL ASSOCIATION OF SOUTHERN FLORIDA)

WORKER CLEARING LAND. (HISTORICAL ASSOCIATION OF SOUTHERN FLORIDA).

"COLORED TOWN"

The black men who came to Dade County to help construct the F.E.C. line were by no means the area's first black residents. Besides the Coconut Grove settlement, a few freed slaves settled here after the Civil War. Prior to emancipation, both the Fitzpatrick and English plantations were operated by relatively large contingents of slaves. Even before that, no doubt, black wreckers and traders from the islands had travelled to the southeast coast. Although they were not the first, the twelve men who came with John Sewell to build the railroad contributed to Miami's history in a very tangible way.

A. W. Brown, a black man and the head of Sewell's crew, threw the first shovel of dirt to begin the Royal Palm Hotel.[31] The construction of Flagler's hotel was only the first of many projects that created a need for an increased labor force. The ensuing activity provided an abundance of jobs where there had

previously been few. Many black men, whose families followed later, moved south to Miami as the call for labor spread. Others came from the Bahamas.

The promise of work was real enough. There were tracks to be laid, roads to be built, hammocks cleared and buildings erected, but as for the weary hopes of those seeking escape from the increasing national trend towards racist violence and deprivation in the bitter aftermath of Reconstruction, the emerging city of Miami would provide little refuge. Through the use of restrictive land deeds and segregation statutes, both of which were standard throughout the nation, many of the white city fathers and mothers forced the establishment of what came to be known as "Colored Town," a small section just west of the railroad tracks, near the Miami city limits.[32] It was the only area in Miami in which black citizens were allowed to buy land.

As the years went by, the black community developed a lively business district and culture of its own, despite the poverty,

BOOKER T. WASHINGTON SCHOOL, BUILT IN 1927, WAS THE FIRST PUBLIC SCHOOL IN THE COUNTY THAT OFFERED BLACKS A HIGH SCHOOL EDUCATION. THE BUILDING IS SIMPLE, WITH SOME CLASSICAL DETAILS, BUT IN KEEPING WITH ITS PRIMARY FUNCTION OF PROVIDING EDUCATION WHERE IT WAS PREVIOUSLY NOT AVAILABLE. THE STRUCTURE IS COMFORTABLE, LIGHT AND AIRY, WITH LARGE WINDOWS ARRANGED IN GROUPS. A NEW SCHOOL BUILDING IS BEING COMPLETED ON THE ADJACENT SITE AND THE ORIGINAL STRUCTURE IS SCHEDULED FOR DEMOLITION.

congestion, and municipal neglect. Avenue G (now N.W. 2nd Avenue) was one of the earliest thoroughfares forged by Flagler's men. It ran through the center of Colored Town. By 1905 the half mile strip of Avenue G in the black district boasted a number of businesses including various general stores, a grocery, an ice cream parlor and a drugstore. Dr. Solomon Frazier, one of the earliest black physicians in Miami, operated the pharmacy out of a building that also served as his home.[33] Dr. William B. Sawyer and others, started the Christian Hospital in 1914, the only hospital in Miami that would care for blacks.[34] *The Industrial Reporter*, the first local black community newspaper was also established by 1904.[35] The Mt. Zion Baptist Church, the Greater Bethel A.M.E. Church, and St. Agnes Episcopal Church were three of the earliest places of worship. Kelsey Pharr came to Miami in 1914, and later opened a funeral parlor serving all of Miami's black communities. He also started the Lincoln Memorial Park, where many of the area's pioneers are buried.[36] During the next few years, many more stores as well as social and spiritual centers would open their doors.

There was a public school in Colored Town in 1896, known as "School Number Two," but it was crowded and severely lacking in sanitary and educational facilities. Not until 1927, with the opening of Booker T. Washington School, did the area have a senior high school. Much of the slack left by the city in the development of public amenities was taken up by public spirited residents of the area such as Florence Gaskins, Julia Bayler and

BUSTLING STREETS OF COLORED TOWN IN THE 1920s. (BLACK ARCHIVES)

THE DORSEY HOUSE IN THE 1920's. NOTICE THE SPIN-
DLE BALUSTRADE DETAILS ON THE FRONT PORCH,
LATER REMOVED. D.A. DORSEY USED HIS INFLUENCE
AS A BUSINESSMAN AND PROPERTY OWNER TO
MAKE SIGNIFICANT CONTRIBUTIONS TO THE BLACK
COMMUNITY. (BLACK ARCHIVES)

goods store on Avenue G. Through wise investments he went on to amass the largest real estate holdings of any black man in the county. Dorsey became the community's first black millionaire. His numerous enterprises included the Dorsey Hotel, a popular gathering place in the 1920s.[38]

Because it was forced to be, in large part, self-sufficient, a more heterogeneous blend of economic levels existed within Colored Town. Richard Toomey opened a law office on Avenue G and was involved in several other projects. The Rev. Samuel Sampson, Dr. Alonzo P. Kelly, M. J. Bodie and Henry Reeves formed a printing company and put out a newspaper called the *Miami Sun*. It was the forerunner of the still active *Miami Times* which was started in 1923.[39] The Mary Elizabeth Hotel, opened in 1918 by Dr. Sawyer, soon became the center of social functions in the community in addition to providing relatively luxurious accommodations for its guests. Also opened in the early years of the twentieth century was Geder Walker's Lyric Theatre which offered movies and live performances.[40]

others who founded a variety of social and service clubs.[37]

Dana Albert Dorsey, who came to Miami in 1896 with the railroad, opened a dry

Race relations, however, from the beginning of the city of Miami, were conducted

THE DORSEY RESIDENCE AS IT APPEARED IN THE 1950s. THE ORIGINAL PORCHES AND FINE DETAILS WERE REPLACED
BY A SIMPLE ONE STORY PORCH. THE TWO STORY, HIPPED ROOF STRUCTURE STILL STANDS, VACANT AND BOARD-
ED UP, AWAITING DEFINITE PLANS FOR ITS RESORATION AND INCORPORATION WITH THE PROPOSED OVERTOWN
HISTORIC VILLAGE. (BLACK ARCHIVES)

THE CHAPMAN RESIDENCE, IN ITS HEYDAY. WILLIAM CHAPMAN WAS A BLACK PHYSICIAN IN COLORED TOWN. (BLACK ARCHIVES).

THE CHAPMAN RESIDENCE WAS BARELY SPARED BY CONSTRUCTION OF I-95.

with the same prejudice prevalent everywhere. Blacks had voted at the incorporation meeting in July 1896, but as instruments of Henry Flagler's political will. Within a few years, Dan Hardie was elected sheriff by advocating "arresting suspicious characters first, and letting them explain afterwards."[41] Most of those he arrested were black men charged with nebulously defined offenses such as vagrancy, vice, and disorderly conduct.[42] In 1915, the same year the Ku Klux Klan was revived in Georgia, a booklet distributed to attract peo-

THE HOUSE HAS BEEN FULLY RESTORED THROUGH A STATE GRANT.

38

FUNERAL IN COLORED TOWN. NOTICE LYRIC THEATER IN THE BACKGROUND, WITH LARGE OPEN ARCHWAY ENTRANCE, BEFORE ITS ALTERATION. (BLACK ARCHIVES)

ple to Miami advised prospective visitors to leave their black drivers at home "as most of the local garages unite in refusing to give service to automobiles driven by colored chauffeurs."[43]

In spite of the economic adversities, racial tensions and oppression, Colored Town developed a cultural identity to be proud of. Inspired carpenter — built houses of Bahamian influence, a successful business district, and in later years, a vibrant entertainment center, all served to make Colored Town one of the most enterprising, interesting and least recognized suburbs of the young city of Miami.

BLACK ARCHITECTURE IN MIAMI

The black workers who helped build white Miami also built their own community. Although there was often a white landlord who provided the initial capital for housing, these houses would later be sold or rented to the same men who built them. In other cases, a black family might manage to save enough to afford to buy a lot to build their own house. This often made the relationship of the owner, the builder and the carpenter a very

close one, if all three were not one and the same. Hulles L. Bragg, an early black contractor in Miami, built his house before 1914 of sturdy Dade County pine, with a deep shaded porch and a generously pitched hip roof, creating a classical sense of proportions and simple detailing.[44]

THE LYRIC THEATER OPENED IN 1919 AS ONE OF THE MAJOR CENTERS OF ENTERTAINMENT FOR THE BLACK COMMUNITY. REGARDED AS THE MOST BEAUTIFUL BUILDING IN THE AREA, IT OFFERED LEGITIMATE THEATER, MOVIES, AND MEETING SPACE IN A COMFORTABLE WELL-APPOINTED INTERIOR. THE EXTERIOR STILL SHOWS EVIDENCE OF ITS FORMER ELEGANCE, THROUGH THE THREE PART COMPOSITION OF THE FACADE AND THE APPLIED CLASSICAL DETAILS.

THE BRAGG RESIDENCE, BUILT BEFORE 1914, IS WELL PRESERVED AND SOLIDLY BUILT. THE VISUAL WEIGHT OF THE LOW HIP ROOF AND WIDE CORNICE IS IN SHARP CONTRAST WITH THE LIGHT, OPEN FEELING OF THE DEEP PORCH AND ITS SLENDER WOOD POSTS. HULLES BRAGG WAS A PROMINENT BUILDER-CONTRACTOR, RESPONSIBLE FOR THE CONSTRUCTION OF MANY SIGNIFICANT BUILDINGS IN THE BLACK COMMUNITY, INCLUDING THE MOUNT ZION BAPTIST CHURCH AND THE NEW MACEDONIA BAPTIST CHURCH.

The early Miami City Directories' listings in the Colored Town section show a number of black carpenters, builders and contractors.[45] It is therefore not uncommon for their work to be patterned after the building vernacular of their hometowns.

Many of the building types found in the early days of Colored Town closely resemble the typical Conch houses of the Bahamas and Key West. These in turn are quite similar to the "cracker" houses of north Florida and the deep South, where Bahamian Conch type had its origins. The conch, a local hard shell mollusk, lends its name to the islanders who lived as wreckers, spongers, fishermen and merchants. The Bahamians who migrated to Key West during the nineteenth century brought with them the knowledge of shipbuilding and applied their experience to the construction of their homes. These houses were built to withstand violent weather. Structures were elevated off the ground on wood posts or stone piers, a measure against storm floods and wood rot, allowing air circulation underneath the house.[46]

The early Conch houses used a post and beam structural system, crossbraced for reinforcement, with mortise and tenon joints pegged together. The houses were generally two stories, with balustraded porches across the front or around two or three sides, on both the first and second story. Gable roofs, door and window shutters and exterior staircases were among other notable features of this building type.[47]

The houses in Miami, and also, Charles Avenue in Coconut Grove, inspired by the Conch vernacular employed the simpler, balloon frame construction method. The elaborate "gingerbread" decorations, pride and trademark of the carpenter-builders in the conch houses after the 1880s, were eliminated for economy. The porches and exterior staircases facilitated circulation for these multi-family dwellings. Buildings were faced with horizontal weatherboards and were basically unadorned.

Another prevalent building type of Colored Town was the shotgun house. Believed to have originated in West Africa, these houses were found in the Bahamas, Key West and throughout the American South.[48] Intended as workers' cottages, they were usually built in rows, very close together and on very small lots. As single family units, they were sub-standard, small and narrow, only one room wide, with gable roofs. Inside, they are normally three rooms deep, arranged one after the other, with circulation directly through

MIAMI CONCHS

THIS BAHAMIAN STYLE BUILDING HAS RETAINED ITS ORIGINAL FEATURES IN SPITE OF ITS AGE. THE WOOD LOUVER WINDOWS THAT REACH ALMOST FLOOR TO CEILING AND THE DOUBLE TIERED PORCH WITH SIMPLE WOOD BALUSTRADE ARE TYPICAL OF THE CONCH BUILDING VOCABULARY. ▶

IN THIS 1915 BUILDING AN OCTAGONAL CORNER TURRET ADDS ANOTHER DIMENSION TO THE BAHAMIAN INFLUENCE ON THE PORCH. THE STRUCTURE WAS DEMOLISHED IN JUNE, 1982. ▼

THE WRAP-AROUND, SHALLOW PORCH OVER THE SIDEWALK IN THIS PRE-1913 GROCERY STORE IS AN EXCELLENT RESPONSE TO ENVIRONMENTAL CONCERNS. IT ABATES THE HOT AFTERNOON SUN, KEEPS THE RAIN OFF THE FRONT AND SERVES AS A VISUAL PIVOT TO THE STREET INTERSECTION. NOTE THE SIMILARITIES WITH ANDERSON'S GENERAL STORE IN SOUTH DADE. ▲

TWO STORY BAHAMIAN STYLE HOUSES SERVE AS BACKDROP TO FUNERAL PROCESSION. (BLACK ARCHIVES) ◀

SHOTGUN HOUSES ARE ONE ROOM WIDE, THREE ROOMS DEEP. THESE SIMPLE, MODEST ROW HOUSES WERE BUILT BY THE HUNDREDS BY LARGE REAL ESTATE DEVELOPERS DURING THE EARLY YEARS OF COLORED TOWN. (ROMER COLLECTION, MIAMI-DADE PUBLIC LIBRARY)

THE FORMER HOME OF ARTEMUS BROWN, BUILT IN 1918, HAS A LARGE DEEP PORCH ACROSS THE FRONT, SUPPORTED ON WOOD POSTS AND DECORATED WITH "GINGERBREAD." THESE BARGEBOARDS, NAMED FOR THE JIGSAW CUT DESIGNS, WERE POPULAR IN THE CONCH HOUSES OF KEY WEST, THE BAHAMAS AND THE VICTORIAN COTTAGES OF THE U.S. MAINLAND, BUT WERE NOT WIDELY USED IN THE MORE MODEST BUILDINGS OF COLORED TOWN. MR. BROWN, WHO CAME TO MIAMI IN 1904, WAS THE FIRST BLACKSMITH IN THE CITY.

the rooms. This linear arrangement of interior spaces gave these houses their name. It was popularly said that one could fire a shotgun through the front door and the shot would go out the back door without even touching any part of the house. Several small groups of the original shotgun houses still stand. Although simple and highly repetitive in appearance and structural expression, they serve as evidence of the humble, struggling beginnings of Miami's black community.

RAILROAD TOWNS

A few years after the F.E.C. line to Miami was completed, work began on extending the railroad farther south. Flagler wanted to make the Florida line an outlet for commerce and tourism from the U.S. to Cuba, the West Indies, and South America. It has been speculated that it was Flagler's intention from the inception of the Miami extension to continue the railroad to a deep water port further south.[49] Flagler himself once said that Miami would "never be more than a fishing village for my hotel guests."[50] A "fishing village" was hardly a good reason to build a railroad. Key West, on the other hand, was already a well established city, had the deepest harbor south of Norfolk, Virginia, and was three hundred miles closer to the

THE FIRST SCHOOL IN LARKINS WAS BUILT ON LAND DONATED BY HOMESTEADER ADAM RICHARDS, IN 1896. THIS BUILDING WAS ERECTED IN 1915 AND IS NOW PART OF THE SUNSET ELEMENTARY SCHOOL. (ROMER COLLECTION, MIAMI-DADE PUBLIC LIBRARY)

proposed Panama Canal than any other U.S. port.

Soon after Flagler's men established themselves in Miami, a corps of engineers was dispatched to conduct exploratory surveys of South Dade, the Everglades and the Florida Keys. They found southwest Dade County almost completely devoid of human habitation. The main exception south of Coconut Grove, besides Cutler, was the small settlement known as Larkins. There, Wilson A. Larkins ran a post office and trading post for the few homesteaders in the area that is now South Miami.[51]

The settlement of most of the southwest Dade region occurred later than that of Miami. Because of its inaccessibility and the undesirable quality of the land, settlers preferred land in other parts of the county when it was still available. Much of South Dade was swampy for a large portion of the year. The federal Swamp Act of 1850 gave each state the right to petition for title to swamp lands. Florida acquired much of southwest Dade in the late 1800s and early 1900s through this legislation. A great deal of it was then bought by large scale realtors who anticipated the

railroad and the partial drainage of the Everglades which began a few years later.[52] There were several homesteads claimed in this area, however, most of the early settlers purchased their land from the U.S. government, the State of Florida, or real estate firms such as the F.E.C.'s Model Land Company.

The Model Land Company was the real estate division of the Florida East Coast Railway. Its representatives controlled a great deal of land in South Dade County; some of it was acquired from the state and other parcels through an agreement with the heirs of Dr. Henry Perrine. The terms of the 1840 land grant to Perrine stipulated that to obtain a final patent to the prescribed township, he had to establish a settler in each 360 acre section of the parcel.[53] James Ingraham, Flagler's representative, assisted the family in complying and obtained a significant portion of the grant for the F.E.C. Once the title to the land was secured, Flagler proceeded with the railroad extension, and the Model Land Company sold excess tracts to other prospective settlers who would in turn provide business for the railroad in both produce shipping and passenger travel.

By 1904, most of the South Dade F.E.C. line was completed. Along the track, usually at the section lines, railroad sidings were constructed. The sidings, some with station houses, became the focal points of the small communities that began to develop around them. Some of these settlements have completely disappeared, but other F.E.C. stops are still familiar names; from north to south the F.E.C. South Dade stations were Kendall, Benson, Key, Rockdale, Perrine, Peters, Goulds, Princeton, Naranja, Modello and Homestead.[54]

For the most part, the railroad towns of Benson, Key, Rockdale and Peters no longer exist. Kendall, the first F.E.C. stop south of Larkins, developed around the station and some early groves. A large portion of land in the Kendall area was purchased from the state in 1883 by the Florida Land and Mortgage Company, which was owned by four British merchants.[55] After plans for the railroad were announced, John Boughton Kendall, a trustee of the company, settled in the area to manage the company's holdings and operate a grove. Most of the residents of Kendall, in the first years of the twentieth century, were Seminole Indians who had two villages in the vicinity.

Goulds, Modello and Naranja grew around the F.E.C. sidings or platforms built for shipping agricultural produce. Perrine was one of the more significant stops on the South Dade line. The F.E.C. built a full sation at Perrine, a home for the section foreman, and another for the station agent. In 1903, the "Town of Perrine" was platted by the Model

Land Company.[56]

The Drake Lumber Company developed the town of Princeton. Gaston Drake's lumber company opened in South Dade as soon as the railroad made shipping possible. Drake's mill provided lumber for much of the building in South Florida including Vizcaya, the Collins bridge to Miami Beach and the Flagler railway extension from Homestead to Key West. Drake named the railroad stop where his company was situated, Princeton, after his alma mater, and built housing near the mill for over one hundred fifty employees. Most of the earliest settlers in the area came as employees of the mill. The Drake mill was dismantled in 1923.[57]

A short distance west of the tracks was the Silver Palm area, established in the late 1890s and named for the beautiful little palm with its silver-backed fronds that grew profusely in the pine forests. Most of the land was covered by slash pines, their huge trunks up to six to eight feet in girth. Clearing enough land to build a home and put the required area under cultivation to "prove-up" a homestead was a back-breaking task. The community grew up around Will Anderson's general merchandise store at the corner of present day S.W. 232nd Street and 157th Avenue. The store supplied a variety of goods to residents who came from many miles around to shop and fraternize at this remote commercial outpost. The intersection now known as Anderson's Corner soon grew to include the Silver Palm Schoolhouse and Lowry Anderson's blacksmith shop. Silver Palm remains one of South Dade's most characteristic and intact rural communities.

BUILT CIRCA 1907 BY PIONEER CHARLES GRAHAM AND NEWLYWED WIFE EMMA LINDGREN, THIS IS ONE OF THE FINEST EXAMPLES OF EARLY FRAME VERNACULAR ARCHITECTURE IN THE SILVER PALM AREA.

SILVER PALM DRIVE

THE SILVER PALM SCHOOL HOUSE WAS BUILT IN 1904. BY CHARLES GROSSMAN, A CARPENTER. IT WAS THE FIRST SCHOOL IN THE SILVER PALM AREA. IT IS PRESENTLY USED AS A PRIVATE RESIDENCE.

ANDERSON'S GENERAL MERCHANDISE STORE WAS BUILT ABOUT 1911. ITS CROSSROADS LOCATION MADE WILL ANDERSON'S STORE A POPULAR STOPPING OFF PLACE. THE BUILDING WAS RESTORED IN 1985.

Further to the west of the railroad tracks lies the area known today as the Redlands. This was the second area open to homesteading in South Dade to attract settlers. Farmers looking for tillable land found deposits of a red soil with a clay and marl compostion in the Redland area — singular so as not to be confused with Redlands, California. The land was high enough not to be flooded in the summer, which made the area more conducive to agriculture. The intersection of S.W. 248th Street and 187th Avenue is a designated local historic district representative of a rural crossroads. Included in the district are three private residences, a church and the Redland Fruit and Spice Park. Contained within the park is the Redland Schoolhouse from 1906 and a horticultural research station built in 1915 and used by the Red Cross in World War I. Also in the park is the oldest house in South Dade, the Mitchell-Bauer House, built in 1902 near S.W. 268th Street and 159th Avenue, and moved to the park in 1982.

TYPICAL RESIDENCE IN THE REDLAND HISTORIC DISTRICT.

REDLAND HISTORIC DISTRICT

THE REDLANDS POST OFFICE AND CANDY STORE STOOD IN WHAT IS NOW THE REDLAND FRUIT AND SPICE PARK. BUILDINGS CONSTRUCTED OF "LOG ENDS" WERE A COMMON SIGHT IN SOUTH DADE BECAUSE THE LOCAL MILLS GAVE THEM AWAY FREE. (ROMER COLLECTION, MIAMI-DADE PUBLIC LIBRARY)

THE MITCHELL-BAUER HOUSE WAS BUILT IN THE REDLAND AREA IN 1902. THE STRUCTURE WAS MOVED TO THE REDLAND FRUIT AND SPICE PARK IN 1983 AND IS UNDERGOING RESTORATION AS A PIONEER HOUSE MUSEUM.

THE REDLAND METHODIST CHURCH WAS BUILT IN 1914 AND IS A BEAUTIFUL EXAMPLE OF A SMALL FRAME CHURCH BUILDING. WILLIAM JENNINGS BRYAN, THE FAMOUS THEOLOGIAN AND ONETIME PRESIDENTIAL CANDIDATE, ONCE SPOKE FROM ITS STEPS.

THE T.A. CAMPBELL RESIDENCE IN HOMESTEAD WAS BUILT IN 1912. THE CAMPBELLS MOVED TO HOMESTEAD IN 1909. THE HOUSE IS A RARE EXAMPLE OF VICTORIAN ARCHITECTURE IN DADE COUNTY. ITS CORNER TOWER IS ITS MOST SIGNIFICANT FEATURE.

In June of 1904, after the first leg of the railroad extension was completed, F.E.C. surveyor J. S. Frederick laid out another new town thirty miles south of Miami at the end of the line.[58] The town, incorporated in 1904, was named Homestead. One of the first pioneers in Homestead was W. D. Horne, who in 1904 opened Homestead's first store to serve the needs of the F.E.C. railroad workers. Horne is credited with many Homestead "firsts." Not only did he open the first store, he was the town's first postmaster, first real estate agent, he opened the first packing house, and he was the first president of the Bank of Homestead.[59]

Florida City, although not planned by the F.E.C., was also spawned by the railroad. Prior to the completion of the F.E.C. line, the Tatum brothers, who within a couple of years would become prominent Miami developers, purchased 22,000 acreas of swampland from the state and subdivided the Miami Land and Development Company subdivision south of Homestead.[60] They dug a canal for drainage,

but long before the job was done, their sales representative, Edward Stiling, began selling the seasonally inundated ten acre farm sites at fifty dollars per acre. Mr. Stiling went to Detroit, Michigan, to sell the Florida lots and attracted thirty families. The settlement was originally named "New Detroit." On November 19, 1911, a plan for "Detroit" was filed in the public records of Dade County, but the name was changed when the citizens voted a preference for "Florida City." Florida City was incorporated in 1914, and one year later had 368 residents.[61]

By the date the first train arrived in Key West on January 22, 1912,[62] families were building homes all the way from the north to the southernmost end of the county and from the Everglades to Biscayne Bay. Curiously, the F.E.C. souvenir brochure commemorating the completion of the railroad to Key West still considered the best thing to be said about Miami was that it had "… no malaria, very few mosquitoes, and an average temperature of seventy-four degrees."[63]

THE MAIN BUSINESS STREET IN HOMESTEAD, FLORIDA, IN 1925. THE OLD TOWN HALL CAN BE SEEN ON THE LEFT, WITH CANVAS AWNINGS. (ROMER COLLECTION, MIAMI-DADE PUBLIC LIBRARY)

SAME SCENE OF KROME AVENUE TODAY. OLD TOWN HALL IN THE FOREGROUND AWAITS RESORATION AS CITY'S POLICE AND FIRE MUSEUM ON THE GROUND FLOOR, WITH COMMUNITY MEETING ROOMS UPSTAIRS.

SOUTH DADE ARCHITECTURE

Among the houses these South Dade settlers built during the railroad era are some of the finest, best preserved and lesser known examples of the early vernacular architecture of Dade County. Proportions and massing are still reminiscent of the Victorian and Queen Anne styles that were popular around the country, but decoration is simple or not used at all. Local buildings date back only to the later phases of those national architectural styles. The difficulties in obtaining building supplies in such a remote location also kept these houses down to a minimum in decorative refinements. The turn-of-the-century residences built in the city of Miami adhered more closely to the esthetic dictates of their urban environment. In South Dade, however, builders let the bold forms, sharp roof contours and the broad porches create a different, simpler beauty. These houses are generally wood frame, balloon construction, two stories in height, with gable and hip roofs. Large windows, often in cross ventilation arrangements, wide porches and spacious interiors, all combine to take advantage of breezes, abate the heat and the sun, and reflect the detached, rural character of the surroundings. The natural environment seems to be part of this architecture, as man and nature complement each other's work.

The slow pace of life in South Dade has changed little. The rural character has prevailed, and although development activity has increased over recent years, density is still relatively low. The early buildings are aging gracefully; the groves still abound around them. The last frontier in Dade County was conquered, but its beauty has not been lost.

THE LINDGREEN RESIDENCE IS ONE OF THE MOST ADMIRED HOUSES IN SOUTH DADE. THE LINDGREEN FAMILY MOVED FROM CENTRAL FLORIDA IN 1895, CLAIMED THE HOMESTEAD IN 1903, AND BUILT THE HOUSE IN 1912.

THE MOBLEY/WOOD HOUSE WAS BUILT IN 1910 OF DADE COUNTY PINE. THE EXTERIOR EXPRESSES FUNCTIONAL BEAUTY THROUGH MULTIPLE MASSES OF TALL GABLE AND HIP ROOFS. THE DEEP PORCH AROUND THREE SIDES OF THE MAIN MASS IS THE MAJOR ELEMENT IN THE SIMPLE BEAUTY OF THE HOUSE, OTHERWISE DEVOID OF ANY DECORATION.

THE PRESTON LEE HOUSE, BUILT IN 1910, HAS MANY SIMILARITIES WITH ITS NEIGHBOR, THE MOBLEY HOUSE. ON BOTH HOUSES THE MAIN MASS HAS THE RIDGE OF THE TALL GABLE PERPENDICULAR TO THE FRONT AND THE SAME ARRANGEMENT OF OPENINGS. HERE THE OPENING OF THE PORCH EXTENDS HORIZONTALLY, PARALLEL TO THE FRONT, BEYOND THE HOUSE'S MORE SOLID AND VERTICAL MASS. MR. LEE WAS A COUNTY COMMISSIONER WHOSE CONTRIBUTIONS INCLUDE THE BUILDING OF THE TAMIAMI TRAIL.

AT CAULEY SQUARE A TWO STORY COMMERCIAL BUILDING AND A SERIES OF SMALL COTTAGES, MOST DATING FROM THE 1920s, HAVE BEEN CONVERTED TO AN ENCLAVE OF ANTIQUE SHOPS, BOUTIQUES, RESTAURANTS AND AN ICE CREAM PARLOR. THE OFFBEAT ARRANGEMENT OF ARCHITECTURAL DETAILS AND FOUND OBJECTS ON THESE SIMPLE STRUCTURES ADD A NEW DIMENSION OF FUN AND IRREVERENCE TO HISTORIC PRESERVATION.

AT CORAL CASTLE, ED LEEDS-KALNIN CREATED A SCULPTURE GARDEN WHICH HE DEDICATED TO HIS "SWEET SIXTEEN" LOST LOVE. ALMOST SINGLE-HANDEDLY AND WITH LIMITED TOOLS, HE SCULPTED MOONS AND PLANTS OUT OF STONE MONOLITHS WEIGHING SEVERAL TONS EACH, BETWEEN 1921 AND THE TIME OF HIS DEATH IN 1951.

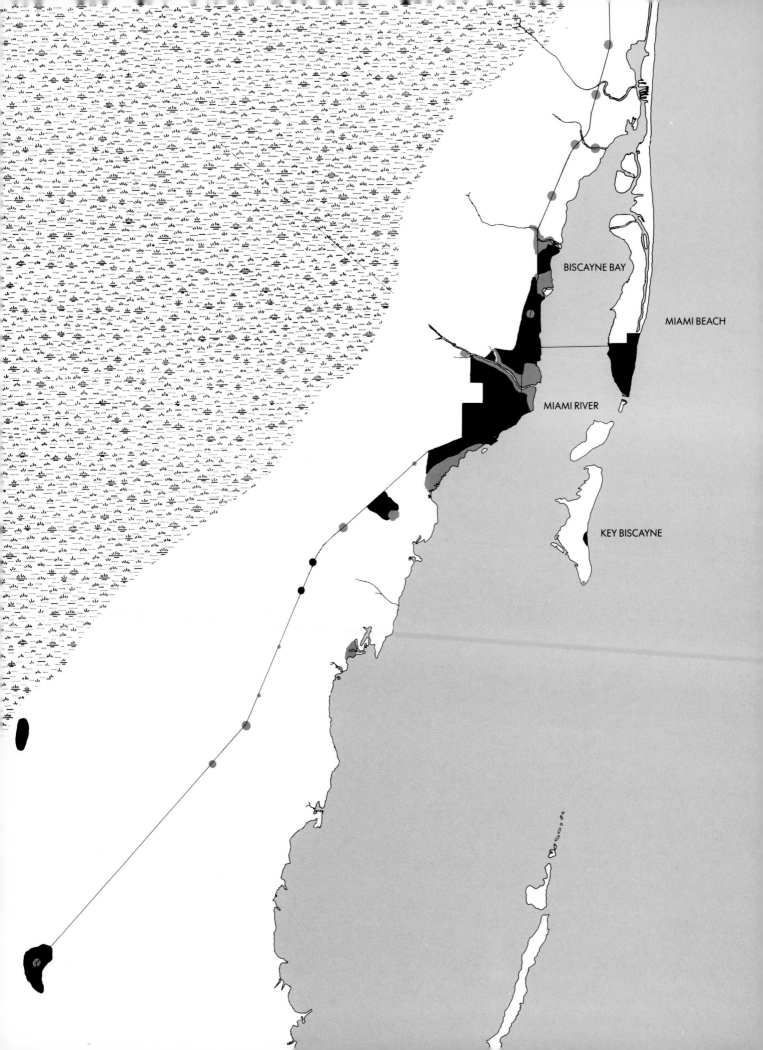

BISCAYNE BAY

MIAMI BEACH

MIAMI RIVER

KEY BISCAYNE

AN EARLY SUBURBAN STREET IN MIAMI. (HISTORICAL ASSOCIATION OF SOUTHERN FLORIDA)

SUBURBIA COMES TO THE FRONTIER

Miami is drawing to itself thousands of the better class of American citizens, men and women of education and character thus building a citizenship made up of the very cream of the population from nearly all the states in the Union. People who have made their wealth elsewhere are seeking Miami in ever increasing numbers for either a winter or a permanent home.[1]

So read *The Lure of the Southland*, a promotional booklet published in 1915. It was one of many pamphlets and brochures distributed in the early 1900's by realtors, builders, banks, businessmen and the F.E.C. extolling the virtues of the new city. These publications described Miami's subtropical beauty in the purplest of prose and laced it with such enticing statistical claims as "the world's greatest per capita consumption of cement," and "a mile of sidewalk laid a month."[2]

After the city of Miami was laid out by Flagler's surveyors, a few small residential subdivisions were platted on its outskirts. As each new passenger train arrived at the Miami station packed full of eager young families, expansion beyond the city limits continued and suburban neighborhoods were planned to accommodate new residents. With Julia Tuttle gone and Henry Flagler preoccupied with the Key West extension, the path was cleared for a second generation of land promoters to take advantage of the appeal of the mainland United States' first subtropical urban area.

Until 1903, when the Miami Avenue bridge was built across the Miami River, the only way to cross the river was by ferry or small boat. The bridge facilitated the development of the south bank. In 1903,[3] the Patterson and Olive subdivision was platted as a residential neighborhood. Soon sturdy, unpretentious, two-story homes were erected there, contructed of Dade County pine, or rusticated blocks with details such as oolitic limestone piers, leaded windows, and fishscale shingles.

It was not the construction of middle-class neighborhoods that captured the inter-

THE BRICKELL FAMILY ON THE PORTICO OF THEIR BRICKELL AVENUE HOME. THE HOUSE WAS DEMOLISHED IN 1963. (HISTORICAL ASSOCIATION OF SOUTHERN FLORIDA)

est of the public and business community though. The large estates along the bayfront and their glamorous winter inhabitants did. Prior to the advent of the railroad, the Miami area was a crude frontier in the eyes of the more refined. After 1900, it was proclaimed exotic.

BRICKELL AVENUE

The most desirable bayfront land south of the Miami River down to Coconut Grove was owned by the Brickells. Mary Brickell, William's wife, directed the family real estate interests. She was a shrewd woman and her cautious, but sometimes eccentric methods of doing business significantly increased the family fortune. Mrs. Brickell was also extremely generous. Described as looking something like Queen Victoria and as being every bit as imperious,[4] Mary Brickell was reputed to have doled out thousands of dollars in cash from her cupped apron to families

"VILLA SERENA," BUILT BETWEEN 1911 & 1915, WAS THE HOME OF WILLIAM JENNINGS BRYAN, FAMOUS ORATOR & THREE TIME PRESIDENTIAL CANDIDATE. THE HOUSE EXPRESSES AN EXCELLENT ENVIRONMENTAL DESIGN. IT IS BUILT AROUND A CENTRAL COURTYARD THAT FACES BISCAYNE BAY, WITH BROAD, OVERHANGING TILE ROOFS AND AN ABUNDANCE OF WINDOWS, GROUPED TOGETHER FOR MAXIMUM VENTILATION.

THIS BAYFRONT HOUSE WAS BUILT IN 1916 BY L.T. HIGHLEYMAN, A MIAMI CITY COUNCILMAN AND DEVELOPER OF THE POINT VIEW SUBDIVISION.

THE HIGHLEYMAN HOUSE WAS DISFIGURED IN THE 1970's BY AN UNSYMPATHETIC ADDITION ACROSS THE FRONT, DURING THE TIME WHEN IT WAS KNOWN AS THE COMMODORE ROWING AND SAILING CLUB.

ABANDONED AND DETERIORATED FOR SEVERAL YEARS, THE HIGHLEYMAN HOUSE WAS DEMOLISHED IN THE SUMMER OF 1988.

desirous of building homes. At the time of her death in 1922, she had $98,543.80 outstanding in unsecured loans.[5]

In 1905, the Brickell Addition to Miami was subdivided,[6] breaking up the bayfront land into large estate sized lots which fronted on Brickell Avenue. The scenic bayfront property had always been the most sought after. Soon large private homes rose along the bayshore. Until recent years, Brickell Avenue displayed a beautiful variety of splendidly individual estates which blended with the lush, natural subtropical setting. The street came to be called "Millionaires' Row." Louis C. Tiffany built a home there, as did William Jennings Bryan, and Carl Fisher of Illinois who had just built the Indianapolis Speedway and would soon begin developing a small strip of land opposite Biscayne Bay known as "the Beach." The most prominent resident of the Brickell area was James Deering, whose Villa Vizcaya became a national showcase even before it was completed.

LARGE, ELEGANT WATER FRONT HOMES LINED UP THE EXCLUSIVE POINT VIEW AREA JUST EAST OF BRICKELL AVENUE. THESE HOUSES HAVE BEEN REPLACED WITH HIGH RISE CONDOMINIUMS IN RECENT YEARS, IN ORDER TO TAKE BETTER ADVANTAGE OF THE VALUABLE REAL ESTATE. (HISTORICAL ASSOCIATION OF SOUTHERN FLORIDA)

THE MITCHELL-BINGHAM RESIDENCE, BUILT BETWEEN 1919 AND 1922, IS REMINISCENT OF THE NEW ENGLAND SHINGLE STYLE POPULAR AROUND THE TURN OF THE CENTURY. ANNIE MITCHELL'S BROTHER WAS LOUIS COMFORT TIFFANY, THE FAMOUS GLASS DESIGNER. HIS OWN ESTATE, A FEW HUNDRED FEET AWAY, HAD AN OCTAGON SHAPED HOUSE, DESCRIBED BY A NEIGHBOR IN A MIAMI HERALD ARTICLE AS "ONE OF THE ODDEST LOOKING PLACES" HE HAD EVER SEEN. A PORTION OF THIS HOUSE IS BEING PRESERVED AS PART OF THE ATLANTIS CONDOMINIUM.

"PALM COURT," BUILT IN 1919, HAD A STEEP GABLE ROOF OF SPANISH TILES AND A PROJECTING CENTRAL BAY IN THE SHAPE OF A TURRET. THE LUSH LANDSCAPING AND THE PALM-LINED DRIVEWAY CONTRIBUTED TO THE BEAUTY OF THIS WATERFRONT MANSION.

THIS BAYFRONT MANSION WAS BUILT IN 1920 AS THE HOME OF DR. JAMES M. JACKSON, WHO LIVED THERE UNTIL HIS DEATH IN 1924.

THE BRIGGS RESIDENCE, CALLED "VILLA REGINA," WAS BUILT BEFORE 1920. ITS CLASSICAL DETAILS, SIZE AND ELEGANCE ARE EXPRESSIVE OF THE LIFESTYLE OF BRICKELL AVENUE IN ITS HEYDAY. IT WAS DESIGNED BY ARCHITECT GORDON MAYER.

HIGH RISE CONDOMINIUMS NOW STAND ON THE SITE OF THE HOUSES PICTURED ABOVE.

A 1934 AERIAL VIEW OF THE VIZCAYA PALACE AND GARDENS SHOWS THE DENSE VEGETATION OF THE HARDWOOD HAMMOCK. JUST BEYOND THE MAIN HOUSE IN THE CENTER OF THE PHOTO ARE THE ATTENDANT FARM BUILDINGS. IN THE BACKGROUND IS THE SPARSELY POPULATED "ROADS" SECTION OF THE CITY OF MIAMI. (ROMER COLLECTION, MIAMI-DADE PUBLIC LIBRARY)

THE VILLA VIZCAYA

The Villa Vizcaya epitomizes the Brickell area's display of wealth, quality of construction and sometimes good taste. It is the most grandiose residential building project ever undertaken in Miami. Construction of the villa and grounds took over ten years to complete and employed over one thousand men. The estate covered 180 acres and included a seventy room villa, formal gardens, undisturbed hammock forests, farm and farm buildings.

The family of Vizcaya's owner, James Deering, had made a fortune by merging its farm machinery business, the Deering Harvesting Machine Company, to form International Harvester in 1902. James, an eccentric millionaire bachelor, sailed the world in search of the ideal location to build a home. By 1910, he had purchased from the Brickell family the large bayfront property and had assembled the team or architects to execute his design.

F. Burrall Hoffman, Jr. was the principal

architect and Paul Chalfin was associate architect, responsible for the interiors and furnishings, while Diego Suarez was the landscape architect. Both Hoffman and Chalfin studied at Harvard and L'Ecole des Beaux Arts, which accounts for the classical training expressed in their work. Hoffman, a young man of twenty-eight, was at the time working in New York with the firm of Carrere and Hastings,[7] the architects for Flagler's Ponce de Leon Hotel in St. Augustine. Diego Suarez graduated from the Academia dei Belle Arti in Florence as an architectural designer.[8] Most of his knowledge about Italian gardens came from his apprenticeship in the restoration of the Renaissance gardens of the Villa La Pietra in Florence and other landscape designs executed during his stay in Italy.

Design inspiration for Vizcaya came from Italian villas and gardens, combining features from High Renaissance, Mannerist, Baroque and Rococo styles. The building mass, with four projecting corner towers linked by curtain walls leading to the central courtyard, reflects fifteenth century Renaissance fortress influence, "all the primitive 'donne' of a Sforza stronghold."[9] The variety

60

VILLA VIZCAYA. EAST VIEW FACING BISCAYNE BAY.

VILLA VIZCAYA. MAIN ENTRANCE SHOWING NEW GLASS ROOF OVER CENTRAL COURTYARD.

VILLA VIZCAYA. GARDEN VIEW.

in the building's facades is a Mannerist trait, much practiced in the suburban villa designs of Giulio Romano.[10] But the use of the central courtyard and the cross ventilation it affords to all the spaces opening out to it is an excellent response to the local climate. The gardens, with their expanding axial vistas across parterres and terraces that culminate in a variety of pavilions, fountains and sculpture, clearly portray the movement and theatrics of Baroque design. The controlled views created by the tall trees and the raised casino, however, are Mannerist stylistic features. This manipulation of vistas through landscaping had not been an intentional affectation, but rather, a means of correcting the blinding glare from the lake at the end of the gardens. When Suarez visited the work in progress, he realized his scheme did not translate effectively from the model to the actual site. The design had to be revised by adding the raised casino pavilion in front of the lake in order to ease the sun's reflection created by the southern orientation.[11] The most dramatic effect achieved at Vizcaya occurs on the bayfront elevation. The endless view of the bay is framed through two curved arms that reach out to the water, creating the typical Baroque concave front "piazza," in this case a small harbor for yachts to dock. In front of this space a large stone barge with classical statuary seems to float out on the endless sea, its function actually being to act as a breakwater against storms.

Vizcaya was as contrived a home as it is a successful museum—it was a whimsical showplace to be admired for its grandeur and opulence, not a real home for day to day living. The single major accomplishment of Vizcaya was the contribution it made to the development of Miami. The huge labor force imported for its construction included skilled carpenters, masons, artists and many other fine craftsmen, most of whom remained in the area. This large contingent of high quality workers left its imprint beyond the walls of Vizcaya during the building boom that ensued after its completion.

AERIAL VIEW OF THE CHARLES DEERING ESTATE. DEERING MANSION ON THE RIGHT. ORIGINAL RICHMOND COTTAGE TO THE LEFT.

CHARLES DEERING ESTATE

James Deering's older brother, Charles, also built a beautiful mansion on Biscayne Bay, further to the south, in the pioneer town of Cutler. The Charles Deering Estate is one of the finest bayfront properties in Dade County, a rich treasure trove of history, botany, architecture, and archaeology. The estate is significant for its legacy to pioneer life, as represented in the 1896 Richmond House, but just as important for the glimpse it presents into the life of one of the early industrialists to build their winter homes in Miami.

Charles Deering graduated from Annapolis and served as a naval attache in Spain for several years. Charles studied art in Paris and also pursued the subjects of botany, ornithology, literature, and naval affairs. Compared to his socially-oriented brother, James, Charles was considered reclusive. According to his biographer, Walter Dill Scott, "the idle chatter of many 'social' occasions was to him an unendurable bore." (Scott, p. 7).** While unconfirmed newspaper accounts claimed that James threw lavish parties to show off his Vizcaya palace to the likes of the Ziegfeld Follies, brother Charles found pleasure in his rare books and Spanish art collections. He enjoyed the romantic solitude of his two medieval castles by the sea in Spain, away from his business responsibilities as chairman of the family-owned company, International Harvester.

Charles moved to South Florida circa 1911 and settled in the area then known as Buena Vista, near present-day Northeast 40th Street and Biscayne Boulevard. There he cleared much of the land, planted citrus groves, constructed miles of canals and installed an irrigation system. He cultivated a variety of plants, particularly citrus, mangoes and avocados. Deering conducted horticultural experiments and planted seeds exported from various areas of the world. Charles also enjoyed animals, especially birds, and built several large aviaries on his property. He bred many varieties of waterfowl including ducks, pheasant, geese, cranes, swans, herons, and pelicans. His efforts attracted the attention of naturalists and botanists who visited his Buena Vista estate to photograph and inventory his collections. Plans for a house were drawn by architect Clinton McKenzie, but never materialized, for Charles soon began to feel the pressure of Miami's growth in his own backyard. Miami's northward expansion was primarily centered around the railroad stops. The railroad towns of Buena Vista, Lemon City and Little River would soon grow large enough to fuse into one continuous suburban extension of greater Miami. Talk of a major thoroughfare near his property, connecting Miami with points north, con-

DEERING ESTATE. AERIAL VIEW WITH BOAT BASIN IN FOREGROUND.

vinced Charles to move from Buena Vista. By the time the Dixie Highway rolled into town, Charles Deering was in Cutler, away from Miami and the rumbling of the railroad. Today the walled-in residential development of Bay Point at Biscayne Boulevard has paved over the first Charles Deering Estate.

Mr. Deering had been acquiring property in the Cutler area since 1914. Cutler was one of Miami's earliest recorded settlements, established in the late 1890s. The small town consisted of houses and stores, a post office, a school, and the Richmond Cottage. The rear portion of the cottage, built in 1896, was the residence of the S.H. Richmond family. In 1900 they built an addition facing the bay, and began operation as a hotel. In 1916 Charles bought the Richmond Inn and started to develop the property. The short lived town of Cutler was assimilated by the Deering Estate and all of the early buildings, except the Richmond Inn, were razed. In an act not too often seen in Miami, Deering had reclaimed the wilderness for his own enjoyment.

Charles Deering turned the Richmond Cottage into his residence during his early years of occupancy, while a larger stone house was built by 1922, adjacent to the old inn. The main house was

designed by Phineas E. Paist, an associate architect of Vizcaya, and later one of the principal architects for Coral Gables. The house was built like a fortress, more like Deering's Spanish castles than the graceful, wood frame structures of the Richmond Cottage.

If James Deering's Vizcaya was a showplace of conspicuous wealth, the Charles Deering Estate was a private sanctuary for his treasures. The structure is fireproof, with thick, poured concrete walls and overhangs to keep direct sunlight away from the precious paintings and rare books. There is no kitchen or dining room; both activities were relegated to the old Richmond Cottage. One of the most remarkable features of the building is the cellar, where, behind a door camouflaged as a bookshelf, a 12 inch thick combination safe steel door opens yet another treasure — a large, prohibition era wine cellar, stocked with the finest libations of the times, including rare 19th century European wines.

Charles, like his brother, could afford all the luxury, and excess of Vizcaya. Instead, the stone mansion is somber, austere and even clumsy in its design. In sharp contrast to the fine designs that architect Phineas Paist executed throughout Coral Gables and in the Miami Federal Courthouse

63

DEERING MANSION IN THE FOREGROUND, RICHMOND COTTAGE TO THE LEFT.

building, the Deering mansion has little of the charm of his other Miami buildings. It appears more like a medieval fortress by the sea. The arcaded porch that overlooks the bay combines pointed, flat and semicircular arches, all in one composition. Stucco surfaces on the porch ceiling and high on the walls are crudely detailed with "X" thumb print marks etched into the wet cement.

If the design of the stone house is somewhat tongue-in-cheek and irreverent, Charles Deering's high respect for nature and for the undisturbed beauty of the location are clearly stated. When Charles moved to the property in 1922 he found himself surrounded by over 400 acres of wilderness. The tract included hardwood hammocks, pine woods, mangrove forests and aquatic turtle grass flats, much of which has returned to its relatively undisturbed natural state. Charles extensively landscaped the area around the housing compound with a well-manicured lawn, ornamental plants, and a small orchard of fruit trees. Charles surrounded the boat basin, 200 feet in diameter, with plantings of large royal palms and coconut palms, creating a beautiful grove.

Centuries of life in South Florida lay hidden within the grounds of the Deering Estate. Archaeological excavations indicate the area was first occupied by PaleoIndians as early as 8000

RICHMOND COTTAGE BEFORE ALTERATIONS. CIRCA 1905.

B.C. A recently exposed site nearby has revealed ancient fossils of extinct dire wolves, bison, and sloths which may have once roamed the grounds. Also located within the property is a prehistoric Indian village and burial mound, and the remains of the historic pioneer settlement of Cutler.

Known as the jewel of South Dade, the Charles Deering Estate is one of the most significant and best preserved sites in Dade County. Due to the efforts of preservationists, environmentalists, and concerned officials, the estate was recently saved from development. The State of Florida bought the property and leases it to the Dade County Park and Recreation Department. Plans for re-use are currently in the development stages.

A VETERAN'S DAY PARADE MARCHES DOWN MAIN HIGHWAY IN COCONUT GROVE'S BUSINESS DISTRICT IN 1925. (ROMER COLLECTION. MIAMI-DADE PUBLIC LIBRARY)

COCONUT GROVE

With the constuction of Vizcaya, the bayfront acquired a character of luxury and privilege from the Miami River to Coconut Grove. Although the residents of Coconut Grove discouraged Henry Flagler from building his railroad through their rustic hamlet, the arrival of the railroad in Miami brought a development boom there, too. Large tracts of property along the bay south of the village were sold during those years by J. W. Ewan, former manager of the Fort Dallas property. William Deering, the father of James, built there as did his partners in the International Harvester Company, the McCormicks. William J. Matheson, a chemical dye manufacturer, was introduced to the area in 1904, by his son Hugh who was a student at the Florida Adirondack School, now Ransom-Everglades.[12] He was followed by a slew of wealthy northern industrialists, such as John Bindley, one-time president of Pittsburgh Steel; Arthur Curtis James, another railroad magnate; and Dr. Leon H. Baekland, the in-

ventor of "bakelite," the predecessor of plastic.

Coconut Grove was not only for the wealthy, though. F. C. Bush and Walter C. DeGarmo, residents of the area, formed the Coconut Grove Development Company and subdivided Coconut Grove Park in 1911.[13] It encompassed a large tract of land south of the village between what is now Douglas Road and Main Highway.

In 1912, the Sunshine Fruit Company filed a plat for the Bayview Road Subdivision, formerly lot M of J. W. Ewan's Ewanton Heights.[14] Within a few years, there were a number of cottages erected on this street, mostly by employees of the Sunshine Fruit Company. The first Miss Harris' School opened at the head of Bayview Road in 1914.[15] It was one of the earliest private girls' schools in Dade County.

The Sunshine Fruit Company was founded in 1910 by H. de B. Justison to manage the groves of absentee owners.[16] They soon became involved in real estate and after Bayview Road, subdivided the Sunshine Villas, Justison and Franklin Subdivision (St.

65

THE PLYMOUTH CONGREGATIONAL CHURCH WAS ORGANIZED IN 1897 BY SOME OF THE MOST PROMINENT EARLY CITIZENS OF COCONUT GROVE. THIS BUILDING WAS ERECTED IN 1917 IN A STYLE INSPIRED BY A SPANISH MISSION CHURCH IN MEXICO. IT IS CONSTRUCTED OF LOCAL OOLITIC LIMESTONE.

"FOUR WAY LODGE" WAS THE HOME OF WILLIAM MATHESON, INDUSTRIALIST AND OWNER OF A COCONUT PLANTATION WHICH ENCOMPASSED MOST OF KEY BISCAYNE. THE HOUSE IS REMARKABLY SIMILAR TO BRYAN'S VILLA SERENA. (HISTORICAL ASSOCIATION OF SOUTHERN FLORIDA)

"CHEROKEE LODGE," NAMED FOR THE CHEROKEE ROSES THAT ONCE GREW ON THE PROPERTY, WAS BUILT AROUND 1917 IN AN ENGLISH COTTAGE STYLE. THE HOUSE WAS OWNED BY EMALINA McMILLAN, NIECE OF JOHN BINDLEY, THE PRESIDENT OF THE PITTSBURGH STEEL COMPANY. MR. BINDLEY'S ESTATE, "EL JARDIN," IS LOCATED ACROSS THE STREET AND SERVES NOW AS THE CARROLLTON SCHOOL.

Gaudens Road), and a number of other residential neighborhoods in Coconut Grove. The company also opened the Sunshine Inn and cottages as a hotel for prospective clients, but soon found themselves catering to Northern tourists. James Whitcomb Riley, *"the Hoosier poet,"* was one of the many regular guests to visit the inn.

North of the village of Coconut Grove, the area known as Silver Bluff began as a subdivision in 1911, on land that was formerly part of the estate of J. T. Peacock. The plat for Silver Bluff was filed by John and Edith Gifford and Beverly and Margarita Peacock.[17] The subdivision was named for a geological feature in the area, a limestone bluff, portions of which can still be seen along South Bayshore Drive. Silver Bluff was incorporated in 1919, as was Coconut Grove, but in 1925, both were annexed to the city of Miami.[18]

"THE PAGODA" WAS BUILT IN 1902 BY PAUL C. RANSOM AS THE BAYFRONT WINTER CAMPUS OF THE FLORIDA ADIRONDACKS SCHOOL, NOW KNOWN AS RANSOM-EVERGLADES. CONSTRUCTION IS OF DADE COUNTY PINE, FACED IN VERTICAL BOARD AND BATTEN AND ELEVATED OFF THE GROUND ON LIMESTONE PIERS. THE NAME IS DERIVED FROM THE PAGODA-STYLE MASSING OF THE BUILDING. THE GROUPED WINDOWS AND CORNER PORCHES ARE AMONG THE MANY ASSETS OF THIS HANDSOME SCHOOL BUILDING.

THE TROLLEY ROUTE DOWN PRESENT DAY FLAGLER STREET, STARTED IN 1906. THE TATUM BROTHERS LINKED MIAMI WITH THE AREA WEST OF THE RIVER, BUT THE VENTURE SOON FAILED. THE TROLLEYS WERE REINTRODUCED IN 1915. (HISTORICAL ASSOCIATION OF SOUTHERN FLORIDA)

THE SUBURBS

By the earliest years of the 1900s, most of the bayfront land surrounding the city of Miami was reserved for large estates and their owners. But unlike what publications such as *The Lure of the Southland* implied, the majority of the new population were not members of the leisure class. Many people came to take advantage of the newly created work that was a result of the soaring building industry. Suburban expansion was already extending north and south of the city. During this time, it also began to move farther west, something that was impossible before work began on the Everglades drainage project.

As a result of the 1850 Swamp Act, Florida received 20,000,000 acres of swampland.[19] In 1855, the Trustees of the Internal Improvement Fund, composed of the governor and several cabinet members, was formed by the state to manage public lands. Action was delayed by the Civil War, but between 1888 and 1905, the Trustees received a variety of proposals regarding Everglades drainage. Some individual and corporate interests expressed opposition, or at least reservation at man's contemplated tampering with nature on such a large scale, but with each escalation of price and interest in South Florida real estate, the pressure for action magnified regardless of the potential consequences. In 1904, Napoleon Broward was elected governor on a pro-drainage platform and in 1905 the Board of Drainage Commissioners was founded and endowed with the authority to create a system of drainage canals between the Everglades and Biscayne Bay.[20]

The sale of Everglades land and dredging began at about the same time. Tracts of land were sold in both small and large parcels, some in the tens of thousands of acres. Two of the largest purchasers in Dade County were Richard J. Bolles who bought swampland in North Dade, and the Tatum Brothers in South Dade and around Miami. They immediately subdivided some portions of their holdings and began selling soggy lots on the promise of the infallibility of drainage technology. But drainage produced

THE MIAMI CANOE CLUB WAS A POPULAR ATTRACTION FOR VISITORS TO THE MIAMI RIVER DURING THE 1920s. THE REMAINING STRUCTURES FROM THIS PHOTOGRAPH, NOW PART OF A HISTORIC DISTRICT, ARE BEING REHABILITATED TO SERVE AS A BED AND BREAKFAST COMPLEX.

both less and more than was foretold. Less in the sense that much of the land that was turned over in sales was not rendered entirely habitable as was promised with the opening of the run-off canals. One woman in South Dade was inspired to poetry after a year or two on her "post drainage" property. It began:

> There was a wet man.
> He had a wet wife
> And four wet children
> He lived a wet life....[22]

The Drainage Program resulted in more than was anticipated in the form of environmental damage. Many of the fresh water springs and rivers along the coastal ridge dried up. The Miami River was the most seriously affected. The river had been a key factor in the area's development since prehistoric Indians first established camps and villages along its banks and travelled in dugout canoes between the coast and the Everglades. The first white settlers were also drawn to the river where they built homes, coontie

mills, trading posts, and military forts. Henry Flagler graced the river's mouth with the impressive Royal Palm Hotel in 1896. Local residents and tourists appreciated the beauty of the river, and sight-seeing tours and attractions were popular in the early 1900s. Commercial Indian villages were established along the river, such as Coppinger's and Musa Isle, which offered alligator wrestling and native crafts. However, the Drainage Program called for dredging the river and extending it to lake Okeechobee as the Miami Canal. The rock which formed a natural dam and rapids at the river's head (near present day 27th Avenue.) was dynamited. With that act the clear water of the river was permanently darkened with the flow of Everglades muck, dead fish and alligators that rushed toward Biscayne Bay that day in 1909. Salt water intrusion gradually changed the balance of life in and around the river. Today the Miami River is a "working river," a commercial artery and an international point of entry which still offers a unique perspective on life in Southeast Florida.

THE WARNER RESIDENCE WHEN FINISHED IN 1912 WAS ONE OF THE MOST ELEGANT HOUSES IN THE EMERGING SUBURB WEST OF THE MIAMI RIVER. THE SOUTHERN STYLE NEO-CLASSIC REVIVAL HOUSE HAS POURED CONCRETE COLUMNS AND FINELY CRAFTED INTERIOR WOOD DETAILS, SUCH AS THE WELL PRESERVED CENTRAL STAIRCASE. THE WARNER FAMILY OPERATED MIAMI'S FIRST FLORAL BUSINESS FROM THE DOWNSTAIRS OF THIS HOUSE UNTIL THE 1970's. THE BUILDING IS CURRENTLY USED AS PROFESSIONAL OFFICES. (DOLLY McINTYRE COLLECTION)

THE B. B. TATUM RESIDENCE WAS BUILT BETWEEN 1910 AND 1913. THE TATUM BROTHERS COMPANY WAS ONE OF THE LARGEST REAL ESTATE DEVELOPMENT FIRMS IN MIAMI AT THE TIME. THE HOUSE IS TYPICAL OF THE WOOD FRAME BUILDING VERNACULAR OF SOUTH FLORIDA.

A great deal of easternmost land in the Everglades did dry out and most people saw the events of those years as unmitigated progress. Certainly the path was cleared for further development, even though it would be a few more years before the population demanded the extra space.

In 1906, another bridge was constructed over the Miami River at the foot of Flagler Street. The bridge and a short-lived trolley car line that ran from there east on Flagler and then along N.E. 2nd Avenue to the train depot, were part of the development schemes of the Tatum Brothers Company.[23]

Smiley, Bethel and John Tatum came to Miami at the turn of the century. Bethel Tatum purchased a half interest in the *Miami Metropolis*, but soon joined in a partnership with his brothers to form a real estate development company. Over the next few years, the Tatums filed plans for large subdivisions all over the county. Close to Miami, on a large tract of land near the Miami River, they opened the Lawrence Estate Park Subdivision in 1912.[24] It soon became one of the most popular residential subdivisions around Miami.

In 1913, Mrs. Brickell put lots on the market in the Riverside Subdivision,[25] just east of the Tatum's Lawrence Estate Park. Riverside

MASONRY VERNACULAR RESIDENCE IN THE RIVERSIDE AREA, BUILT BETWEEN 1914 AND 1918, OF RUSTICATED CONCRETE BLOCKS.

JOHN B. McKENZIE, ONE OF THE MOST ACCOMPLISHED STONE MASONS IN MIAMI, BUILT THIS MISSION INSPIRED OOLITIC LIMESTONE HOUSE ABOUT 1913.

THIS WAS THE HOME OF THE ARTHUR BRIGHAM FAMILY, BUILT IN 1916. THE STRUCTURE BECAME WELL-KNOWN IN SUBSEQUENT YEARS AS ONE OF GERTIE WALSH'S HOUSES OF ILL-REPUTE. IT IS STILL STANDING ON WEST FLAGLER STREET AND 29TH AVENUE.

THE ELMIRA CLUB, POPULARLY KNOW AS THE "HUNTING LODGE," WAS BUILT IN 1909, ON N.E. 68TH STREET AND THE BAY, AS THE CLUBHOUSE FOR THE ELMIRA SUBDIVISION, PLATTED THAT SAME YEAR BY A GROUP OF RESIDENTS FROM ELMIRA, NEW YORK.

was a small subdivision between today's S.W. 7th and 8th Avenues, but it was expanded in 1919 by the Brickells and renamed Riverview.[26] Riverside, however, remained as the popular neighborhood name. Modest but comfortable homes were built there, many of them personally financed by Mary Brickell.

North of Miami, homesteads fell like a row of dominoes into suburban conversion. The Mary Brickell, and the Baldwin and Oxar Subdivisions were platted right on the north end of the city in the late 1890s. Between 1910 and 1918, the bayfront land extending to the north was carved up into residential lots. The Biscayne Park, Miramar, Bayside, Bayonne, Edgewater, Bird, Banker's Park, Broadmoor, and Sandricourt Subdivisions[27] were laid out between the city limits and Buena Vista. With the exception of Biscayne Park which was owned by the Tatums, most of these subdivisions were laid out by relatively small landowners who were local residents.

The development of the new subdivisions north of the early city of Miami, was boosted by the reopening of the Tatum brothers' trolley car line. Although the Tatums' first attempt to operate a mass transit system failed, a second trolley line was reintroduced in 1915. It reached as far north as Buena Vista and was soon connected with an adjoining line that crossed the county bridge to Miami Beach.

THIS FINE FRAME HOUSE WAS BUILT IN THE MIAMI KNOWLTON SUBDIVISION IN THE EARLY 1900s. IT WAS DEMOLISHED IN 1988.

THE PATTERSON AND OLIVE SUBDIVISION WAS ONE OF THE EARLIEST RESIDENTIAL SUBURBS SOUTH OF THE MIAMI RIVER. THIS STONE AND WOOD FRAME HOUSE WAS BUILT THERE (NOW S.E. 6TH STREET) BETWEEN 1911 AND 1913. ITS CLASSICAL DETAILS AND LEADED WINDOWS MAKE THE BUILDING PARTICULARLY NOTEWORTHY.

AT THE SAME TIME MIAMI'S SUBURBS WERE DEVELOPING, LOCAL AGRICULTURAL PRODUCTION WAS ALSO EXPANDING. THE WILLIAM MATHESON FAMILY OF COCONUT GROVE PURCHASED MOST OF KEY BISCAYNE IN 1909 AND BEGAN A COCONUT PLANTATION. ABOVE (RIGHT) IS THE PLANTATION BARN, BUILT IN 1917. IT WAS DEMOLISHED IN 1982. ONE WORKER COTTAGE SIMILAR TO THE ONE DEPICTED HERE (LEFT) REMAINS. (ROMER COLLECTION, MIAMI-DADE PUBLIC LIBRARY)

ANOTHER PERSON PROMINENTLY INVOLVED IN PRODUCE FARMING WAS GEORGE B. CELLON. CELLON MOVED TO SOUTH FLORIDA AROUND 1900 AND STARTED LARGE AVOCADO AND MANGO GROVES JUST NORTH OF MIAMI WHERE HE DEVELOPED A NUMBER OF NEW COMMERCIAL VARIETIES OF THE FRUITS. HE BUILT THIS HOUSE IN 1908. ABOVE (RIGHT) IS CELLON'S HOUSE AS IT APPEARD SHORTLY AFTER IT WAS BUILT, AND AS IT LOOKS TODAY, STILL IN ITS ORIGINAL N.W. 7TH AVENUE LOCATION. (PHOTO RIGHT, HISTORICAL ASSOCIATION OF SOUTHERN FLORIDA)

HALISSEE HALL WAS BUILT ON THE OUTSKIRTS OF MIAMI IN 1912 BY JOHN SEWELL. SEWELL CAME TO MIAMI IN 1896 AS ONE OF FLAGLER'S CONSTRUCTION SUPERINTENDENTS AND BECAME A PROMINENT EARLY MERCHANT AND MAYOR OF THE CITY FROM 1903 TO 1907. THE MANSION IS BUILT OF OOLITIC LIMESTONE WALLS 18 INCHES THICK, IN A NEO-CLASSIC REVIVAL STLE. THE FOURTEEN ACRE ESTATE IS NOW PART OF THE JACKSON MEMORIAL HOSPITAL COMPLEX WHERE THE HOUSE STILL STANDS. (ABOVE PHOTO, HISTORICAL ASSOCIATION OF SOUTHERN FLORIDA)

THE HINDU TEMPLE WAS BUILT IN 1920 BY JOHN SEYBOLD, A PROMINENT MERCHANT IN MIAMI SINCE 1896. THE DESIGN IS INSPIRED BY THE MOVIE SET OF "THE JUNGLE TRAIL," FILMED ON LOCATION IN MIAMI IN 1919. WHEN THE SET WAS DISMANTLED, SEYBOLD HAD ARCHITECT AUGUST GEIGER DESIGN THIS HOUSE, ON THE SAME SITE. SOON AFTER, THE HOUSE WAS PURCHASED BY CHARLES RICHARDSON, AN ACTOR. THE PROPERTY IS STILL IN THE RICHARDSON FAMILY. (ABOVE PHOTO, HISTORICAL ASSOCIATION OF SOUTHERN FLORIDA)

A SUNNY DAY ON MIAMI BEACH (HISTORICAL ASSOCIATION OF SOUTHERN FLORIDA)

MIAMI BEACH

When Carl Fisher, a self-made millionaire from Indiana, moved into his new winter residence on Brickell Avenue in 1912, in the distance across the bay, he could see the beginning of the creation of John Collins, an elderly Quaker gentleman who had moved onto an isolated island in the bay a few years before. Between Miami and the island, Collins had begun the construction of a wooden bridge which, at two and one half miles when completed, was the longest wooden bridge in the world.[28] Most people thought he was crazy. Carl Fisher was inspired and invested in the project in exchange for two hundred acres of the island's oceanfront land.

John Collins arrived in South Florida in 1906 to investigate the failure of a coconut plantation he partially financed.[29] Charles Lum began the plantation in 1882, but his efforts were eventually overcome by the elements. Several years after the coconut venture was abandoned, Collins decided the soil there had a favorable composition for the cultivation of tropical fruits and started an avocado grove. Soon he enlarged his land

holdings to include the area of present day 14th Street to 67th Street.[30] In order to facilitate transportation of his produce to the mainland, Collins began work in 1912 on two projects, a canal linking Lake Pancoast with the bay and a wooden bridge. To subsidize building costs, Collins offered lots for sale on the southern end of his property, but within the year, the construction of the bridge came to a halt due to lack of funds. It was then that Carl Fisher entered the picture. He was a peculiar counterbalance to the austere John Collins. Fisher was a man of excess, but also an astute businessman. He had the commercial vision to look at the swampy, tangled land mass in the midst of Biscayne Bay as if it were a blank screen on which he projected in glorious technicolor the quintessence of the millionaires' playground, a production he would name Miami Beach.

Simultaneously with the Collins effort, the Lummus brothers bought land originally owned by the Lum plantation on the southern end of the island. In 1912, the Lummus Subdivision was platted by the Ocean Beach Realty Company,[31] marking the first real estate venture in Miami Beach, only months before Collins' capital-raising land sales project with his

THE COLLINS BRIDGE OPENED THE WAY FOR DEVELOPMENT IN MIAMI BEACH. BUILT IN 1912, IT WAS THE LONGEST WOODEN BRIDGE IN THE WORLD AT THE TIME. (HISTORICAL ASSOCIATION OF SOUTHERN FLORIDA)

Miami Beach Improvement Company. Carl Fisher lent money to the Lummus enterprise for draining and filling of the southern mangrove swamps, in return for 210 acres of bayfront lands. With land holdings on the ocean and bay sides of the island, Fisher opened the third real estate office on the Beach, the Alton Beach Realty Company.

From the beginning there was a marked difference between the Lummus and Fisher subdivisions. The Lummus property was platted with small lots selling at moderate prices to anyone who was 'white, law-abiding and could afford the down payment.'[32] A community of modest beach houses began to form. An earlier ferry boat operation bringing swimming enthusiasts from Miami was taken over by the Lummuses, and land salesmen aboard this boat began promotion pitches before visitors reached the island. Smith's Casino, originally run by the Tatums, was an early recreational bathing spot. In 1914 the first hotel in Miami Beach opened its doors.[33]

Land sales were much slower in the Fisher subdivisions. His property had been divided into much larger lots than the Lummuses'. He included many restrictive covenants and held out for steeper prices to attract

THE MIAMI BEACH POST OFFICE IN 1920. THE BUILDING STILL STANDS ON 5TH STREET AND ALTON ROAD, ALTHOUGH GREATLY ALTERED BY A SHINY YELLOW AND RED TILE FACING. (HISTORICAL ASSOCIATION OF SOUTHERN FLORIDA)

THE OCEAN BEACH FERRY TRANSPORTED SWIMMING ENTHUSIASTS FROM THE FOOT OF FLAGLER STREET TO MIAMI BEACH. THE FERRY WAS OWNED AND OPERATED BY THE LUMMUS BROTHERS OCEAN BEACH REALTY COMPANY, DEVELOPERS OF THE FIRST SUBDIVISION IN MIAMI BEACH. (HISTORICAL ASSOCIATION OF SOUTHERN FLORIDA)

77

THE BLACKMAN FAMILY POSES ON THE PORCH OF THEIR BUNGALOW, BUILT BETWEEN 1915 AND 1918. THE ORIENTAL INFLU-ENCE WAS A POPULAR FEATURE IN THIS TYPE OF HOUSING. E.V. BLACKMAN WAS THE AUTHOR OF A LOCAL HISTORY BOOK ENTITLED *MIAMI AND DADE COUNTY, FLORIDA*. (HISTORICAL ASSOCIATION OF SOUTHERN FLORIDA)

a wealthier clientele. Fisher could afford to be patient.

A few more years were to pass before Miami Beach was transformed into a full-fledged tourist mecca for the elite and those aspiring to follow in their footsteps. Carl Fisher had other interests to keep him busy. On October 15, 1915, he led the Dixie Highway Pathfinders, a fifteen car cavalcade which originated in Chicago, into Miami, announcing the construction of the Dixie Highway, the East coast's first north/south highway.[34] Soon the spoked wheels of the early Fords and Stoddards were rolling off the slick paved road onto the rickety Collins bridge en masse as the automobile became America's most popular form of transportation and Miami and Miami Beach their drivers' favorite destination.

SOUTH FLORIDA BUNGALOWS

One building type found in all the middle class suburbs that grew around Miami is the bungalow. Miami Beach had many bungalow houses in its early years, as did Edgewater, Buena Vista, and what is now Little Havana, but the highest number and the finest bungalows were in the Lawrence Estate

Subdivision area. Bungalows spread through Miami like brush fire between 1915 and 1925. This was not, however, a singular or local phenomenon, as the bungalow became one of the most popular residential styles across the nation during the first two decades of the century.

From the onset of suburban development in Miami, national magazines such as *House Beautiful* advertised mail-order catalogues that offered complete building plans and specifications starting at a mere five dollars. Firms such as California-based E.W. Stillwell Company sold *All-American Homes* books, their pages replete with the same types of bungalows that line the streets of Miami's early subdivisions.[35]

The bungalow is so well suited to the South Florida area that it could easily pass for indigenous architecture. Its origins, however, were in India, where the name refers to a suburban villa or roadside inn. These buildings, often much larger than the American counterpart, have high pitched roofs, using the vast space above the ground floor plan as insulation from the sun, and verandahs on three or four sides, again as a means of shelter from the intense heat.[36]

78

The most direct force influencing the development of the American bungalow came from the Arts and Crafts movement of the turn-of-the-century, which called for a return to the simpler lifestyle of pre-Industrial Revolution days. This principle was best manifested in architecture in the work of brothers Charles and Henry Greene in Pasadena, California, prior to 1910.[37] They used a "back to nature" vocabulary, new honesty in expression through exposed structural elements, wood and field stones, natural colors, a reinforcement of horizontal planes and the finest in hand-crafted details. The woodwork, metalwork, pottery and glasswork displayed in their houses are evidence of their high quality of craftmanship.

The bungalow derived most of its vocabulary from Greene and Greene's work, but in a simpler, more modest scale. Exposed structural members and unfinished surfaces were part of the desired "effect." Combinations of materials and gable roof outlines, abundance of porches and an assortment of models inspired by different styles and regions, all amount to the bungalow's greatest virtues, flexibility, simple inexpensive construction, adaptability to any area of the country and comfort.

This was the ideal lower-middle class home of the early twentieth century. One could not be formal in a bungalow. Space-saving conveniences like built-in furniture, i.e. kitchen cabinets, bookcases, closets and shelves were the rule, not the exception. The low maintenance required by rough textures and natural finishes in the interiors add to the list of praises for the bungalow.

The South Florida bungalow optimized the advantages of the area's natural resources. Construction was of Dade County pine, with horizontal weatherboards and wood shingles often used as exterior facing. Foundation walls, chimneys and porch supports were built of oolitic limestone, usually quarried at the site, although stucco surfaces were widely used also. Large windows, deep-set porches and wide eaves were all fine environmental responses from pre-air condi-

TYPICAL BUNGALOW WITH THE GABLE ROOF PERPENDICULAR TO THE STREET.

STREET SCENE WITH BUNGALOWS IN THE EDGEWATER SECTION OF MIAMI.

TYPICAL BUNGALOW WITH THE GABLE PARALLEL TO THE STREET.

79

THE BELVEDERE BUNGALOW, WITH A SECOND STORY OF SMALLER AREA THAN THE FIRST FLOOR. THE COMBINATION OF MATERIALS, THE MULTIPLE GABLE ROOFS, THE VARIETY OF PORCH SUPPORTS, AND EXPOSED STRUCTURAL DETAILS ARE AMONG ITS MAIN FEATURES. THE BUILDING WAS DEMOLISHED IN NOVEMBER, 1988.

tioning days. The battered stone piers added considerable stability against high winds. By breaking the vertical supports of the porch roof into a broad tapered masonry pier at the bottom and a short wooden post above, commonly referred to as "elephantine" columns, the entire porch was strengthened. These elephantine posts were expressed in a variety of ways, becoming the "gingerbread" of the bungalow, so to speak. Their informal floor plans and their simple construction allowed local builders to give these houses a personal touch. The most distinguishing elements of the style were retained, while their expression and details were treated in a variety of ways, without strict adherence to stylistic dictates. Like the "Carpenter Gothic" houses of the nineteenth century, some of the finest bungalows built in Miami fall into several categories. The most commonly found type has a gable roof, its ridge perpendicular to the street, and a front porch, either contained under the main roof or with a separate gable. Others have the ridge of the gable parallel to the street and the gable facing the front is often pierced by a dormer. Yet another variation has multiple gable roofs, following the contours of more elaborate, sprawling floor plans. The most ambitious ones are the Airplane or Belvedere bungalows, which achieved great popularity in the Lawrence Estates Subdivision. These are larger houses with more articulated masses and multiple roof gables. Their main feature is a central second story mass smaller than the ground floor. The second floor, or "belvedere," might

BUNGALOW WITH MULTIPLE GABLE ROOFS.

BELVEDERE BUNGALOW IN THE EDGEWATER AREA OF MIAMI.

be used as a master bedroom or several smaller rooms, but always considering cross ventilation in the spatial arrangements. The entire building has a three-dimensional quality, rather than a fixed street orientation, a luxury afforded to buildings in the suburbs, due to lower prices and larger lots.

The lessons to be learned from the design of the bungalow are timeless. Their broad gabled overhangs and battered porches were as much bold expressions of architecture as they were climatic features. Today, when energy efficiency and environmental considerations are so important in design, the bungalow is a model for good, inexpensive construction.

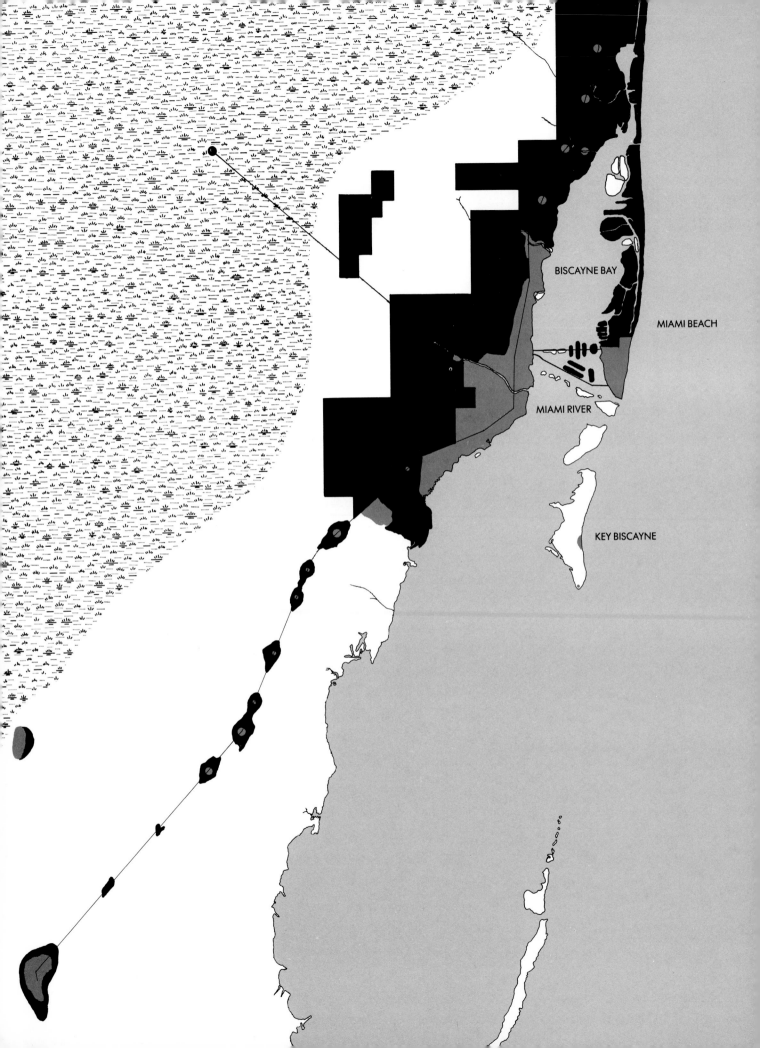

BISCAYNE BAY

MIAMI BEACH

MIAMI RIVER

KEY BISCAYNE

MIAMI FLAPPERS, (ROMER COLLECTION, MIAMI-DADE PUBLIC LIBRARY)

THE BOOM

With the end of the "Great War" in 1919, America was a profoundly different place. The tragedy and technology that enveloped the world in the first global war brought the frightening realization of the potential for destruction in the modern age. "Morality" suddenly became a subjective term. In the decade that followed, Victorian parents looked on in dismay as their daughters bobbed their hair, shortened their skirts, smoked cigarettes, and began drinking alcohol despite the new prohibition laws. They were accompanied in this decadent behavior by young men who were equally disrespectful of the old canons of proper behavior. The condition that helped most to perpetuate the trend were the years of "Coolidge prosperity." Industrial output was expanding without precedent. The stock market soared, and the consumer market was being flooded with an endless array of gadgetry and conveniences. Most prominent among these industrial miracles was the automobile which by the 1920s became a national phenomenon. So, in addition to increased mobility, there were more jobs, more money and more leisure time in which to cultivate a new hunger for fun and pleasure.[1]

This restless and somewhat cynical national psyche was bombarded in the early twenties by the brash and immodest brochures promoting the wonders of Miami and Miami Beach. They depicted moonlit seascapes framed in palm fronds and spoke of places unhindered by tradition. They offered ways to invest one's extra dollars and all but guaranteed a return. What's more, this could be accomplished in an environment of carefree enjoyment. Hotels and real estate developments in Miami had carried on a similar campaign before the war, but it was Carl Fisher who gave new meaning to the phrase "promotional advertisement" in the twenties.

Fisher was one of the most instrumental developers in converting the desolate strip of swamps and mangroves east of Biscayne Bay into the tourist mecca that became Miami Beach. Although his enterprise on Miami

83

THIS UNIQUE METHOD OF GOLFING WAS ONE OF CARL FISHER'S MANY PUBLICITY STUNTS THAT INVOLVED HIS ELEPHANT, ROSIE. (HISTORICAL ASSOCIATION OF SOUTHERN FLORIDA)

Beach had gotten a slow start, it took off with a fury after the war. Its success was partly a matter of being at the right place at the right time, but also, Fisher knew his business. He pioneered the publicity stunt.[2] Fisher had become famous in Indiana promoting his bicycle business and auto showroom. The woman who later married Carl Fisher wrote of first seeing him in 1908 floating above Indianapolis seated ''in a white automobile hung as a basket under a vermilion balloon.''[3] The balloon was emblazoned with the words ''Stoddard-Dayton,'' the name of the automobiles Fisher was trying to sell at his new dealership. It was only one of the many such stunts that gained him free newspaper publicity and had people all over Indiana talking about Carl Fisher.

Fisher built the Indianapolis Speedway and conceived the plan for the Lincoln Highway, the first transcontinental automobile road in the U.S., between New York and San Francisco. Fisher's most successful business venture was the Prest-O-Lite Corporation which manufactured compressed carbridge gas fuel for automobile headlights. The Union Carbide Company bought him out in 1911 for nine million dollars.

Carl Fisher brought Miami Beach to national attention with no less showmanship. In addition to being spotlighted in advertisements for the luxurious new hotels and beachfront estates, Miami Beach began appearing in the news and gossip columns. In 1921, when President Harding played golf on Miami with Fisher's pet elephant for his caddy, photographs of the event appeared in newspapers all over the country.[4] Soon there was a constant stream of socialities, politicians and movie stars, some paid to be there. They were present at hotel openings, parties that rivaled the Great Gatsby's, and sporting events such as power boat racing which was pioneered off the shores of Miami Beach by Fisher's friend, Gar Wood.[5] In 1924, Florida changed the state constitution to prohibit income and inheritance taxes.[6] It was an obvious bid to attract the wealthy and was a big boost to Fisher's similar efforts.

84

THE PANCOAST HOTEL WAS BUILT IN THE 1920s ON COLLINS AVENUE AND 29TH STREET. IT WAS DESIGNED BY RUSSELL T. PANCOAST. (HISTORICAL ASSOCIATION OF SOUTHERN FLORIDA)

THE FLAMINGO HOTEL, COMPLETED IN 1921. IN THE FOREGROUND IS GAR WOOD'S POWER BOAT. (ROMER COLLECTION. MIAMI-DADE PUBLIC LIBRARY)

THE FLORIDIAN COMPLETED IN 1926, STOOD AT THE FOOT OF THE McARTHUR CAUSEWAY & BISCAYNE BAY INTIL 1987. (ROMER COLLECTION, MIAMI-DADE PUBLIC LIBRARY)

THE KING GOLE WAS BUILT BY FISHER AND DESIGNED BY KIEHNEL AND ELLIOTT, ON THE PRESENT SITE OF THE MIAMI HEART INSTITUTE. THE BUILDING WAS DEMOLISHED IN 1982. (ROMER COLLECTION, MIAMI-DADE PUBLIC LIBRARY)

THE BLACKSTONE HAS BEEN IN OPERATION SINCE 1929, WHEN IT OPENED AS THE FIRST HOTEL THAT CATERED TO JEWS IN MIAMI BEACH. THE FISHER HOTELS OBSERVED STRICT RACIAL AND ANTI-SEMITIC RULES. (ROMER COLLECTION, MIAMI-DADE PUBLIC LIBRARY)

THE RONEY PLAZA WAS BUILT IN 1925 BY N.B.T. RONEY AND WAS DESIGNED BY SCHULTZE AND WEAVER. THERE IS A SIMILARITY IN THE DESIGN OF THE TOWER WITH THOSE OF THE BILTMORE HOTEL AND THE FREEDOM TOWER.

THE NAUTILUS, BUILT IN 1924, WAS ONE OF CARL FISHER'S MOST LUXURIOUS HOTELS. THE BAROQUE ENTRANCE, CURVED PARAPETS, AND THE TWIN CHURCH-LIKE TOWERS WERE AMONG THE SPANISH DECORATIVE ELEMENTS EMPLOYED BY THE ARCHITECTURAL FIRM OF SCHULTZE AND WEAVER IN THEIR FIRST COMMISSION IN THE MIAMI AREA. (HISTORICAL ASSOCIATION OF SOUTHERN FLORIDA)

THE SPANISH VILLAGE, NOW ESPANOLA WAY, WAS BUILT IN 1925 BY RONEY AS AN ARTIST COLONY. THE PICTURESQUE AREA HAD A REPUTATION IN ITS EARLY DAYS AS A GAMBLING AND RED LIGHT DISTRICT. (ROMER COLLECTION, MIAMI-DADE PUBLIC LIBRARY)

CURRENT VIEW OF ESPANOLA WAY.

FIRE STATION ON LIBERTY AVENUE AND 23RD STREET. IN THE BACKGROUND IS THE RONEY PLAZA UNDER CONSTRUCTION. (ROMER COLLECTION, MIAMI-DADE PUBLIC LIBRARY)

PUBLIC BUILDINGS IN MIAMI BEACH

THE MIAMI BEACH COMMUNITY CHURCH WAS DESIGNED IN 1921 BY WALTER C. DE GARMO IN A SPANISH COLONIAL REVIVAL STYLE. (HISTORICAL ASSOCIATION OF SOUTHERN FLORIDA) ▶

MIAMI BEACH CITY HALL WAS BUILT IN 1928 IN A MEDITERRANEAN/BEAUX ARTS STYLE. (HISTORICAL ASSOCIATION OF SOUTHERN FLORIDA) ◀

BEACHFRONT ESTATES

FORMER ESTATE ON COLLINS AVENUE. (ROMER COLLECTION, MIAMI-DADE PUBLIC LIBRARY)

THE FORMER ESTATE OF CARL FISHER STILL STANDS ON NORTH BAY ROAD. THE ARCHITECT WAS AUGUST GEIGER.

THE FIRESTONE ESTATE LANGUISHES IN THE SHADOWS OF THE RISING SKELETON OF THE FONTAINEBLEAU IN 1956. (FONTAINBLEAU HILTON PHOTO COLLECTION.)

THE HARVEY FIRESTONE ESTATE WAS ONE OF THE GRANDEST IN MIAMI BEACH IN THE 1920s. IT OCCUPIED THE PRESENT SITE OF THE FONTAINE-BLEAU-HILTON (ROMER COLLECTION, MIAMI-DADE PUBLIC LIBRARY)

FROM LEFT TO RIGHT, IRVING COLLINS, AND FREDERICK SUITE ESTATES. THE FIRST HOUSE WAS DESIGNED BY CARLOS SCHOEPPL, THE NEXT THREE BY RUSSELL PANCOAST, DURING THE 1920s.

RESIDENCE OF IRVING COLLINS, SON OF THE EARLY DEVELOPER OF MIAMI BEACH, IT WAS DESIGNED IN 1924 BY RUSSELL PANCOAST.

THE VANDERBILT ESTATE

AERIAL VIEW OF VANDERBILT ESTATE IN 1937, SHOWING THE YACHT ALVA IN THE FOREGROUND. (ROMER COLLECTION. MIAMI-DADE PUBLIC LIBRARY).

Among the very wealthy families who built their pieds-a-terre in Miami was William Kissam Vanderbilt, Jr., of the well-known New York railroad empire. Mr. Vanderbilt began acquiring tracts on Fisher's Island in the mid-1920s. William was the grandson of Commodore Cornelius Vanderbilt, who made his fortune by promoting steamship and railroad transportation in the mid to late 1800s. Cornelius is regarded as the founder of Vanderbilt University in North Carolina, (formerly Central University), and he donated one million dollars to the college. William's parents, William Kissam Sr. and Alva Murray Smith were married in 1875. William had an older brother, Harold, and a younger sister, Consuelo, who was described as "shatteringly beautiful" and "unquestionably the most magnificent woman of her time." Consuelo reportedly broke hearts on two continents before marrying first, the Duke of Marlborough, and second, the dashing French aviator, Louis Jacques Balsan. A graduate of Harvard, William Jr. was a millionaire who served as president of the New York Central Railroad Company.

The wealth of the Vanderbilt family had traditionally been conspicuously displayed. The family owned two oceanside estates, the Breakers and the Marble House, in Newport, Rhode Island, a mansion on Fifth Avenue in New York, and a 250 room French chateau, the Biltmore, in Asheville, North Carolina. Many of William's friends, including his brother and sister, built winter homes in Palm Beach. But William fell in love with the small island off Miami Beach which was nothing but sand and scrub at the time. Vanderbilt bargained with real estate developer Carl Fisher and traded one of his yachts, the Eagle, for seven acres on the island.

The Vanderbilts were just one of many

91

VANDERBILT MANSION, NOW A RESTAURANT AND CLUBHOUSE FOR THE FISHER ISLAND DEVELOPMENT.

colorful names associated with Fisher's Island through the years. Originally Fisher's Island was created in 1906 when Congress ordered the construction of Government Cut to open a more accessible channel for shipping commerce between the Atlantic and Biscayne Bay. A channel was carved straight across the bay, making an island of the sand and mangroves. Unlike many of the other small islands in Biscayne Bay which were artificially created, at least a portion of Fisher's Island was a natural geological formation that was originally an extension of mainland Miami Beach.

In 1918 most of the island was owned by Dana A. Dorsey, the most prominent businessman in Miami's black community. Dorsey became a millionaire in the real estate business and was the primary benefactor of what was then known as "Colored Town." Dorsey purchased Fisher's Island to provide a public beach for Miami's black citizens who were prevented from visiting "white" beaches. Dorsey's plans for a "high class colored resort" never materialized and he sold the property in late 1919 to the Alton Beach Realty Company which was owned by Carl Fisher.

After Fisher acquired the island he significantly increased its size for development by bulkheading and filling. Fisher more than quadrupled the area of the land mass. He managed to sell over one million dollars worth of property on the island before the disastrous demise of the real estate boom in 1926. Fisher had hoped to develop the island to house commercial docks, but Mayor E.G. Sewell of Miami wanted them on his side of the bay and he was successful. Instead the only structure on the island built by Fisher was a mausoleum for himself and family members. No one was ever buried there, but the empty stone tomb still remains on the island. After Vanderbilt bought the property from Fisher, he retained well-known architect Maurice Fatio to design a winter home for him and his second wife, Rosamund Lancaster Warbuton. Fatio was an extremely talented architect, who followed in the footsteps of Addison Mizner and designed many Spanish style mansions in Palm Beach during the 1920s and '30s. Fatio was already familiar with the Vanderbilt family, having designed large waterfront villas for William's sister and brother in Palm Beach.

Constructed at a cost of 1.5 million dollars, the estate included the nineteen bedroom main house, guest cottages, servants quarters, a pool house, golfcourse, ten-

BOAT HOUSE FOR THE ESTATE, NOW USED AS A BEACHFRONT RESTAURANT AND BAR.

nis court, swimming pool, fire house, pump house and an airplane hangar for Vanderbilt's seaplane. He named his island retreat "Alva Base," after his German-built diesel yacht, Alva, which he docked at the island. Nicknamed "the floating mansion," the 350' yacht contained eight staterooms and required a crew of 49. The entire compound was substantially completed by 1936.

Despite overt displays of wealth by other members of the family, William was known more as a modest millionaire and a shy, self-effacing man. In keeping with his personality, Vanderbilt located his estate on the southeast side of the island, boldly facing out to sea, but quite properly aloof and invisible from the mainland.

The estate is impressive, yet understated. The twelve structure housing compound is surrounded by a wall on the land side, and set on beautifully landscaped grounds. But the individual structures are small in scale and delicate in detail. Other family members built replicas of French chateaux and Italian Renaissance villas such qs the Biltmore and the Breakers. Alva Base, however, is inspired by the architecture of sun drenched, seaside villages along the Mediterranean coasts.

The list of prominent people associated with Fisher's Island continues even after the Vanderbilts sold the property in the 1940s. Ed-ward S. Moore, whose family founded U.S. Steel, was the next occupant of the island. Moore, a stockholder in the Hialeah Race Course, was the owner of the famous thoroughbred horse farm, the Circle M, near Lexington, Kentucky.

After Moore died his widow sold the property to Gar Wood, known as the "speedboat king." Wood, a boat racer and inventor, developed the original hydraulic hoist which revolutionized the trucking industry. He is also credited with the design of what became the PT boat of World War II. He is best known for his speedboat races which won him eight consecutive international Harmsworth Trophies, four U.S. Gold Cups and five world championship records. During the thirty years he lived on the island he worked on various projects such as an electric car and military boat designs. Unfortunately, the more projects he had, the more neglected the estate grew.

Presently, the approximately eleven acres which includes the Vanderbilt Estate have been developed into a private resort community known as Fisher Island. The mansion and outbuildings have been converted into restaurants and offices. Condominium villas have been constructed to the west of the estate, in keeping with the original Mediterranean Revival architecture. The resort includes tennis courts, a golf course, marina and beautifully landscaped grounds.

A TYPICAL SCENE IN FRONT OF A BOOMTIME REAL ESTATE OFFICE. (ROMER COLLECTION, MIAMI-DADE PUBLIC LIBRARY)

The statistics of the Miami real estate boom were staggering. The population more than doubled in a five year span from 1920 to 1925, and the prices of plots of land could double or triple in a day during the height of the boom.[7] The time for reasonable speculation had long since passed in 1924. Word of South Florida was no longer spread through in the major newspapers.

The real estate action was not limited to investors with substantial capital, because many sellers were willing to take a small cash deposit known as a "binder" with the balance due later. The binder became the standard means of conducting land sales transactions, and the "binder boys," as their promoters were known, the conduit of the commotion. Historian Frederick Lewis Allen noted:

There was nothing languorous about the atmosphere of tropical Miami during the memorable summer and autumn of 1925. The whole city had become one frenzied real estate exchange…The Dixie Highway was clogged with automobiles from every part of the country; a traveller caught in a traffic jam counted the license plates of eighteen states among the sedans and flivvers waiting in line. Hotels were overcrowded. People were sleeping wherever they could lay their heads, in station waiting rooms or in automobiles.[8]

By 1925 most of the new arrivals were middle and lower middle class people. Despite the fact that great fortunes had been made in industry and the stock market, the majority of Americans, over seventy percent, lived on incomes of less than $2,500.00 a year, according to figures compiled by the Brookings Institution on the era of the 1920s.[9] Many of these people grew up with the stories of Horatio Alger and as adults lived in a culture permeated by a romantic fascination with the "good life." Plenty of stories were circulating in the early 1920s of people who became rich overnight in the Florida real estate market with only a small initial cash investment. But by the time the masses arrived, South Florida real estate's reputation as a wise investment was beginning to sour.

The boom reached its height in the fall of 1925;[10] however, it had done so on too many empty promises. There were hundreds paid advertisements, but by front page stories of small developments attempting to imitate Miami Beach and the equally prominent Coral Gables, which was begun in 1921, but many were fraudulent ventures. Too large a number of people bought lots in subdivisions like Manhatten Estates advertised as being "not more than three-fourths of a mile from the prosperous and fast growing city of Nettie," to find that Nettie was nothing more than an abandoned turpentine camp.[11]

Early in 1926, national publications were filling their pages with stories on the situation in Miami and its victims. In March, the *Saturday Evening Post* ran a fictional short story entitled, "Land of Promise" about the adventures of Mr. and Mrs. Preevoe on a Florida home buying expedition.[12] It is a farcical tale of the prospective clients' experiences in the mythical "Atlandixie City," which was fashioned after the typical South Florida boom development of the 1920s. The Preevoes are wined, dined and entertained by a variety of lesser celebrities who are placed randomly around the pink stuccoed premises. A salesman does admit that there had been some swampy places within the city limits, but proudly declares that "these have been dredged and deepened and now form a continuous chain of lakes." The Preevoes, enticed but not seduced, decide to take a look at the next development down the road before sinking the family fortune into Atlandixie, but when they try to leave without purchasing a lot, their luggage is impounded by the management.

The Post story was a case of the ridiculous being very close to the truth. Thousands of people found that out when they bought lots in "cities" in Florida such as Atlandixie only to discover that they were not incorporated, had no public utilities or municipal improvements, and that the swamps, come the rainy season, did indeed form a continuous chain of lakes.

The "Land of Promise" story was one of many: in the *Saturday Evening Post* later that spring, a story by Will Rogers entitled "Florida Versus California: A Debate Held

MANY TOURISTS IN THE 1920s WHO COULD NOT AFFORD THE LUXURY OF MIAMI BEACH STAYED IN TOURIST CAMPS SUCH AS BROYHILLS ON WEST DIXIE HIGHWAY, PICTURED IN 1925. (ROMER COLLECTION, MIAMI-DADE PUBLIC LIBRARY)

Before the Prevaricator's Club of America;"[13] in *McCall's Magazine*, a series by noted economist Ida Tarbell, "Florida and Then What?";[14] and in *The Magazine of Wall Street*, on March 27, 1926, "Salvaging Florida's Wrecked Boom," by A. R. Pinci.[15] Interestingly, Mr. Pinci speculates on the connection between the Florida boom and the stock market. He indicates that there was present on Wall Street at that time a fear that those who had invested in both might eventually have to sacrifice one to salvage the other.

Regardless of that relationship, by the spring of 1926, Florida real estate prices began to sink, buyers disappeared and more and more people found themselves holding binders on property they could not afford to pay off. While the situation looked bleak that spring, it was nothing compared to the way things looked on the morning of September 19, 1926, after a severe hurricane struck the southeast coast. Three hundred and ninety-two people were dead, over six thousand injured, and 17,784 families were affected by the loss of valuable property.[16] Whatever remained of the real estate boom came to a dead halt that day, and South Florida was plunged into a depression a good three years before the rest of the country.

(ROMER COLLECTION, MIAMI-DADE PUBLIC LIBRARY)

Pioneers Who Made Fortunes in Florida Playland Hardest Hit by Terrible Disaster

1926 HURRICANE

PROPERTY LOSS WORSE THAN AT FIRST REPORTED IS IN

THEIR DREAMS CAUGHT IN CHAOS

PROPERTY DAMAGE REACHES MILLIONS

THE WRECKAGE OF A SILVER BLUFF HOME WHERE ONE PERSON DIED. (ROMER COLLECTION, MIAMI-DADE PUBLIC LIBRARY)

BISCAYNE BOULEVARD, LOOKING NORTH TOWARD THE MC ALLISTER HOTEL IN THE AFTERMATH OF THE 1926 HURRICANE. THE STEEL SKELETON TO THE LEFT OF THE PICTURE IS THE INGRAHAM BUILDING.

96

CUSHMAN RESIDENCE IN MORNINGSIDE PARK, 1927. (ROMER COLLECTION, MIAMI-DADE PUBLIC LIBRARY)

ORIGINS OF THE MEDITERRANEAN REVIVAL STYLE IN MIAMI

The single most significant expression of South Florida's lifestyle during the boom years is the legacy of the Mediterranean Revival architecture it created. The style represents all the excess and extravagance of the Roaring Twenties in the Miami area. It is ornate, pompous, and flamboyant like the wealthy industrialists and speculators who built their winter residences on the shores of Biscayne Bay. It is deeply rooted in the Spanish heritage of the Florida peninsula, yet in tune with contemporary national trends. It is a good regional adaptation of an architectural vocabulary removed from its original environment by hundreds of years and thousands of miles. But most important it is playful, tossing aside strict adherence to academic dictates, truly meant for "the good life" of a tropical playground as reflected in a 1925 issue of *The House Beautiful*:

To say that the new Florida architecture lacks seriousness is unwittingly to compliment its architects on the attainment of their real aim. They do not mean it to be serious. While they do not intend it to be frivolous, they definitely intend its picturesque informality to express the spirit of a land dedicated to long, carefree vacations.[17]

A number of factors were involved in the creation of the Mediterranean Revival style of architecture and its introduction to South Florida. L'École des Beaux Arts in Paris and the Mission and Spanish Colonial Revival styles, popularized in the southwestern United States in the first two decades of this century, were the most direct forces in the formation of Mediterranean architecture. The Paris École des Beaux Arts had a great influence in turn-of-the-century American architecture. Many well known architects from the period studied at the Beaux Arts. The Beaux Arts movement was rooted in the study of classical architecture putting an emphasis on rigorous academic exercises aimed at sketching authentic reproductions of fastidiously crafted architectonic details. The products of this school of architecture lean toward monumentality in design and derive their inspiration from a variety of styles, mainly Renaissance, Baroque and Neo-Classical, and a variety of countries, chiefly France, Italy and England. The Beaux Arts theories advocated keeping the different styles separate, but the architects often juxtaposed stylistic features in new combinations, resulting in the eclecticism tipical of the times. The Chicago Worlds Columbian Exposition of 1893 was the greatest single display of Beaux Arts architecture in the United States. This "White City," in all its classical splendor, was only a temporary vision, executed in paper maché and plaster of Paris.

THE MISSION STYLE

One of the few buildings at the Columbian Exposition to depart from the European classics was the California State Building. In typical Beaux Arts tradition, the design did look to old models for inspiration, but in this case the models came from their own backyards. It was the old Californian missions, particularly the old Mission Church in San Diego that inspired this design.[18] The building was sober in ornamental details, relying on massing, arched openings, Mission roof tiles and a bellcast central parapet for decoration. The vocabulary it created became known as the Mission style.

The Mission style is simple, inexpensive to build and of quiet, unobtrusive design. It achieves its expression through minimal decoration. "Being so classically simple, there is a style about them that will always be good, no fads of a passing day in evidence to mar their future worth."[19]

Mission architecture employs flat roofs with parapets, usually curved or bell-shaped, the same parapet detail often repeated over porch roofs. Arched openings for windows, doorways and porches are commonly used. A simple stucco molding surrounds the arches. Construction may be of block or wood frame faced in rough textured stucco. Sloping red tiled roofs provide one of the few contrasting elements, and applied ornament is sparsely used. Parapets are often interrupted by a single row of sloping tiles, creating simple two dimensional compositions. Scuppers, or roof drains, pierce the parapets at rhythmic intervals.

In 1914, when August Geiger designed the Homestead Public School,[20] he described it as a Mission style building,[21] although earlier works such as William Jennings Bryan's Villa Serena, William Matheson's Four Way Lodge and H.H. Mundy's Coconut Grove Public School all have a distinctive Spanish Colonial influence. Mission styled houses, along with the bungalows, became the most popular building types for the moderate income subdivisions that spread throughout the metropolitan Miami area during the twenties decade. Many streets in the northwest and southwest areas of the city of

TYPICAL MISSION STYLE RESIDENCE. SUBTLE ACCENTS OF ROOF AND FLOOR TILES AND STRIPED AWNINGS BECOME MAJOR DECORATIVE ELEMENTS. (ROMER COLLECTION, MIAMI-DADE PUBLIC LIBRARY)

MRS. FRANK T. VALENTINE POSES IN FRONT OF HER MISSION STYLE HOME IN SOUTHWEST MIAMI. (ROMER COLLECTION, MIAMI-DADE PUBLIC LIBRARY)

DETAIL OF HOMESTEAD PUBLIC SCHOOL, DESIGNED BY AUGUST GEIGER IN 1914. THE ARCHITECT DESCRIBED THE BUILDING AS MISSION STYLE, ALTHOUGH THE ROOFS ARE COVERED IN ITALIAN "LUDOVICI" TILES.

Miami are still lined with these buildings, modest in size and construction, but rich in character and charm.

SPANISH COLONIAL REVIVAL ARCHITECTURE

The California Building at the San Diego exposition of 1915, by Bertram Goodhue, clearly established the Spanish Colonial Revival style. This was the next step in the development of the Spanish idiom of architecture in the West Coast. A more elaborate version of the Mission style, it put heavier emphasis on applied decoration. Ornate sculptural details inspired by the Spanish "Churriguresque" of Mexican Baroque architecture, were often applied, especially around entrances, or highlighting windows, balconies and cornices. The Spanish Colonial Revival became popular in California and quickly spread its influence to a national scale. Magazines of wide distribution and Hollywood movies played a major role in the promotion of Spanish Colonial Revival architecture during the 1920s.

Similarities with Southern California in weather conditions and Spanish heritage

made Florida a popular area for the same building forms. The Spanish flavor in Florida architecture goes back to Carrère and Hastings' designs for Henry Flagler, especially the Ponce de Leon Hotel in St. Augustine, finished in 1888. Their Beaux Arts training is clearly seen in their scholarly, albeit naive interpretation of Moorish architecture.

August Geiger designed the Miami City Hospital in 1915. The first building of what later became Jackson Memorial Hospital, it was nicknamed "the Alamo" in later years, although the reason for this name remains a mystery. The Alamo and the Miami Beach Municipal Golf Course House, now the Miami Beach Community Center, are very similar in appearance. In both buildings, rather than the sober simplicity of the Mission-inspired Homestead Public School, Geiger employed a classical sense of design through elements like scale, proportion and symmetry, befitting the architect's Beaux Arts training.[22] These elements were expressed in a Spanish idiom of applied stucco ornaments, arcaded ground floor loggia and tile roof. Not truly Spanish, it is rather inspired by the architecture of California, Texas and New Mexico during the

MIAMI CITY HOSPITAL, NICKNAMED "THE ALAMO," WAS DESIGNED BY AUGUST GEIGER IN 1915 AS THE FIRST BUILDING OF WHAT IS NOW JACKSON MEMORIAL HOSPITAL. THE BEAUX ARTS INSPIRED SENSE OF PROPORTIONS AND COMPOSITION ARE EXPRESSED IN A SPANISH COLONIAL REVIVAL IDIOM. (ROMER COLLECTION, MIAMI-DADE PUBLIC LIBRARY)

years of Spanish territoriality. Geiger had actually created the earliest traceable example of Spanish Colonial Revival architecture in Miami.

THE ALAMO, AFTER ITS RESTORATION AS A VISITORS CENTER.

WASHINGTON AVENUE COMMUNITY CENTER, AFTER ITS RESTORATION VIEWED FROM THE NORTH ELEVATION.

THE MIAMI BEACH MUNICIPAL GOLF COURSE BUILDING, ALSO BY AUGUST GEIGER, BEARS A STRONG SIMILARITY TO THE ALAMO. COMPLETED IN 1916, IT NOW SERVES AS THE WASHINGTON AVENUE COMMUNITY CENTER. (ROMER COLLECTION, MIAMI-DADE PUBLIC LIBRARY)

EL JARDIN, BUILT IN 1917, IS NOW THE CARROLLTON SCHOOL. ONE OF THE EARLIEST MEDITERRANEAN REVIVAL WORKS IN MIAMI, DESIGNED BY THE FIRM OF KIEHNEL AND ELLIOTT. ENTRANCE DETAIL.

MIAMI MEDITERRANEAN

Mediterranean Revival architecture escapes precise definition or description. It is eclectic, whimsical, overstated and beautiful to behold. One element is always present in Mediterranean architecture—sunlight. The varying contours of juxtaposed masses and roof lines, the picturesque arrangements of details such as balconies, arches and red tiled roofs against the blue skies and white clouds of South Florida, the rough textured stucco surfaces painted in bright whites and soft pastels, the sharp contrasts of light and shadow constantly playing against ever-changing outlines; they owe it all to the sun.

The Mediterranean style was as much at home in Florida and California as in its native European shores. No one seemed to mind the incongruities of a brand new old building where six months earlier there was only swamp, and if anyone did, they stained the walls, cracked the stucco and installed second-hand roof tiles imported from Cuba in order to achieve the desired aged effect. That the climate was much more tropical, and thick solid walls were inappropriate was of no consequence, since grouped windows, arcaded loggias, porches, balconies and central courtyards made up for any other inconveniences. That flatlands, palm trees and tall pines were foreign to the natural environment where the style originated did not stop the growing popularity of the Mediterranean in Miami.

It is no surprise that there is no "Mediterranean Style" along the coasts of Spain or France or Italy or Greece. The style is, in fact, more native to Florida and California than it is to the Mediterranean. It borrows from different styles, interprets, combines, adapts them and arrives at a synthesis that responds to local factors in the fashionable vocabulary of the day as confirmed by Rexford Newcomb:

> Spanish, Italian, Moorish, Byzantine... are under this orchestrated process merged... into a sun-loving style which, while eminently American in its plan and utilities, is never-the-less distinctly Mediterranean in its origins and spirit.[23]

"El Jardin" is the earliest known full-fledged Mediterranean Revival work remaining in Miami. Designed by the firm of Kiehnel and Elliott, it was the winter home of John Bindley, president of the Pittsburgh Steel Company.[24] Kiehnel and Elliott's firm, established in Pittsburgh, in 1906,[25] specialized in Neo-Tudor, Neo-Classical and Beaux Arts architecture executed in red brick. In the design for El Jardin, one of the first commissions that brought Richard Kiehnel to Miami in 1917,[26] the firm breaks away from their former patterns. A rectangular plan with an open courtyard and the generous overhang of the low pitched roof establish the backdrop of classical understated elegance of a Renaissance palace design. It is the applied decoration that breaks the classical serenity of the building and elevates it to the ornate extremes of the Spanish Churriguresque, a Moorish-influenced interpretation of the Baroque style. Kiehnel was able to control the powerful dec-

EL JARDIN; BAYFRONT VIEW

oration by using it sparingly on the front elevation, as dramatic accents around the central doorway, the second story balconies and the deep-set frieze, while giving it full rein on the rear bayfront elevation. The building thus maintains a more private, solid front as small openings and the double Spanish door of thick wood panels encrusted with large bronze studs indicate, and a more playful open facade toward the bay. Here the building mass is articulated into two corner pavilions slightly projecting from the rear wall of the central courtyard. The first story of this central wall is pierced by three large elliptical arches which repeat the rhythm of the four interior courtyard elevations. The second story appears as an open loggia sparkling with elaborate detailing, like delicate Spanish lace cast in stone.

The fine craftsmanship of the intricate cast stone decoration and wrought iron grillwork is a trademark of John B. Orr, builder of some of the major construction projects in the Miami area during the boom years.[27] The mastery of the Kiehnel/Orr combination produced special cosmetic effects which gave the brand new surfaces a weathered, aged

look. Paint coats were overlapped letting colors underneath show through. Cast stone was given artificial veining and porous surfaces while solutions were applied to promote mildew growth.[28] The anachronism created in transporting the ancient works of the Mediterranean shores to the warm golden sands of Biscayne Bay had been successfully accomplished by Richard Kiehnel in his creation at El Jardin. The Miami area had been introduced to the most influential style of its history, but it was Coral Gables that adapted this style as its own trademark.

GROTTO DETAIL. (ROMER COLLECTION. MIAMI-DADE PUBLIC LIBRARY)

103

MEDITERRANEAN STYLE IN PUBLIC BUILDINGS

CORAL GABLES CONGREGATIONAL CHURCH, BUILT IN 1925 BY KIEHNEL AND ELLIOTT WAS THE FIRST CHURCH IN CORAL GABLES. THE DESIGN IS BASED ON THAT OF A CHURCH IN CENTRAL AMERICA. (ROMER COLLECTION, MIAMI-DADE PUBLIC LIBRARY)

MIAMI SENIOR HIGH SCHOOL; 1928, KIEHNEL AND ELLIOTT. THE BUILDING HAS NORMAN/ ROMANESQUE DESIGN FEATURES. (ROMER COLLECTION, MIAMI-DADE PUBLIC LIBRARY)

MIAMI SENIOR HIGH SCHOOL. AUDITORIUM. (ROMER COLLECTION, MIAMI-DADE PUBLIC LIBRARY)

CORAL GABLES ELEMENTARY SCHOOL, BUILT IN 1926 BY KIEHNEL AND ELLIOTT, IS STILL ONE OF THE MAJOR LANDMARKS ON PONCE DE LEON BOULEVARD. (ROMER COLLECTION, MIAMI-DADE PUBLIC LIBRARY)

MIAMI FIRE STATION NO. 4. BUILT IN 1922 ON SOUTH MIAMI AVENUE AND 10TH STREET. (ROMER COLLECTION, MIAMI-DADE PUBLIC LIBRARY)

FIRE HOUSE FOUR WAS SUCCESSFULLY ADAPTED TO A RESTAURANT IN 1988.

THE RIVIERA THEATER WAS THE MAJOR FOCUS OF ENTERTAINMENT IN THE SOUTH MIAMI AREA WHEN IT WAS BUILT IN 1925. THE BUILDING SERVED AS THE HOLSUM BAKERY SINCE THE 1930's. IT WAS DEMOLISHED TO MAKE WAY FOR THE BAKERY CENTER. (ROMER COLLECTION, MIAMI-DADE PUBLIC LIBRARY) ▼

COURTYARD VIEW OF THE U.S. POST OFFICE AND COURT-HOUSE, BUILT IN DOWNTOWN MIAMI IN 1931 BY THE FIRM OF PHINEAS PAIST, SHOWS RENAISSANCE INSPIRED DETAILS. (ROMER COLLECTION, MIAMI-DADE PUBLIC LIBRARY) ▶

THE CORAL GABLES HOUSE WAS BUILT BY THE MERRICK FAMILY IN 1907, YEARS BEFORE DEVELOPMENT OF THE CITY.

CORAL GABLES

Although South Florida lost its reputation for quality on some of the shoddy real estate developments of the later boom years, that reputation was made on the better projects such as Coral Gables. For years after its opening, Coral Gables' financial and aesthetic success was cited countless times by less scrupulous builders to sell inferior homes in other poorly planned and nominally executed subdivisions.

Coral Gables was envisioned and developed by George Merrick.[29] He first came to Miami in 1898 with his father, the Reverend Solomon Greasley Merrick, a New England pastor. The Reverend Merrick had purchased the 160 acre Gregory homestead, and he and his son quickly set about clearing and planting the land. Young George soon became a familiar sight around the seedling city of Miami with his mule and wagon full of citrus produce which he sold door to door.

Before long Merrick's lovely manicured grove became a tourist attraction as well as a successful grapefruit growing operation. The original 160 acres increased to 1600 acres. The first modest Merrick residence was replaced by the house Merrick named "Coral Gables," after its coral colored gabled roof.

By this time Merrick was attending Rollins College in Winter Park, Florida. He later entered Columbia University, but was forced to withdraw because of the declining health of his father who died two years later in 1911. By 1909, George Merrick ran the largest produce farm in South Florida. Later he was assisted in his endeavors by his wife, Eunice Peacock, whom he married in 1916. Eunice was a member of the Coconut Grove pioneer family.

After his marriage, Merrick began drawing up blueprints to convert the family plantation into a suburban development, Coral Gables. The project envisioned was a fully planned community following a Spanish Mediterranean theme. The first lot sales were made in 1921, and in 1925 at the height of the boom, Coral Gables was incorporated as a city. Coral Gables had become the biggest single real estate venture of the boom. Sales reportedly reached $150 million.[30]

William Jennings Bryan, the famous orator, politician and theologian, was hired to tout the virtues of "beautiful Coral Gables." Bryan made a number of rousing speeches to prospective buyers while standing on the casino steps of Merrick's Venetian Pool. He was not the only celebrity present at the pool, which had been a rock quarry before its conversion and opening in 1924. Paul Whiteman played jazz for the dances at the pool, and Johnny Weismuller and Esther Williams swam there.[31]

The years 1924 and 1925 were the most prosperous for Coral Gables, but even though the venture had a solid reputation, it too was effected by the "bust" of the real estate market. The costly hurricane and the stock market crash wiped out Merrick's personal finances, leaving Coral Gables on its own to develop at a slower less frantic pace.

CORAL GABLES, "THE CITY BEAUTIFUL"

Coral Gables was a model city. Many of the sprouting developments tried to imitate or compete for attention and sales, but none could rival Merrick's city. While others fell short of their promises, Coral Gables delivered in high quality planning, design and public amenities that doubled as advertising gimmickry. The city plan was developed by Denman Fink, Merrick's uncle and artistic consultant, with Phineas Paist as principal architect. The landscape artist was Frank Button, who designed Lincoln Park in Chicago. Several other locally renowned architects and designers, such as H. George Fink, Paul Chalfin and Walter De Garmo, participated in this creation. Other major architectural firms making significant contributions to the architectural legacy of Coral Gables included Kiehnel & Elliott and Schultze & Weaver.

The city plan provided for separate residential and commercial areas, golf courses, churches, a private beach accessible through a canal and special "theme" residential villages. Street names like Granada, Santander, Toledo and Alhambra evoked Old Spanish towns and regions. Architects and artists were

THE FLEET OF BUSES USED TO SHOW CORAL GABLES LOTS TO POTENTIAL BUYERS. (ROMER COLLECTION, MIAMI-DADE PUBLIC LIBRARY)

THE VENETIAN POOL, BUILT IN 1924, WAS DESIGNED BY DENMAN FINK AND PHINEAS PAIST. IT LOOKS MUCH THE SAME TODAY AS IT DID IN THE 1920s. (ROMER COLLECTION, MIAMI-DADE PUBLIC LIBRARY)

GEORGE MERRICK, LIKE CARL FISHER, REALIZED THE PUBLICITY VALUE OF SPECIAL EVENTS. "MISS MIAMI" OF 1926 WAS SELECTED AT THE BILTMORE HOTEL POOL. (ROMER COLLECTION, MIAMI-DADE PUBLIC LIBRARY)

THE UNIVERSITY OF MIAMI OPENED IN CORAL GABLES IN 1925. ONE OF ITS FORMER MAIN BUILDINGS IS NOW THE SAN SEBASTIAN APARTMENTS ON LE JEUNE ROAD. (ROMER COLLECTION, MIAMI-DADE PUBLIC LIBRARY)

sent to Spain to study the original European models that served as inspiration to this new Mediterranean city on the American continent. The old world charm being created from the ground up won architect H. George Fink a special recognition from King Alfonso XIII of Spain for the promotion of the Spanish theme in the city of Coral Gables.

Outdoor spaces, landscaping and "street furniture" were key elements of the overall development scheme. Entrances were designed to greet visitors, residents and prospective buyers. Seven entrances were planned, among them the Alhambra and Granada entrances, with large archways over the streets, built of oolitic limestone effectively softened through landscape. The Douglas Entrance, dubbed "La Puerta del Sol," was designed at the northeast corner of the city as a grand gateway leading from the closest point of access from the city of Miami, into a walled-in, residential and community complex of townhouses, meeting rooms and shops. The project, though only partially completed, managed to achieve the desired effect of an impressive approach to "The City Beautiful." Of the entrances that were built, the Douglas Entrance and the Country Club Prado Entrance still stand in sharp contrast to

each other. The Douglas Entrance is a very urban scheme, reflecting its close proximity to Miami. On the other hand, the Prado Entrance at the northwest corner of Coral Gables relies primarily on landscaping and open space planning for its design. It consists of a number of pylons in an elliptical arrangement, typical of Baroque spaces, leading to a stepped Spanish-styled fountain in a reflecting pool. The plazas contribute to the old world ambience created through cracked stucco, old fashioned lamps, bougainvillea or trickling waters like the De Soto plaza and fountain.

THE DE SOTO FOUNTAIN ON GRANADA BOULEVARD WAS ONE OF THE MEDITERRANEAN STYLE PLAZAS THAT THE QUARTET OF GEORGE MERRICK, DENMAN FINK, GEORGE FINK, AND PHINEAS PAIST PLANNED TO GIVE CORAL GABLES A EUROPEAN FLAVOR.

THE BILTMORE HOTEL, BUILT IN 1925 AT A COST OF TWO MILLION DOLLARS, WAS THE GRANDEST SCHEME OF MERRICK'S CORAL GABLES DEVELOPMENT. SCHULTZE AND WEAVER DESIGNED THE BUILDING WITH A TOWER REMINISCENT OF THOSE OF THE RONEY PLAZA AND THE FREEDOM TOWER. (ROMER COLLECTION, MIAMI-DADE PUBLIC LIBRARY)

THE BILTMORE

THE BILTMORE COUNTRY CLUB, NOW THE METRO-POLITAN MUSEUM AND ART CENTER. (ROMER COLLECTION, MIAMI-DADE PUBLIC LIBRARY)

STAIRCASE DETAIL. (ROMER COLLECTION, MIAMI-DADE PUBLIC LIBRARY)

COLISEUM WAS BUILT AT THE END OF THE CORAL GABLES DEVELOPMENT'S HEYDAY AS A CULTURAL AND SPORTING CENTER. ITS FACADE WAS NEVER FINISHED. (ROMER COLLECTION, MIAMI-DADE PUBLIC LIBRARY)

ORIGINALLY A FURNITURE FACTORY AND SHOWROOM, CHARADES DEMONSTRATES A FINE ADAPTATION OF AN OLDER BUILDING TO A NEW USE WITHOUT LOSS OF VISUAL OR HISTORICAL INTEGRITY. (ROMER COLLECTION, MIAMI-DADE PUBLIC LIBRARY)

THE DOUGLAS ENTRANCE WAS DESIGNED IN 1924 BY WALTER DE GARMO, PHINEAS PAIST AND DENMAN FINK AS A RESIDEN-TIAL, COMMERCIAL, AND CULTURAL COMPLEX CALLED "LA PUERTA DEL SOL" OR GATE OF THE SUN. ITS INSPIRATION CAME FROM SPANISH WALLED-IN TOWNS, REFLECTING ITS URBAN SURROUNDINGS. (ROMER COLLECTION, MIAMI-DADE PUBLIC LIBRARY)

EL PRADO ENTRANCE WAS DESIGNED AND BUILT IN 1927 BY DENMAN FINK. THE PARK SETTING OF FOUNTAINS, PYLONS AND TRELLISES REFLECTS THE CHARACTER OF THE UNDEVELOPED AREAS THAT ONCE SPREAD JUST BEYOND THE NORTHWEST EDGE OF THE CITY OF CORAL GABLES.

THE COLONNADE BUILDING. (ROMER COLLECTION, MIAMI-DADE PUBLIC LIBRARY)

THE COLONNADE BUILDING

Visitors who in 1925 were arriving by busloads were greeted at the Coral Gables Sales Corporation building. It was only appropriate for the headquarters of such an aggressive real estate venture to be as vocifer-

THE COLONNADE BUILDING HAS BEEN BEAUTIFULLY RESTORED, ALTHOUGH THE NEW CONSTRUCTION BEHIND IT DWARFS IT.

ONE OF THE FINEST EARLY HOUSES IN THE CORAL GABLES, ITS 1913 CONSTRUCTION PREDATES THE MEDITER-RANEAN DEVELOPMENT OF THE 1920S. THE BOLD, SLOPING ROOF OF CUBAN BARREL TILES IS SUPPORTED OVER THE PORCH ON SQUARE PIERS OF OOLITIC LIMESTONE.

ous through its architectural statements as the salesmen inside the building were through their mouths. The Colonnade Building, as it was called, was the best possible advertisement for the land sales office. Its architectural sensationalism was as irresistible as the sales pitch that accompanied it. Phineas Paist, chief architect for the city of Coral Gables, is credited with the design and Walter De Garmo and Paul Chalfin as design collaborators.[32] Spanish Baroque elements are used in an exciting, eclectic composition. A two story colonnade climaxes at the central entrance, a whipped cream fantasy realized in stucco. Above, a shallow dome owes its inspiration to

Hadrian's Mausoleum in Rome.[33]

The Colonnade Building has survived the years as motion picture studio, pilot training school, basketball courts and bank offices. Its architecture is yet unrivalled in the changing commercial arteries of Coral Gables.

RESIDENTIAL ARCHITECTURE

In spite of the excellence of commercial buildings and public improvements in the city of Coral Gables, the most impressive accomplishment remains the high quality of residential architectural design. When the Merrick

113

THE STRONG SPANISH INFLUENCE IS SEEN IN THE TILE ROOFS, GALLERIES, ARCHES, COLUMNS AND TRELLIS WORK THAT ADORN THIS CORAL GABLES HOUSE.

family built their home, they combined the gables and classical details such as Palladian windows and Tuscan columns they were accustomed to in Northern houses with a Southern style wrap-around veranda and employed the oolitic stone gathered from the site as principal construction material. The coral

IN THE DORN RESIDENCE, BUILT IN 1926, THE ARCADED LOGGIA RESTING ON DELICATE COLUMNS IS OF ITALIAN INSPIRATION, WHILE THE SECOND STORY TERRACE AND THE TWISTED COLUMNS ARE OF SPANISH ORIGIN. FRENCH DOORS AND A CLASSICAL SENSE OF PROPORTION ADD TO THE MEDITERRANEAN ECLECTICISM OF THE DESIGN. THE DORN FAMILY WAS INFLUENTIAL IN DADE COUNTY REAL ESTATE, BUSINESS AND CIVIC ACTIVITIES SINCE 1896.

colored tiles of the gabled roofs gave the house, and eventually the city, its name of Coral Gables. Merrick's houses for other members of his family and the early houses of the nascent development were also built of oolitic limestone with spacious interiors, bold roof-lines and well landscaped grounds. When the city plan turned in the direction of Spanish Mediterranean design, residential architecture became more elaborate, more self-conscious. Some of the finest examples of Mediterranean architecture are still found in Coral Gables, the product of owners and professional designers with discriminating tastes.

Coral Gables' residential architecture offered something for everyone. Old world escapism through chic living did not have to mean a Spanish Mediterranean house design nor its Moorish or Italianate deviations. The villages offered "alternative styles" for those a breed apart—Chinese, French City, French Country, French Provincial, Dutch South African inspired villages were actually built. Plans for an assortment of other residential areas with design themes from around the world were dashed by Merrick's late financial decline.

THEME VILLAGES

RESIDENCES IN THE FRENCH CITY VILLAGE ARE OF SOBER, ELEGANT DESIGN, WITH TOUCHES OF CLASSICAL DETAILS.

HALF TIMBER DETAILS, NARROW STREETS, SMALL TOWN SCALE AND HIGH GABLE ROOFS ARE MAJOR ELEMENTS OF THE FRENCH PROVINCIAL VILLAGE.

BRIGHT COLORS AND FLARED PAGODA ROOFS ARE AMONG THE MAIN FEATURES OF HOUSES IN THE CHINESE VILLAGE.

CURTISS-BRIGHT DEVELOPMENTS

Coral Gables was not the only planned development of this era. Simultaneous with the Merrick enterprise, Glenn Curtiss and James Bright were planning new communities in the northwest section of Dade County.

Glenn Curtiss, born in Hammondsport, New York in 1878, grew up to become one of the most influential men in aviation history.[34] He invented the aileron, a mechanical part without which no airplane could fly. He was the first man to fly from and land on water, the first to land on the deck of a ship, the first to fly from Albany to New York City, and on and on. He also won the first international aviation race in Rheims, France in 1909. During World War I, ninety-five percent of all American pilots were trained in planes designed by Glenn Curtiss.

In 1912, Curtiss sent a representative to the Miami area to open a flying school. Curtiss himself did not come until 1916. Curtiss moved his school to northwest Dade in 1917, and within a couple of years the Curtiss-Bright Ranch was in existence.[35]

James Bright was a Missourian who came to South Florida in 1909. By 1910 he began acquiring large tracts of land in northwest Dade.[36] The portions that were still wet were planted in Para grass which helped reclaim the land, and consequently established Bright in the cattle ranching business. By the time Curtiss joined the operation, the ranch had expanded to 12,000 acres and the two men agreed to develop some of their holdings into residential communities. From this partnership came the towns of Hialeah and Miami Springs. Glenn Curtiss followed the partnership with the development of Opalocka.

HIALEAH

Hialeah was the first Curtiss-Bright development in Dade County. Like most of the rest of west Dade County, habitable land became available in the Hialeah area after the state drainage program was under way.

In 1908, Richard J. Bolles purchased 500,000 acres from Florida for two dollars an acre.[37] As a result he owned most of what today is Hialeah. Bolles subdivided the land into ten acre tracts and put the parcels up for

"WELCOME TO HIALEAH" PROCLAIMS THE SIGN ON THE INDIAN BILLBOARD FIGURE ON OKEECHOBEE ROAD. ACROSS THE STREET IS THE REAL ESTATE OFFICE BUILDING. (ROMER COLLECTION, MIAMI-DADE PUBLIC LIBRARY)

sale. Bolles' project, like many others begun in the Everglades before drainage was complete, came under attack when the land proved to be less fertile and more wet than promised.[38]

In 1921, the Curtiss-Bright interests announced the creation of the town of Hialeah where they sold ten acre tracts. Within a year there were forty-one families living in Hialeah which was soon dubbed "the Gateway to the Everglades."[39] As the momentum of the real estate boom gathered, Hialeah's character began to change from rural to suburban with the construction of more homes, entertainment and sport facilities including a greyhound race track, a horse track, a jai-alai fronton, and an amusement park.

Among the more interesting of Hialeah's early businesses was the Miami Studios, a motion picture company. In 1922, the company erected a large building on West Ninth Street between Second and Third Avenues.[40] Many of the silent screen's most famous stars made pictures there. One of D.W. Griffith's classic films, "The White Rose" was made, in part, at the Hialeah studio.[41]

Both Glenn Curtiss and James Bright built homes in Hialeah, but they soon turned their attention to subsequent developments

designed in grander schemes as they, too, became intoxicated by the apparently limitless financial and architectural possibilites of the South Florida real estate market.

THE PADDOCK AREA BEHIND THE GRANDSTAND AT HIALEAH RACE TRACK. (ROMER COLLECTION, MIAMI-DADE PUBLIC LIBRARY)

THE HIALEAH DEPOT OF THE SEABOARD COASTLINE RAILWAY, STILL STANDING, REPRODUCES THE STREET ELEVATION OF A SPANISH VILLAGE. (ROMER COLLECTION, MIAMI-DADE PUBLIC LIBRARY)

THE SEMINOLE LODGE, WHICH DOUBLED AS POLICE STATION, HAS THE CURVED PARAPETS, SIMPLE MOLDINGS AND SLOPING TILE DETAILS TYPICAL OF THE MISSION STYLE. (ROMER COLLECTION, MIAMI-DADE PUBLIC LIBRARY)

HIALEAH MISSION

Hialeah was not a planned development with a well defined, central architectural theme like the subsequent plans for Miami Springs and Opa-locka. The predominant building types of the early years in Hialeah, however, show a strong tendency to the Mission style. Hialeah did not introduce the Mission vernacular to Dade County, as pointed out earlier when August Geiger refers to his designs as Mission in style, but it was the earliest residential area to make widespread use of it. The first houses in Hialeah were designed in the Mission style. The largest, best example of Mission architecture in Hialeah, however, is the building of the City of Miami Water Plant. The interpretation of the style in local limestone makes a powerful statement, capturing the simple boldness of Mission architecture at its best.

THE JAMES BRIGHT RESIDENCE, BUILT IN 1921 IN THE MISSION STYLE, WAS ONE OF THE EARLIEST HOUSES IN HIALEAH.

THE MIAMI WATER PLANT, BUILT IN HIALEAH IN 1924.

COUNTRY CLUB ESTATES IN ITS EARLIEST DAYS MAY NOT EXACTLY HAVE LIVED UP TO ITS NAME, BUT THE DEVELOPMENT LATER BECAME THE VERY ATTRACTIVE MIAMI SPRINGS. (ROMER COLLECTION, MIAMI-DADE PUBLIC LIBRARY)

MIAMI SPRINGS

Dismayed by the rapid, uncontrolled growth of Hialeah, Curtiss decided to build a second residential community on another Curtiss-Bright tract of land, featuring strict building and zoning codes. Miami Springs was the end result of this plan. In 1922, Curtiss surveyed his tract from the air and began laying out streets. The early city plan included a wide boulevard lined with Australian pines, a small business district centered around a circular plaza, a golf course and the residential area clustered about winding drives. Lots were expensive; many sold for $1,200.00 apiece.[42] In some instances, however, Curtiss gave away land to aviator friends with the stipulation that homes would be constructed immediately on these lots. No roofs except those lined with tiles could be visible over the trees, and houses were required to be set back from the street and contain backyards. No industry and few businesses were permitted. Moreover, every effort was made to preserve and enhance the area's natural beauty.

In 1926, the development was incorporated as a town. It was originally named Country Club Estates. Four years later, its name was changed to Miami Springs in recognition of the fifteen wells of spring water (located primarily under the golf course) which provided the city of Miami with its water supply.

MIAMI SPRINGS PUEBLO

Curtiss and Bright were both familiar with the American Southwest. Curtiss' involvement in the aviation business had exposed him to more regions of the United States than most of his contemporaries. James Bright's business interests prior to moving into Florida had concentrated in the Southwestern states and in Mexico. It is therefore no coincidence that the first two residential developments planned by the Curtiss-Bright team should be based on architectural themes influenced by the Mission and Spanish Colonial vernacular popular at that time in the Southwest.

Plans for Miami Springs were left less to chance than in Hialeah. With a more exclusive planned development to face the fierce competition of the times, Curtiss and Bright adopted an architectural theme of quaint,

119

THE "MIAMI SPRINGS VILLAS" WAS ORIGINALLY THE RESIDENCE OF GLENN CURTISS, WHICH HE DESIGNED IN 1925.

BUILT IN 1926 AS THE PUEBLO HOTEL, THIS IS THE LARGEST, MOST EXTRAVAGANT PROJECT OF CURTISS' DEVELOPMENT IN MIAMI SPRINGS. IN 1929, JOHN HARVEY KELLOGG, OF CEREAL PRODUCTS FAME, PURCHASED THE BUILDING AND CONVERTED IT TO THE MIAMI BATTLE CREEK SANITARIUM. DURING WORLD WAR II IT SERVED AS A REST FACILITY FOR SOLDIERS, LATER AS A HEALTH SPA AND MORE RECENTLY AS THE FAIRHAVEN RETIREMENT HOME. (ROMER COLLECTION, MIAMI-DADE PUBLIC LIBRARY)

"THE ALAMO," SO NAMED FOR ITS VAGUE RESEMBLANCE TO THE TEXAS LANDMARK, WAS BUILT IN 1926 FOR GLENN CURTISS' MOTHER. ◄

ARABIAN NIGHTS FESTIVAL IN OPA-LOCKA. (ROMER COLLECTION, MIAMI-DADE PUBLIC LIBRARY)

picturesque quality in order to lure prospective land buyers. The Pueblo style was selected as the architectural theme of Miami Springs. Pueblo architecture had become a popular local vernacular particularly in New Mexico and Arizona in the 1920s. It combined Indian, Spanish Colonial and Mission features, all native to the region. It was an architecture at home in the desert, where the natural environment along with available materials and methods of construction had created the style. In South Florida, it was picturesque but foreign, more of a conversation piece or sales gimmick. The soft forms of the earlier adobe dwellings were translated to modern building techniques of cement blocks (sometimes wood balloon frame) faced with hand molded stucco instead of the original sun dried mud. Exposed roof beams (vigas) projecting from the soft curved parapet walls are among the most recognizable effects. The beam ends were often attached to the exterior of the building rather than being actually exposed structural members. The intense sun of the Southwest deserts with little help from breeze or rain and the primitive building technology account for the thick walls and small

openings of the style. In South Florida, a style of large openings, central courtyards, overhanging and sloping roofs might have been more practical and appropriate.

The popularity of Pueblo architecture in Miami Springs was short lived. Construction was slow in the early years and was virtually halted with the real estate collapse that followed the hurricane of 1926. When building activity resumed, the original architectural theme was abandoned.

OPA-LOCKA

Glenn Curtiss independently embarked upon a third development which was originally named "Opatishawockaloca," from an Indian word meaning "big island covered with many trees in the swamps." By 1921, Curtiss had shortened the name to "Opa-locka" and began planning the city on the 120,000 acre Curtiss-Bright Ranch. The shortened version of the name first appeared as the name of present day East Second Avenue in Hialeah.[43]

Curtiss idealistically wanted Opa-locka to be "the most perfect city that planning and

THE HURT BUILDING, LATER KNOWN AS THE OPA-LOCKA HOTEL, WAS BUILT IN 1926. THE BUILDING HOUSED SHOPS, GUEST ROOMS, OFFICES, A SOCIAL HALL, A GAS STATION AND THE FIRST OPA-LOCKA POST OFFICE (ROMER COLLECTION, MIAMI-DADE PUBLIC LIBRARY)

engineering could achieve, and the most beautiful that the art of man could conceive."[44] He hired architect Bernhardt Muller of New York, who in keeping with the romantic fantasy of the era, selected a medieval English village motif with a castle at its center. Curtiss later decided he preferred an Arabian theme and sent a copy of the book *The One Thousand and One Tales From the Arabian Nights* to Muller with a note that instructed him to design an Arabian Opa-locka.

While Muller was working on the plans for Opa-Locka in 1925, Glenn Curtiss became aware that the real estate boom was subsiding. Even so he decided to continue with the project and in February of 1926, began construction. Several of the Curtiss/Muller Arabian fantasies were erected, but after the devastating repercussions of the '26 hurri-

cane and the Depression, Curtiss was forced to abandon his efforts to complete the city as planned.

OPA-LOCKA MOORISH

The architecture Bernhardt Muller created for Opa-locka was not Moorish in the Mediterranean Revival spirit of the Islamic period of domination over North Africa and Southern Spain. The style was out of the pages of a fairy tale, and the product was as unreal as "the Arabian Nights" themselves.

The Opa-locka development was barely started when the real estate boom began its decline. In the summer of 1926, the Administration Building (City Hall) was completed, only weeks before the devastating

122

OPA-LOCKA ADMINISTRATION BUILDING, NOW THE CITY HALL, WAS BUILT IN 1926. ONLY ONE OF THE ORIGINAL FIVE DOMES REMAINS. (ROMER COLLECTION, MIAMI-DADE PUBLIC LIBRARY)

OPA-LOCKA ADMINISTRATION BUILDING, NOW THE CITY HALL, WAS BUILT IN 1926. ONLY ONE OF THE ORIGINAL FIVE DOMES REMAINED BEFORE ITS FULL RESTORATION IN 1988. (ROMER COLLECTION, MIAMI-DADE PUBLIC LIBRARY)

THE OPA-LOCKA RAILROAD STATION IS ONE OF THE FIRST BUILDINGS OF THE CURTISS DEVELOPMENT. ITS MULTI-COLORED GLAZED TILE DETAILS IN A VARIETY OF PATTERNS ARE ONE OF ITS FINEST FEATURES. THE REAR PORTION OF THE BUILDING WAS SERIOUSLY DAMAGED BY FIRE IN 1982. IT PRESENTLY AWAITS RELOCATION AND REHABILITATION.

hurricane struck. It may be speculated that the modest scale and construction during the early development phases might have been a reaction to the economic slump that ensued the hurricane bust. The small lot size and the stucco over the wood frame construction in residential areas seem to indicate that the Curtiss scheme was planned as a lower priced suburb than Merrick's Coral Gables, whose concept it tried to emulate while falling far short of it. The Moorish buildings needed a larger scale to be effective. The style is best seen in the City Hall buildings, with their array of domes, minarets, watchtowers and other special effects such as crenellated parapets, cracked stucco showing a fake brick structure, quaint balconies and a variety of arches. In the small residential buildings the same features became overpowering and comical, bordering on the absurd.

Opa-locka stands as evidence of the fantasies and excesses of the times in a dream gone sour before it began. The remnants of its early days make up one of Dade County's most fascinating architectural exhibits.

OPA-LOCKA HOUSE, DESIGNED IN THE MOORISH STYLE.

124

WILLIAM JENNINGS BRYAN ELEMENTARY SCHOOL WAS BUILT IN NORTH MIAMI IN 1930, ON THE ORIGINAL SITE OF THE ARCH CREEK SCHOOL. THE MEDITERRANEAN STYLE BUILDING WAS DESIGNED BY E. L. ROBERTSON.

NORTH MIAMI AREA

Prior to the 1920s, north Dade County was sparsely settled, but as the real estate boom created an increased demand for land, remote groves were soon being converted to subdivisions. While a concentrated settlement and steady development of North Dade is relatively recent in comparison to some other areas of South Florida, what is now North Miami has a fairly long human history. To the first known settlers, besides the Tequesta Indians, the area known as Arch Creek, was the most consistent focal point of activity. After several name transitions, the city of North Miami was the end result.

The one geographic feature that attracted people to the area throughout the latter part of the nineteenth century was the naturally formed limestone bridge that extended across the creek. The bridge became a favorite spot for early picnickers and tourists, but the rich soil eventually brought permanent settlement. Among the first successful farmers in the area was C.G. Ihle who raised a rich variety of garden vegetables and tropical fruits.[45] During the last years of the nine-

teenth century, Arch Creek began to take on the trappings of a community. Julia Tuttle, and later Fred Muller, subdivided their land holdings in the area and began to sell lots to newcomers. By 1912, Arch Creek contained eighteen homes, a population in excess of one hundred, a post office, a one room grammar school, the United Congregational Church of Arch Creek, and a small business district, which included two tomato packing houses near the railroad station.

In the 1920s, the land boom soon transformed this picture of agrarian harmony into a fast-paced town. The major boomtime developers in the community north of Miami were Arthur Griffing, D.F. Baker, and Earl Irons. Griffing, the most important of this group, came to the area in 1903, and purchased a large parcel of farmland. Baker and Irons platted a number of lesser subdivisions which also contributed to the development of the area.

The success of these developments created a demand for incorporation. On February 5, 1926, Arch Creek was incorporated as "The Town of Miami Shores." The name came from the title of a popular song of the day and was believed to be more alluring.

125

This action created a confusing situation because just south of the declared limits of the "Town of Miami Shores" was the large subdivision also known as "Miami Shores."

The preferred means for municipal incorporation was by act of the state legislature. The Town of Miami Shores incorporated by declaration so it would not have to wait until the State Legislature reconvened. The developers were anxious for incorporation because it meant that they would not have to foot the bill for improvements such as water, sewer lines, and paved roads. The town originally included part of Miami Beach and extended south to the northern limit of the city of Miami. The rapid development of the North Miami area, like the rest of the county, was brought to an abrupt halt by the hurricane of 1926. Despite this fact, the town fathers continued to expand the town limits, annexing Sunny Isles, Golden Beach, and all of the ocean front to the Broward County line.

However, the bust and hurricane had affected the town too severely. The rapid expansionism and methods of selling property employed by developers of the Town of Miami Shores caused the area to be devastated by the bust of the real estate market. People defaulted on payments for lots, many houses under construction at the time the hurricane struck were a complete loss, and a bridge over to the town's ocean frontage also was destroyed, cutting off all services to the area. It was not long before there were several moves for secession from the town.

Despite the fact that the town of Miami Shores (North Miami) received a large federal loan to help repair hurricane damage, the community remained in financial trouble. Local banks were reluctant to loan money to a town that was so closely associated with the bust. In March of 1927, Councilman Griffing proposed that the name of the town of Miami Shores be changed to "North Miami," the name which passed through an Act of the Legislature on June 6, 1927.

North Miami entered a period of lengthy economic depression. During the next decade the township lost about one half of its area and all its ocean frontage. Outlying regions began complaining of lack of services and started withdrawing from the town either by lawsuit or simple secession. The real estate bust and the depression years considerably

A SPANISH STYLED RESIDENCE IN NORTH MIAMI, BUILT IN 1926.

TWO STORY MISSION STYLE HOUSE IN BISCAYNE PARK.

slowed the growth of North Miami.

Other boomtime residential developments in northeast Dade County include Biscayne Park, a subdivision of Arthur Griffing's, nestled between Miami Shores and North Miami, and El Portal, just south of Miami Shores. El Portal existed before the boom as an area of sprawling groves. Its major period of development, like Biscayne Park, was begun on the verge of the financial bust. Their early growth was slow and their architecture followed in the footsteps of the larger trendsetters. The older buildings in these areas are individual examples without the same uniformity of style or scale that was apparent in the planned developments.

ONE OF THE PUREST MISSION STYLE RESIDENCES IN BISCAYNE PARK, BUILT AROUND 1929.

THE OLDEST KNOWN HOUSE STILL STANDING IN EL PORTAL. IT WAS BUILT AROUND 1910 IN THE AREA OF MIAMI SHORES AND RELOCATED TO ITS PRESENT SITE BEFORE 1925. THE HOUSE WAS FULLY REHABILITATED IN 1988 AND ITS SECOND STORY PORCH WAS RE-OPENED.

THE SHERWOOD FOREST SUBDIVISION IN EL PORTAL CONTAINS HALF TIMBER STYLE HOUSES, INSPIRED BY ENGLISH COTTAGES, IN A DENSELY VEGETATED SETTING.

MIAMI SHORES

The Miami Shores subdivision, which had created some identity problems for the town of Miami Shores, was a development of the Miami Shores Company, a subsidiary of Hugh Anderson's Shoreland Company. Hugh Anderson moved to South Florida around 1908 and quickly amassed a fortune in real estate development. In 1924, Anderson's Shoreland Company purchased a 1,600 acre tract north of Little River and proceeded to build the community of Miami Shores.[46]

The site of the future Miami Shores contained a colorful history long before its purchase by the Shoreland Company. In the decades following the Civil War, several homesteaders, including Edward Barnott, Richard Potter, and William Brooks, settled in parts of this area of thick piney woods and palmetto scrubs. In the early 1870s, William Gleason and William H. Hunt, two carpetbaggers who took over local politics after the Civil War, moved from the tiny village of Miami to the present site of Miami Shores and founded the community of Biscayne. They brought with them the permit to operate the Miami Post Office and renamed it the Biscayne Post Office. In the ensuing years, Biscayne served frequently as the county seat, while many settlers, including E.T. Sturtevant, father of Julia Tuttle, settled in the community.[47]

Biscayne failed to sustain its early growth and promise. In the 1880s, many early residents had departed and the post office was closed. Construction of a county road through the area led to a brief revival in its fortunes near the end of the century. Later, a railroad depot and school were constructed.

At the beginning of the twentieth century, T.V. Moore, a Miami furniture retailer who was also president of the Biscayne Fruit Company, purchased a piece of the old Brooks' homestead and transformed it into a pineapple plantation. Moore's parcel would later become the nucleus of Miami Shores. After World War I, L.T. Cooper, a wealthy patent medicine manufacturer, purchased Moore's property with the intention of marketing it under the name of Bay View Estates. Before Cooper's scheme advanced very far, however, Anderson and the Shoreland Company bought the tract. By the latter part of 1924,

THE MIAMI SHORES ELEMENTARY SCHOOL, DESIGNED BY ROBERT LAW WEED, IS ONE OF THE EARLIEST ART DECO BUILDINGS IN THE MIAMI AREA.

Anderson had provided his envisioned community with a name, Miami Shores. Originally, the area was only a series of subdivisions, not a town. But two years later, when North Miami chose the same name, it created considerable rivalry.

To promote his development, Anderson embarked on an ambitious advertising campaign. A full page ad in the *Miami Daily News and Metropolis* for November 24, 1924, in behalf of "America's Mediterranean" insisted, perhaps prematurely, that "Miami Shores absolutely dominates South Florida's development activities." On December 4, 1924, the first day of sales, land-hungry customers purchased more than 2.5 million dollars of real estate. Ten months later, as boomtime speculation reached hysterical heights, the Miami Shores Company sold an incredible 33.7 million dollars in land.[48] Altogether for 1925, Miami Shores recorded 75 million dollars in sales, second only to Coral Gables.

During the year of 1925, a community emerged on the site of old fruit groves. Elaborate two-story residences arose, each closely patterned after the Mediterranean Revival style of architecture so popular in Coral Gables. Miami Shores also featured broad sidewalks and sweeping thoroughfares. The hub of development was the intersection of Shoreland Boulevard (N.E. 2nd Avenue) where a small business district arose.

In August 1925, the Shoreland Company announced plans for a 35 million dollar building and development program. The plan included acquisition of additional acreage and construction of several grand hotels, Miami Shores Island, a 600 acre community in Biscayne Bay connected by a causeway to the mainland, and elaborate structures along the bay on recently purchased waterfront property. Only part of this plan was completed before the collapse of the boom.

In 1925, when the boom was still at its height, the Shoreland Company subdivisions were annexed by the city of Miami.[49] At this time, the company had platted numerous subdivisions within their 2,800 acres. They were inhabited by a population of 1,389 persons. Another plan initiated by the Shoreland

THE TYLER RESIDENCE, BUILT IN 1925, WAS THE FIRST HOUSE IN THE MIAMI SHORES DEVELOPMENT.

THE WRIGHT HOUSE, DESIGNED IN 1925 BY KIEHNEL AND ELLIOTT. IT WAS BUILT FOR A VICE-PRESIDENT OF THE SHORELAND COMPANY.

THE JEFFRIES HOUSE, COMPLETED IN 1927, IS ONE OF THE FINEST WORKS OF MEDITERRANEAN REVIVAL IN MIAMI SHORES. IT WAS THE HOME OF THE SECRETARY AND TREASURER OF THE SHORELAND COMPANY.

THE SPEARS HARRIS HOUSE WAS BUILT IN 1925 FOR A VICE-PRESIDENT OF THE SHORELAND COMPANY.

THE PHILLIPS HOUSE WAS BUILT IN 1925 AS CENTERPIECE OF THE BELMAR DEVELOPMENT, JUST SOUTH OF MIAMI SHORES ON THE BAY.

MORNINGSIDE

COURTYARD VIEW OF THE CUSHMAN SCHOOL ERECTED IN 1926 FROM A DESIGN BY RUSSELL PANCOAST CREATED TO THE SPECIFICATIONS OF THE SCHOOL'S FOUNDER, DR. LAURA CUSHMAN. (ROMER COLLECTION, MIAMI-DADE PUBLIC LIBRARY)

RESIDENCE DESIGNED BY MARION MANLEY, MIAMI'S FIRST WOMAN ARCHITECT.

THE STRONG DIAGONAL OF THE EXTERIOR STAIRCASE ROOF IS THE MOST SALIENT FEATURE OF THIS MEDITERRANEAN STYLE HOUSE.

BUENA VISTA

STRONG ITALIAN INFLUENCE IN THE ARCADED PORCH AND SQUARE TOWER ARE STILL STRIKING FEATURES OF THIS HOUSE IN SPITE OF YEARS OF NEGLECT.

DETAIL OF T.V. MOORE'S HOUSE IN BUENA VISTA. (ROMER COLLECTION, MIAMI-DADE PUBLIC LIBRARY)

132

EDGEWATER

NEO CLASSIC REVIVAL RESIDENCE WITH A SPANISH TILE ROOF SHOWS TYPICAL ECLECTICISM OF THE 1920'S.

A PROFUSION OF WINDOWS AND WIDE ROOF OVERHANGS MAXIMIZE THIS HOUSE'S BAYFRONT LOCATION.

GROVE PARK

THE GROVE PARK SUBDIVISION WAS DEVELOPED BY THE TATUM BROTHERS IN THE 1920S. MISSION AND SPANISH INFLUENCED HOUSES, RATHER THAN THE FORMER BUNGALOWS OF LAWRENCE ESTATES PARK COMPOSE THE MAIN BUILDING STOCK OF THIS SUBURBAN AREA OF MIAMI.

SHENANDOAH

TYPICAL RESIDENTIAL STREET OF THE SHENANDOAH SUBDIVISION IN THE SOUTHWEST AREA OF THE CITY OF MIAMI. (ROMER COLLECTION, MIAMI-DADE LIBRARY)

MISSION INFLUENCED HOUSE IN SHENANDOAH AREA, WITH THE POPULAR STRIPED CANVAS AWN-INGS. (ROMER COLLECTION, MIAMI-DADE PUBLIC LIBRARY)

DOWNTOWN SKYLINE IN 1925. (ROMER COLLECTION, MIAMI-DADE PUBLIC LIBRARY)

Company in 1925, was the construction of Biscayne Boulevard. Hugh Anderson wanted a major thoroughfare connecting downtown Miami to Miami Shores and other intended North Dade developments. Anderson and his partner, Roy C. Wright, commissioned a survey and began purchasing tracts along the proposed route. Quite a few people did not fancy a 100 foot wide road coming through their property, but that did not stop Anderson, Wright, and the M.R. Harrison Construction Company who waited until one Saturday midnight and bulldozed through private property to which they had no legal title. The Anderson enterprises were eventually ruined by the bust of the real estate market, but Biscayne Boulevard was opened officially on November 11, 1926, prominently linking Miami Shores to the rest of the county. In the aftermath of the boom, the financially troubled Shoreland Company turned over ownership of their tract to Bessemer Properties, a large land development corporation. In 1932, the Miami Shores community withdrew from Miami and incorporated as the "Village of Miami Shores."

DOWNTOWN

The center of Miami easily matched suburban construction during the boom years. In 1921, the Chaille Street Plan divided the city into four sections, S.E., N.W., N.E., S.W., enabling expansion that soon extended to other municipal boundaries.[50] The local political climate was supportive as well. By 1924, the City Commission was known as the "Banker Commission"[51] because everyone of its members, including the mayor, were bankers.

By 1925 the Miami city skyline was a mass of skeletal structures in various stages of completion. The amount of construction during this period was phenomenal. Such a large volume of building material was flooding the city that on August 18th, the F.E.C. announced an embargo on shipments, because 851 freight cars loaded with supplies were backed up on side tracks and 700 more were enroute or waiting.[52]

The boom was not just relegated to real estate and the railroad. As a result of the increased population and activity, all businesses were expanding at a rapid pace. The *Miami Herald* became the primary mouthpiece of the boom and leapt to national prominence in the process. In contrast many of the other publications, mostly tabloids, that suddenly appeared on newsstands during these years died with the boom's demise.[53]

There was a marked increase in the demand for the services of public utilities as well, in the mid-1920s. The American Power and Light Company purchased the Miami Beach Electric Company, Miami Electric Light and Power Company, the Miami Gas Company and the Southern Utilities Company which had plants as far north as St. Augustine. The new system changed its name to Florida Power and Light on December 28, 1925.[54] In a similar fashion, South Bell took over the South Atlantic Telephone and Telegraph Company during those years.[55]

In downtown Miami there were new banks, new offices, government buildings, retail businesses, hotels and apartments. Flagler Street emerged as the center of town. Frederick Rand, an attorney and real estate developer, devised a plan to redirect the center to N.E. 2nd Avenue because he owned property at twenty-five street corners between 1st and 14th Streets.[56] *The Miami News* building was erected in the area, the new Burdine and Quarterman's store opened its doors and Rand began the Roosevelt Hotel, later renamed Lindsey Hopkins. The plan was not completed in time to avoid the repercussions of the bust. Soon the frantic construction in downtown Miami abated, leaving the city in a stillness not familiar to most of the new population.

BURDINE AND QUARTERMAN DEPARTMENT STORE OPENED ITS DOORS IN 1926 AS PART OF FREDERICK RAND'S DEVELOPMENT OF N.E. SECOND AVENUE. THE BUILDING STILL STANDS, ALTHOUGH THE FINE GOTHIC STYLE DETAILS AND THE ARCHED PORTALS HAVE BEEN ELIMINATED. (ROMER COLLECTION, MIAMI-DADE PUBLIC LIBRARY)

EARLY DOWNTOWN HIGHRISES PHOTOGRAPHED FROM THE MIAMI RIVER. NONE OF THESE BUILDINGS REMAIN. (ROMER COLLECTION, MIAMI-DADE PUBLIC LIBRARY)

HIGH-RISE BUILDINGS

As the ten story height restriction was removed from the building code in 1925,[57] a new type of architecture rose in downtown Miami. High-rise office building designs, inspired by Neo-Classical, Mediterranean and Beaux Arts styles, were built utilizing methods of construction developed by the Chicago School during the 1880s. After the Chicago Fire, a new fireproof building technique made possible higher buildings with non load-bearing walls, resulting in the first "skyscrapers." Architects of the Chicago School searched for an esthetic expression for the skyscraper, but it was Louis Sullivan who perfected the vocabulary of the high-rise. His buildings were divided vertically into a base, a main body and a bold, projecting cornice. This construction technique and the forms of expression it employed became known as the "Commercial Style" of architecture. Miami buildings, although not true representatives of the Chicago School, did use the steel frame structural system and the three-part, classical composition.

A. Ten Eyck Brown designed courthouses in cities across the United States, including Albany, Atlanta, and Athens in Georgia, and New Orleans, in Neo-Classical and

NEW COURTHOUSE SKELETAL FRAME RISES AROUND THE 1904 BUILDING. (ROMER COLLECTION, MIAMI-DADE PUBLIC LIBRARY)

DADE COUNTY COURTHOUSE, BUILT BETWEEN 1925 AND 1929 BY ARCHITECT A. TEN EYCK BROWN WITH AUGUST GEIGER AS ASSOCIATE. (ROMER COLLECTION, MIAMI-DADE PUBLIC LIBRARY)

THE INGRAHAM BUILDING, DESIGNED BY SCHULTZE AND WEAVER, WAS COMPLETED IN 1927 AND IS STILL ONE OF THE MOST ELEGANT OFFICE BUILDINGS IN DOWNTOWN MIAMI. THE COMMERCIAL STYLE TYPICAL OF THE CHICAGO SCHOOL IS EXPRESSED HERE IN THE VOCABULARY OF THE ITALIAN RENAISSANCE PALACE. (ROMER COLLECTION, MIAMI-DADE PUBLIC LIBRARY)

THE HUNTINGTON BUILDING WAS COMPLETED IN 1926. THE GARGOYLE-TOPPED BASE WAS REMODELLED IN THE 1950S, BUT THE SCULPTURED BUSTS ON THE PARAPET STILL PROVIDE ONE OF THE MOST INTERESTING ROOF LINES IN MIAMI. (ROMER COLLECTION, MIAMI-DADE PUBLIC LIBRARY)

Beaux Arts idioms. For the Dade County Courthouse, Brown and collaborator August Geiger retained the stylistic features and details of the other courthouse designs but introduced a tower, elevating the building to a height of twenty-seven stories,[58] without losing its "classicism" in composition or detail.

Schultze and Weaver's Ingraham Building was designed in the Beaux Arts tradition patterned after the Florentine palace of the Renaissance. This elegant office building displays the rusticated stone facing diminishing in texture toward the top, typical of the "quattrocento" palaces. Proportions, however, depart from the Italian models, as the main body is increased, joining the ranks of the New York skyscraper and Chicago School buildings, but at a height of only thirteen stories.

THE ORIGINAL TWO STORY SEYBOLD ARCADE WAS BUILT IN 1921. IN 1925 IT WAS ENLARGED TO A TEN STORY BUILDING BY ARCHITECTS KIEHNEL AND ELLIOTT. JOHN SEYBOLD WAS A PROMINENT MERCHANT IN MIAMI SINCE 1896.

THE OLYMPIA THEATER IS NOW THE GUSMAN CULTURAL CENTER. BUILT IN 1925 BY THE CHICAGO FIRM OF EBERSON AND EBERSON, IT WAS THE SECOND IN A SERIES OF ATMOSPHERIC THEATERS IN THE COUNTRY, COMPLETE WITH TWINKLING STARS. IT WAS ORIGINALLY ONE OF THE FINEST VAUDEVILLE THEATERS OF ITS TIME. (ROMER COLLECTION, MIAMI-DADE PUBLIC LIBRARY)

▶ EXTERIOR OF GUSMAN HALL.

THE CAPITAL BUILDING, ORIGINALLY THE SECURITY BUILD-ING, WAS DESIGNED IN 1926 BY ROBERT GREENFIELD OF NEW YORK. ITS COPPER-FACED MANSARD ROOF, TRIMMED IN GLAZED TERRA-COTTA, IS THE ONLY FRENCH SECOND EMPIRE DESIGN IN DOWNTOWN MIAMI. ▲

138

FREEDOM TOWER, BUILT IN 1925 AS THE HOME OF *THE MIAMI DAILY NEWS.* **(ROMER COLLECTION, MIAMI-DADE PUBLIC LIBRARY)**

DAILY NEWS TOWER

The Miami Metropolis was the first newspaper printed in Miami, established in 1896 with the support of Henry Flagler. Later renamed the *Miami Daily News*, it had grown in size and stature at a pace equal to that of the city of Miami. Under the ownership of James M. Cox, a former Governor of the State of Ohio and presidential candidate in 1920,[59] a new building was erected in 1925 to accommodate the paper's increased circulation. The prestigious New York firm of Schultze and Weaver was selected for the work, based on their excellent credits. Leonard Schultze was the chief designer for New York's Grand Central Terminal in 1903 and later, in partnership with S. Fullerton Weaver, the firm was responsible for the design of the Waldorf-Astoria and New York Biltmore, the Los Angeles Biltmore, the Breakers in Palm Beach, the Miami Biltmore in Coral Gables and the Roney Plaza in Miami Beach.[60]

The News Tower is inspired by the Giralda Tower in Seville, Spain. The Giralda shows its 800 years of construction in a pro-gression from Moorish at the base to Palladian and finally Baroque influences at the top. The News Tower, on the other hand, achieved a more unified composition through details of Spanish Plateresque vocabulary.[61] The emphasis of the applied ornament at the top, and around main openings is in typical Spanish Baroque fashion.

The classical influence is evident in the building mass—a three story base, mounted by a twelve story tower on which rests a two story cupola structure. The three part composition carries through horizontally also, as the base is interrupted by engaged pilasters which visually continue the mass of the central tower down to the ground. The decorative elements show exceptional craftsmanship throughout the building. Outside ornamental detailing, executed by the John B. Orr Construction Company, is in cast travertine, artificial stone veined and dyed to a pink color, similar to the surface treatment at El Jardin by Kiehnel and Elliott.[62] The interior is embellished by vaulted ceilings, stone bas reliefs, murals and multi-colored handmade ceramic tiles imported from Spain, Africa, South America and Cuba.[63]

FREEDOM TOWER, ENTRANCE DETAIL.

139

BISCAYNE BOULEVARD LOOKING SOUTH FROM 19TH STREET. MEDITERRANEAN STYLE BUILDINGS ON THE LEFT OF THE PHOTOGRAPH STILL STAND. THE CHRISTIAN SERVICE CHURCH, SEEN ON THE RIGHT OF THE PICTURE, WAS DESIGNED BY AUGUST GEIGER.

The Freedom Tower, renamed after its use as Cuban Refugee Center between 1962 and 1974, still stands as one of the most impressive monuments in the downtown skyline. The building underwent extensive restoration in 1988 and now serves as offices, club and banquet facilities.

LOW-RISE COMMERCIAL BUILDINGS

The real estate boom of the 1920s was well on its way to oblivion in 1926 when the hurricane certified its passage. The previous decline in buyers combined with the natural disaster financially wiped many developers out of the real estate market, and others deserted it as land values slid down the scale that measured speculators' fantasies.

At least one major development scheme was enacted in the aftermath of the boom. Henry Phipps of the U.S. Steel Corporation bought out the financially troubled Shoreland Company of Miami Shores in 1926 when its owners found themselves unable to complete Biscayne Boulevard. The Phipps family formed

the Biscayne Boulevard Company, later known as Bessemer Properties, and completed the construction of the thoroughfare. They also obtained most of the property fronting on the boulevard between 13th and 40th Streets with the intention of making that stretch one of the area's finest commercial sections. At 13th Street and the boulevard, they constructed a wide traffic circle and just north of it, in the next decade, rose the elegant Sears Tower, the Mahi Shrine Temple, the Mayfair Theatre, the Hirsch-Faith Furniture Company among many others, built by, or built on property owned by the Biscayne Boulevard Company.

Contrary to the high-rise architecture downtown, buildings constructed in the area of the new Biscayne Boulevard were low in scale and gaily decorated, dressed up to receive the well-garbed clientele for which they were designed. Real estate values considerably lower than in the already densely built downtown area allowed developers to spread the interior spaces over large lots with generous street frontage. It was estimated that the Phipps family still owned eighty-five percent of the commercial property north of 13th Street even as late as the 1950s.[64]

THE CENTRAL CHRISTIAN CHURCH WAS COMPLETED IN 1925, DEMOLISHED IN 1987. (ROMER COLLECTION, MIAMI-DADE PUBLIC LIBRARY)

A miniscule number of people, such as the Phipps, retained and even multiplied staggering personal wealth during the years of the Great Depression which were to follow, but in stark contrast many more would be standing in very long bread lines. The buildings that went up along Biscayne Boulevard just as the Depression was beginning must have been reassuring symbols to those already struggling to wait out the faltered economy. Their style of architecture certainly reflected the modern age, or at least held out the hope that a new age might come to Miami.

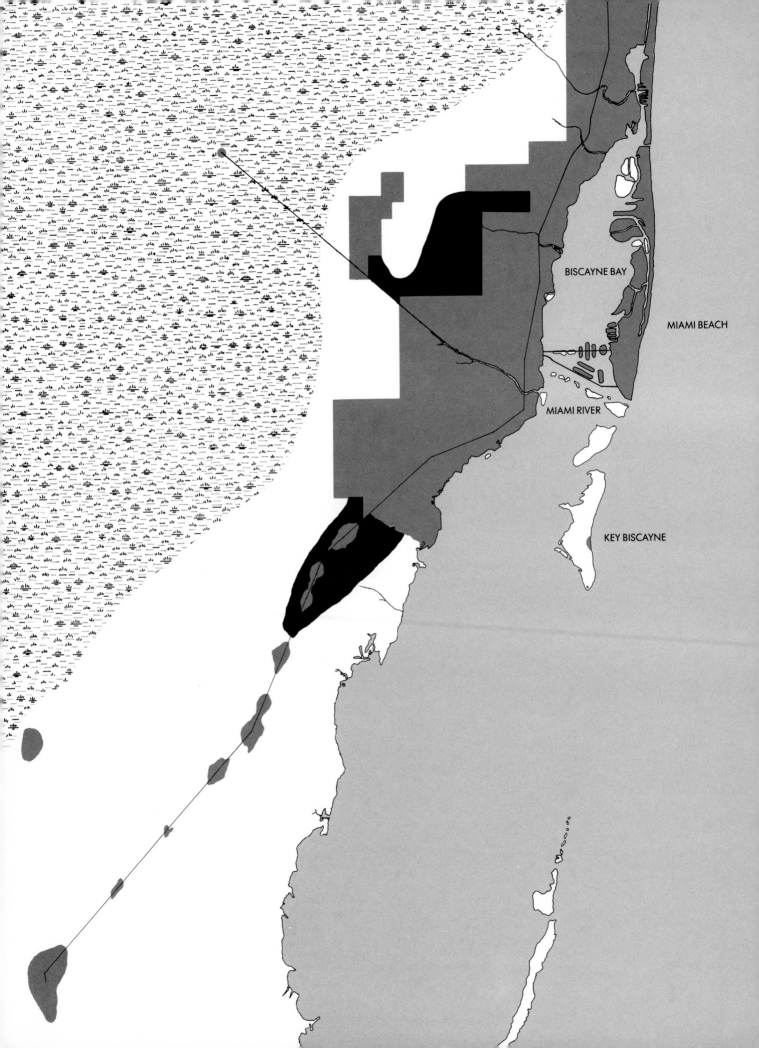

BISCAYNE BAY

MIAMI BEACH

MIAMI RIVER

KEY BISCAYNE

MARATHON DANCERS AT THE CINDERELLA BALLROOM IN DOWNTOWN MIAMI. (HISTORICAL ASSOCIATION OF SOUTHERN FLORIDA)

DADE COUNTY IN THE GREAT DEPRESSION

"These really are good times, but only a few know it."—Henry Ford, March 15, 1931[1]

The stock market crash of 1929 sent the nation into the worst economic depression of its history. Statistically, Florida seemed to suffer less in the Great Depression than the rest of the country; however, that is primarily because economic indicators had already been seriously depleted by the real estate bust of 1926. Between 1926 and 1930, assessed real estate values in Florida dropped from 623 to 441 million dollars.[2] That figure was heavily influenced by Dade County where the boom and bust of the 1920s had been most strongly felt. In 1925, 336 banks in the state reported resources of 943 million dollars, but their assets fell by some 30 million in 1926, and more than forty banks closed that year,[3] long before the stock market crash.

If one were to judge by the headlines of *Miami Herald* articles in late 1927, Miami was pretty much business as usual. "Miami is Ready for Greatest Winter Season,"[4] "Recovery of City from Disaster Year Ago Has Been Complete,"[5] "Work Proceeds on Coral Gables Coliseum,"[6] are only a few of the optimistic headlines. The *Herald* editorial staff were not the only ones feigning optimism. In the September 18th edition of the *Herald* were full page advertisements for Coral Gables, and a new venture of the Tatum brothers, the Florida Petroleum Exploration Company, which was soon to begin drilling for oil two miles south of Florida City.[7]

The details in smaller print in the newspapers are more revealing, though, of the real situation. Daily under the heading "Courthouse News" were several columns of foreclosure notices.[8] There were frequent advertisements for bankruptcy sales of various retail businesses and small back page articles that announced such things as "receiver appointed to handle closing of Bank of Homestead."[9]

It is not fair to expect that the population of Miami who had so recently been swirled around in the seemingly limitless expectations of the boom, could have the foresight to see that the downswing was more than a temporary aberration. But land development in Miami continued to decline. New subdivisions were platted in the late 1920s, but not in numbers that came close to rivaling the previous years. The subdivision plans filed in the County Land Division office between 1923 and 1926 take up well over twenty plat books, whereas, the last two years of the 1920s and the entire decade of the 1930s fill the pages of less than ten.[10]

In 1932, Franklin Roosevelt was elected to the presidency. When he was campaigning, political analyst Walter Lippmann commented that Roosevelt was "a pleasant man who, without any important qualifications for the job, would very much like to be president."[11] It's true that Roosevelt had more of a philosophy than a platform before his election, but his belief that what the country needed to rout it from the depression was "bold, persistent experimentation"[12] proved to be an effective assessment. Economic conditions in the United States were so desperate in early 1933, that for the first few months of his administration there was no organized opposition to his programs. Franklin Delano Roosevelt's "New Deal" for the American people was rapidly put into effect. Public agencies were established to address many of the nation's ills.

During the 1930s, a number of New Deal projects were implemented in Miami. The Civilian Conservation Corps. (CCC) began work on Matheson Hammock and Greynolds Park.[13] The Works Progress Administration (WPA) produced artistic embellishments for the Miami Beach Post Office, the Coral Gables Fire Station, and the Coral Gables Women's Club. The Public Works Administration (PWA) built the Liberty Square Housing Project just north of Colored Town.[14]

Florida: A Guide to the Southernmost State, compiled by the WPA, noted that the black residential district, although it had expanded, was still relegated to the western side of the railroad tracks and stopped abruptly at Fifth Street, even though the black citizenry comprised thirty percent of the population of the city of Miami.[15] Many of the residents of the back streets of Colored Town still suffered in extreme poverty and congestion. The area between Thirteenth and Fourteenth Streets, for example, was known as Good Bread Alley and had a notorious reputation for low quality shot gun housing and crime.[16] Father Culmer and other spirited citizens formed the Negro Civic League and worked very hard during these years to improve the standard of living for black people. By soliciting the *Miami Herald's* interest in their community's plight and getting public attention, some attempts were made to improve conditions.

Liberty Square was planned and built to address the severely overcrowded and substandard living conditions in Colored Town.[17] It gave Miami the first public housing project in the state of Florida. The buildings, in a park setting, were simple and sober, but not

MIAMI BEACH SENIOR HIGH SCHOOL, NOW IDA M. FISHER JUNIOR HIGH SCHOOL, WAS BUILT BY THE P.W.A. IN 1936. IT WAS DESIGNED BY AUGUST GEIGER IN THE MEDITERRANEAN STYLE. (ROMER COLLECTION, MIAMI-DADE PUBLIC LIBRARY)

THIS ALLEYWAY BETWEEN N.W. 3RD AND 4TH AVENUES AT 14TH STREET SHOWS CLEARLY THE CONDITIONS FATHER CULMER AND THE NEGRO CIVIC LEAGUE FOUGHT TO RECTIFY. (ROMER COLLECTION, MIAMI-DADE PUBLIC LIBRARY)

LIBERTY SQUARE. AERIAL VIEW

LIBERTY SQUARE. IN THE FOREGROUND ARE THE REMAINS OF THE WALL THAT ONCE SEPARATED THE ALL-BLACK AREA FROM THE SURROUNDINGS.

LIBERTY SQUARE WAS SO POPULAR THAT THE WAITING LIST SPILLED OVER INTO NEAT MIDDLE-CLASS BLACK NEIGHBORHOODS AROUND THE COMPLEX. ALONZO KELLY, HERE IN FRONT OF HIS LIBERTY CITY HOME, WAS A REALTOR WHO SOLD LOTS IN THE AREA. (BLACK ARCHIVES)

austere nor uninviting. Liberty Square's popularity was immediate, due to the appeal of such amenities as the Central Community Building with a recreational hall, nursery, and doctor's office, as well as a consumer cooperative store, a federal credit union, and classes for tenants.

Greater Miami weathered some devastating years during the depression, but its recovery was more swift than the rest of the nation. The area did not lose its appeal for the few who could afford vacations. Tourism was encouraged during the lean years by the legal and illegal gambling activity.

Ever since Miami and Miami Beach became predominantly reliant on tourist dollars, officials turned a blind eye to gambling and bootlegging activities. During the twenties, these illegal amusements were undertaken in a relatively friendly atmosphere. Casino and racetrack betting were run by the local gentry. Although there were occasional police raids, their effect lasted barely twenty-four hours, and their perpetrators were rife with apologies to the bejewelled customers.

The naughty and somewhat naive approach to these forms of entertainment began fo change radically in 1928 when Al Capone bought a house on Palm Island and

145

AERIAL VIEW OF AL CAPONE'S PALM ISLAND HOUSE IN 1930. (ROMER COLLECTION, MIAMI-DADE PUBLIC LIBRARY)

moved to Miami Beach.[18] Capone was at his home on Palm Island February 14, 1929, throwing a lavish party for local officials and newspaper people when seven hoodlums were lined up in a Chicago garage and, as one imaginative reporter put it, "hem-stitched,"[19] supposedly on his orders. The event came to be known as the St. Valentine's Day Massacre.

Soon after Capone's arrival, other mobsters began wintering in Miami and the fun and games of the vacation industry took on a decidedly sinister character. Relatively honest entrepreneurs were forced out by gangsters who were setting up shop in all the best hotels.

While the illegal operations were flourishing, one form of gambling was legalized in 1931, pari-mutuel betting. The Miami Jockey Club at Hialeah was opened in 1925.[20] Originally the track was less than lavish, but nonetheless popular. The illegality of track betting at the time was circumvented by the patrons' buying "stock" in the horse they favored. In 1929, Philadelphia millionaire Joseph Widener took over the track. He spent two years renovating the operation and made a con-

centrated effort to get pari-mutuel wagering legalized.[21]

Despite the objections of Governor Doyle E. Carlton, on May 15, 1931, the State Senate approved a bill legalizing pari-mutuel betting at horse and dog tracks.[22] The Governor vetoed the bill, but on June 3rd, Doyle's veto was overriden. That action paved the way for the Miami Jockey Club, now Hialeah Race Track, to legally promote track wagering. The bill did the same for dog tracks and jai-alai frontons. On January 14, 1932, the new Hialeah Race Track opened in grand style.[23] There was little evidence there that day that the rest of Dade County and the country were at the rock bottom of the depression.

Despite the attraction of the illegal gambling interests there was a serious decline in tourism after the stock market crash, particularly on Miami Beach. Visitors did not disappear entirely though. As one observer noted:

...people who had always stayed at the Roney [Plaza] for a month or two, and simply couldn't let it be said that they no longer were able to, stayed three or four days, departed with a ream of Roney stationery and sent their letters down from the north to be mailed with a Miami post mark.[24]

While the tourist business did not completely disappear, it did get lean. Within a few years, the situation started to improve. The decline and revival of the beach economy is reflected in the increasing amount of dollars spent on new buildings, mostly hotels, during those years:

1925	$17,702,532.00
1926	$ 5,039,625.00
1927	$ 2,491,308.00
1928	$ 3,374,349.00
1929	$ 7,856,951.00
1930	$ 4,043,039.00
1931	$ 1,947,774.00
1932	$ 1,445,128.00
1933	$ 2,172,515.00
1934	$ 5,478,559.00
1935	$ 9,487,345.00
1936	$12,526,107.00[25]

Most of this development was taking place on the south end of Miami Beach. It was a very different type from the grandeur of Carl Fisher's endeavors. Fisher was financially decimated by the bust and the stock market crash, and by the late 1930s building on Miami Beach was taken over by developers with less capital, for tourists with less vacation money. The growth of Miami Beach followed this pattern until World War II. In the interim, architects and builders produced some of the most vivid and unique architecture in the history of Dade County.

ARCHITECTURE AND THE DEPRESSION

The Depression dealt a severe blow to the construction industry across the United States. Building activity in South Florida slowed down dramatically during the 1930s. But Miami did not lose its national appeal; it just became less accessible. Miami Beach was still a tourist mecca, but its role shifted from millionaire's playground to vacationland for those who could afford to travel. By 1935, Miami Beach was on its way back. Rather than the waterfront Mediterranean mansions

and the luxury hotels of the Fisher days, smaller hotels and apartment buildings characterize the thirties decade. The clientele was now mostly part of a working middle class who managed to escape the national gloom to "get away" temporarily to a semi-tropical paradise. A few days surrounded by the sun, swaying palm trees, and music on a starlit patio did wonders for the body and spirit of those who were weathering the hard economic times. The illusion of paradise was the setting in which the architecture of the Depression years developed. Buildings were modest in scale, but rich in expression of locale and of a new world that rejected the past and embraced the future in the name of Modernism.

TOWARDS A NEW ARCHITECTURE[26]

Art Moderne, the popular catch-all name for a number of stylistic movements intent on creating a new vision, was in no way a local innovation. Even a national architectural vocabulary was only apparent in a broad context. Its origins go back to the European arts scene of the late nineteenth century.

Art Nouveau was a stylistic movement of the 1890s aimed at achieving a compatibility between the romantic traditionalism of nineteenth century Victorian society and with the new products of the industrial revolution. Art Nouveau raised more questions than it answered, created more confusion over the relationship between the Arts and Crafts and the new Industrialism than it achieved solutions. Its sinuous, soft organic curves and subject matter were incongruous in the hard, cold medium of iron and glass. It reinterpreted existing artistic models based on natural motifs through new materials and methods, but never arrived at a constructive synthesis. Instead, the results were more effective as commentary and criticism of the contradictions between the society of the times and its artistic and architectonic representations.

The new century saw the emergence of a new design source based on machine

ART DECO DETAIL ON WASHINGTON AVENUE, MIAMI BEACH.

aesthetics. World War I jolted the arts from its last vestiges of complacent traditionalism. The new movements rejected society's centuries-old rules of convention and double standards veiled under layers of applied decoration. Forms were stripped to bare bones, their structures re-examined and the components arranged in statements of new architectural honesty and integrity. The radical, the avant-garde, the abstract, replaced historicism as artistic vehicles of expressions. Mass, space, line, plan, solid, void, light and color rather than context, story symbolism and detail were new major elements of the new aesthetics. Forms came under different labels: the German Bauhaus, the Dutch De Stijl, the Russian Constructivism all had the same back-to-basics simplicity in their architectural vocabulary as a trademark. In architecture, roofs were flat, surfaces were finished in smooth, white stucco, glass and metal, while applied decorations became non-existent. In an article written in 1908 and titled "Ornament and Crime," Viennese architect Adolf Loos had proclaimed: "Cultural evolutions means that we have to eliminate any ornament from our artifacts. It shows the greatness of our age

that it is unable to produce a new ornament."[27] This new attitude toward design spread throughout Europe and under the leadership of men like Walter Gropius, Mies Van der Rohe, and Le Corbusier, became known as the International Style some years later.

ART DECO

The new architectural austerity certainly left many admirers and practitioners of the traditional design schools unimpressed. An attempt at a reconciliation of the two factions came in the 1920s with an art form inspired by mechanical interpretations of natural forms, geometric patterns, hard line techniques and two dimensional designs. At the "Exposition Internationale des Arts Decoratifs et Industriels Modernes" held in Paris in 1925, a solution was offered—a remarriage of the Arts and Crafts movement with industrial techonology. This movement was dubbed Art Deco in the late 1960s, a shortened version of the name of the exposition where it was first publicized.

Art Deco caught on rapidly in America where the historicist tradition in the arts was too deeply ingrained to accept the radically

FINE EXAMPLE OF STREAMLINE ARCHITECTURE ON COLLINS AVENUE AND ESPANOLA WAY.

new concepts associated with the International Style. Art Deco was a compromise, still dependent on applied decoration for expression, but the subject matter was now highly stylized or abstracted to simple geometric forms. Building forms were angular and facades often stepped back. The architectural vocabulary used symbols from industry, machinery, geometry and speed. The Chrysler Building in New York, designed in 1928, uses automobile hood and hub cap ornamental motifs as part of its corporate architectural symbolism. But designers were experimenting with other historical themes. Mayan and especially Egyptian motifs were favored, all part of the national craze for treasures and ruins from these cultures that followed the discovery of King Tutankhamen's tomb in 1922. Art Deco was soon recognized as yet another variation on the long-line of decorative themes that had embellished "national" styles for over a century. Its popularity began to decline in the same cities where it had been introduced only a few years earlier. The search for a true honest expression of American architecture in the modern age was still on.

STREAMLINE ARCHITECTURE

The economic shock waves of the Great Depression had a similar effect on American architecture to that of the political and social revolutions of the early years of the twenties decade on European art. Architects in the 1930's turned their attention to the simple lines and clean surfaces of the International Style, but softened the effects in order to accommodate American tastes. Partly the need for sobriety and no-nonsense in architecture during the lean years of the Depression, partly the result of the increasingly recognized European modernist influence, a new American style was emerging.

The new iconography was greatly inspired by the revolutionary technological strides in global communications and transportation since World War I. The earlier Art Deco forms expressed a keen interest in the same themes through the symbolism of its applied ornament. Designers in the 1930s instead applied the concepts of the new technology to their abstracted forms and stripped off the surface ornaments. Time and speed were modern age preoccupations which now

149

emerged as architectural motifs derived from laws of aerodynamics. The automobile, the train, the ocean liner and the airplane were primary sources of inspiration in this new architectural language. The industrial designer acquired the importance of the craftsman in former years. The streamline effect of a body rapidly moving though air or liquid was the symbol that appeard on everything including toasters, teacups, jewelry, fashions, cars, airplanes and buildings. The Italian Futurists planned cities, prior to World War I, where vertical and horizontal transportation systems at different levels and speeds became the focal elements of their designs. The German Bauhaus, the Cubists and the Dutch De Stijl, since the 1920's, had provided the abstraction, fragmentation and reorganization of forms and spaces through simple two and three dimensional compositional elements and geometrical forms. The German Expressionists contributed the bold statements of interior functional and spatial arrangements expressed as exterior design determinants. Eric Mendelsohn's Einstein Tower designed in 1919 in Potsdam, Germany, evokes in its fluid, streamlined forms elements of speed and time that transcend earthly comprehension. Le Corbusier's Villa Savoye, built in 1929, used a juxtaposition of right angle and curvilinear, solid and plane geometries, flat roofs and continuous horizontal banding of windows as major design elements. These were all chief components of 1930's American Streamline architecture.

Buildings relied on massing, rounded corners, horizontal fenestration and racing stripes, flat parapet roofs and simple color schemes as decoration. The angularity of Art Deco was replaced by soft, flowing forms. Three-dimensional compositions rather than intricate bas-relief detailing became the new tools for architectural expression. Colors and textures of new materials, like vitrolite, chrome, stainless steel, glass blocks and terrazo, all played under the neon and indirect lighting popular in the Art Moderne. Such was the national climate under which the architectural rebirth of Miami Beach in the mid-thirties flourished.

Art Deco architecture first appeared in Miami at the close of the 1920's, as new buildings were added to the commercial developments along Biscayne Boulevard. The Biscayne Boulevard Company had secured the construction of a Sears Roebuck store, which opened in 1929, as anchor building to this early shopping center area.

The Sears store was built at the foot of Biscayne Boulevard and Thirteenth Street, where a traffic circle, criss-crossed by trolleys, cars, and buses, marked one of the most important intersections in the city of Miami. The east-west artery connected the beaches, through the County Causeway built between 1916 and 1917, with the mainland, and westward along N.W. 14th Street through Overtown. Biscayne Boulevard connected downtown Miami with developments in the northeast area of the county.

The circle is gone, but the major focus of urban activity remains, and the Sears Tower still boldy states the significance of the intersection. The building is clipped at the corner to facilitate circulation, while the resulting plane serves as base to a seven-story tall octagonal tower. The tower was by then a

SEARS TOWER AT NIGHT. (HISTORICAL ASSOCIATION OF SOUTHERN FLORIDA/MIAMI NEWS COLLECTION)

150

TRAFFIC CIRCLE AT THE FOOT OF THE SEARS BUILDING. THE TROLLEY CONNECTED MIAMI BEACH WITH THE MAINLAND VIA THE COUNTY CAUSEWAY. (ROMER COLLECTION, MIAMI-DADE PUBLIC LIBRARY)

SEARS ROEBUCK, BUILT IN 1929, IS THE EARLIEST KNOWN ART DECO BUILDING IN THE MIAMI AREA. (HISTORICAL ASSOCIATION OF SOUTHERN FLORIDA)

THE MAHI SHRINE TEMPLE, NOW THE BOULEVARD SHOPS, WAS BUILT IN 1930 BY THE BISCAYNE BOULEVARD COMPANY. DESIGNED BY ROBERT LAW WEED, IT IS ONE OF THE EARLIEST AND MOST REPRESENTATIVE ART DECO BUILDINGS IN MIAMI BY A LOCAL ARCHITECT.

BOULEVARD SHOPS, SCULPTURAL DETAIL.

corporate symbol of Sears Roebuck and Co. across the country. The verticality of the low rising tower in this case was emphasized by a tall, slender sign, later replaced by a more modern Sears logo. The four story mass that spreads along both main streets has engaged fluted piers to emphasize the vertical thrust of the tower, typical of the Art Deco style. All decoration, such as the vertical fluting and the low-relief organic forms that adorn the tower, are abstracted to geometric designs. Yet at the top of the tower a circular, floral-inspired detail is reminiscent of one of Louis H. Sullivan's favorite decorative motifs for his buildings in Chicago around the turn-of-the-century. The Chicago firm of Nimmons, Carr and Wright, corporate architects for Sears Roebuck, brought to Miami an Art Deco design, Chicago style.

Just two blocks north, Robert Law Weed's Mahi Shrine Temple, now the Boulevard Shops, is an early local interpretation of Art Deco architecture. An almost classical feeling in the horizontal, symmetrical composition is offset by turrets with multi-faceted planes on the upper corners of the building. The angularity and step-back facade typical of the style are very much present. Outer corners are detailed with engaged sculpted figures of Seminole Indians. This adds a local perspective to the national vogue for native American motifs that was part of the Art Deco

THE MIAMI BEACH PUBLIC LIBRARY, NOW THE BASS MUSEUM OF ART, WAS DESIGNED IN 1930 BY RUSSELL T. PANCOAST.

vocabulary. Balconies cantilever over the sidewalk, supported on stepped horizontal slabs. Cast or artificial stone imitating local coral rock is used as surface finish. Metal spandrels between the windows have elaborate low relief designs of abstracted organic forms. The building contributes to the elegance and human scale of Biscayne Boulevard as originally planned.

Another building in the forefront of South Florida's introduction to Art Deco is the old Miami Beach Library, now the Bass Art Museum, designed in 1930 by Russell T. Pancoast.[28] Corners are clipped and faceted, and although the mass is long and horizontal, there is a vertical arrangement in the composition. The bas-relief applied decoration includes Columbus' three ships and airplanes. The structure is faced in keystone, a type of coral rock from the Florida Keys, quarried and cut into slabs, that became a very popular building material in the thirties decade.

BASS MUSEUM. BAS-RELIEF DETAIL.

HOTELS ALONG OCEAN DRIVE.

MIAMI BEACH ART DECO

The uniformity in style, scale and quality of design evident today in the Miami Beach Historic District area is no coincidence. It is the product of a brief, intensive period of building activity to provide accommodations for the renewed tourist influx. A relatively small number of architects, many from New York, many European born, were responsible for the hundreds of buildings that went up in Miami Beach between 1935 and 1940. Their experience with current national and international design trends made up for their general lack of formal architectural training in the classical sense. The architecture they produced, if not correct and academic, was "street wise." They could design in the latest fashion and were able to give buildings identity among their neighbors and yet fit within their tropical setting.

Miami Beach Art Deco has become a popular, acceptable term to describe the architectural products of this period in local history. The new clean sweeping masses of Streamline design were accented with Art Deco applied ornamentation, such as bas

relief panels, fountains, sculpture, murals and etched glass. These decorative elements provided playful, festive allegories of tropical scenes depicting moonlit beaches, palm trees, flamingoes, fish and other exponents of South Florida's flora, fauna, land and seascapes. A central bas-relief panel at the Savoy Plaza Hotel depicts a pink flamingo surrounded by stylized lush vegetation. At the entrance of the Senator Hotel a free-standing fountain of a pelican once spewed water onto a catch basin in the form of a seashell. The etched glass windows of the Primrose Hotel include a full beach scene with palm trees, birds, fish, and a sailboat.

The spirit of travel and speed is captured in the aerodynamic forms and applied racing stripes which are the major form of decoration in hotels like the Cardozo and the Essex House while ocean travel is evoked through the use of porthole windows, pipe railings and sun decks. The Senator Hotel combined all of these elements by the swimming pool, where a horizontal row of porthole openings and the distinctive railings all helped to create the atmosphere of an ocean liner.

Environmental reponses are seen in the use of overhanging flat canopies or "eye-

ART DECO BUILDINGS

CHARLEY'S PADDOCK GRILL, NOW A CLOTHING STORE, WAS BUILT IN 1934 AS PART OF A BLOCK-LONG COMMERCIAL DEVELOPMENT, DESIGNED BY E.L. ROBERTSON.

▶ BAS-RELIEF DETAIL.

◀ BEACON HOTEL.

THE SAVOY PLAZA HOTEL, BY ARCHITECT V.H. NELLEN-BOGEN IN 1935, HAS A STRONG ART DECO THEME. THE BUILDING RETAINS MOST OF ITS ORIGINAL FEATURES, INCLUDING THE CANOPY OVER THE ENTRANCE AND THE BAS-RELIEF PINK FLAMINGO AT THE TOP. (ROMER COLLECTION, MIAMI-DADE PUBLIC LIBRARY)

THE WHITELAW HOTEL, DESIGNED BY ALBERT ANIS IN 1936, HAS THE BAS-RELIEF DECORATIVE PATTERNS AND STEPPED FACADE TREATMENT TYPICAL OF ART DECO ARCHITECTURE.

MARINE LIFE DEPICTED ON THE ETCHED GLASS WINDOWS OF THE PRIMROSE HOTEL (1935, V.H. NELLENBOGEN) GIVE THE IMPRESSION OF LOOKING ACROSS THE STREET THROUGH A FISH BOWL.

Spanish Mediterranean style of the previous decade. Thus, a Streamline building mass with Art Deco bas-relief panels and a sloping tile roof or a colored ceramic tile detail would not be an uncommon sight. The Franklin Hotel uses a classical composition of rusticated base, body and cornice, with fanlight arched porch windows, and adds Art Deco details in the low-relief applied decorative panels. The Peter Miller, on the other hand, combines the rounded corners of the Streamline with a Spanish tile roof and window shutters. The variety of visual cues offers a random sampling of stylistic details to break the monotony of the otherwise uniformly scaled, set back, compacted urban density that emerged from this rapid development period in Miami Beach.

THE NEW YORKER HOTEL, BUILT IN 1940 BY HENRY HOHAUSER, COMBINED THE FINEST FEATURES OF THE ART DECO AND STREAMLINE STYLES IN A HIGH-RISE DESIGN.

brows" over the windows to reduce the penetration angle of the sun, ground floor porches, and the building masses articulated to form courtyards. Local materials such as keystone slabs, often dyed in shades of pink or green, are popular in this period. In the Cardozo Hotel, for instance, pink stone, used for the columns and railings of the front porch, is the building's main source of decoration and built-in color. Terrazo floors in multi-colored patterns also provide some of the pastel hues that went into the design scheme of these hotels. A touch of futurism and fantasy is added through finials inspired by the space age needles or "trylons" of Buck Rogers movie lore. A number of hotels along Collins Avenue display these spires, particularly the 1100 block where four hotels in a row are topped with these towering ornaments.

Designers were uninhibited enough to throw in even occasional highlights from the

THE CARDOZO HOTEL WAS DESIGNED IN 1939 BY HENRY HOHAUSER. ITS SYMMETRICAL FACADE RELIES PRIMARILY ON MASSING, CANTILEVERED CANOPIES AND DYED KEYSTONE FOR DECORATION, IN TYPICAL STREAMLINE FASHION.

THE CARLYLE HOTEL, ONE OF THE FINEST EXAMPLES OF STREAMLINE ARCHITECTURE ALONG OCEAN DRIVE, WAS DESIGNED BY KIEHNEL AND ELLIOTT IN 1941.

SCALE, SETBACK, CORNER SPIRES AND THE HORIZONTALITY OF WINDOWS UNDER EYEBROW CANOPIES CONTRIBUTE TO THE STREAMLINE EFFECT AND COHESIVENESS OF THE 1100 BLOCK OF COLLINS AVENUE.

THE SENATOR HOTEL WAS DESIGNED IN 1939 BY L. MURRAY DIXON. THE ROUNDED CORNER WAS COMPOSED OF A CONVEX MASS JUXTAPOSED ON A CONCAVE PLANE. PORTHOLE WINDOWS, PELICAN FOUNTAINS, ETCHED GLASS AND DYED KEYSTONE WERE AMONG THE FEATURES OF THE MIAMI BEACH STYLE REPRESENTED IN THIS BUILDING. THE SENATOR HOTEL WAS DEMOLISHED IN 1988 TO PROVIDE PARKING SPACE FOR OTHER HOTELS ALONG OCEAN DRIVE.

157

IN THE COMMODORE HOTEL (HENRY HOHAUSER, 1939) SUBTLE CHANGES IN THE DEPTH OF THE WALL PLANE AND THE INTERRUPTION OF HORIZONTAL ELEMENTS BY A VERTICAL PANEL WITH APPLIED MEDALLIONS CREATES THE ILLUSION OF A CYLINDRICAL CORNER SHAFT. (ROMER COLLECTION, MIAMI-DADE PUBLIC LIBRARY)

IN THE WALDORF TOWERS, DESIGNED IN 1937 BY ALBERT ANIS, FLUTING ON THE CURVED CORNER PLANE AND A CIRCULAR SOLARIUM OVER THE PARAPET CREATE THE VERTICAL THRUST OF A TOWER MASS. (ROMER COLLECTION, MIAMI-DADE PUBLIC LIBRARY)

THE FRANKLIN HOTEL (1934, V.H. NELLENBOGEN) USES ART DECO APPLIED ORNAMENTS IN A MEDITERRANEAN INSPIRED COMPOSITION OF RUSTICATED BASE, MAIN BODY AND DECORATED CORNICE, AND ARCHED OPENINGS ON THE PORCH. ▶

THE SIMPLE, ABSTRACTED, RIGHT-ANGLE GEOMETRY REMINISCENT OF THE INTERNATIONAL STYLE IS COMBINED WITH AN ENGAGED PILASTER OF ART DECO DETAILED CAPITAL, MOUNTED ON A BASE OF SPANISH MULTI-COLORED GLAZED TILES IN THE GALAXY BUILDING. ◀

THE PETER MILLER HOTEL (RUSSELL PANCOAST, 1936) COMBINES THE ROUNDED CORNER DESIGN OF STREAMLINE ARCHITECTURE WITH THE LOW HIP TILED ROOFS TYPICAL OF THE MEDITERRANEAN STYLE.

159

APARTMENT BUILDINGS

FLUTED RACING STRIPES PROVIDE A HORIZONTAL FLOW THAT TIES BOTH BUILDINGS TOGETHER. STRIPES ALSO CREATE A UNIFIED WINDOW/PLANE RELATIONSHIP AND SERVE AS DECORATIVE ELEMENTS ON DOOR SCREENS. THE SAME THEME IS APPLIED VERTICALLY AT THE ENDS OF THE BUILDING MASS TO BALANCE THE STRONG HORIZONTAL COMPOSITION. DESIGN IS BY HENRY HOHAUSER, 1938.

IN THIS EUCLID AVENUE BUILDING (1935, ROY F. FRANCE) SLIGHTLY ROUNDED CORNERS, HORIZONTAL STRIPES, PORT-HOLD WINDOWS AND SCUPPERS ON THE PARAPET SERVED AS SUBTLE DECORATION.◀

THE DECORATIVE THEME OF THE FACADE IS REPEATED ON THE SIDE ENTRANCES TO THIS APARTMENT BUILDING BY GENE E. BAYLISS, 1939.▶

160

THE 1500 BLOCK OF MERIDIAN AVENUE HAS A QUIET-ING HARMONY OF DESIGN IN SPITE OF THE VARIETY OF DETAILS AND STYLES REPRESENTED BY THESE APART-MENT BUILDINGS.

HORIZONTAL RACING STRIPES AND CANTILEVERED CAN-OPIES OVER OPENINGS EMPHASIZE THE DEPTH OF THIS COURTYARD.

LANDSCAPING AND SUBTLE DETAILS OF SPANISH INFLUENCE, SUCH AS BALCONETTES AND THE CURVED PARAPET HIGHLIGHT THIS COURTYARD THAT SERVES AS ENTRANCE TO ALL APARTMENTS.

THE BARNETT BANK BUILDING (ALBERT ANIS, 1940) TO THE LEFT OF THE PHOTOGRAPH, HAS A POWERFUL SENSE OF MASS REINFORCED BY CURVED CORNERS AT BOTH ENDS OF ITS BLOCK-LONG LINCOLN ROAD FACADE, AND AT THE TALLER CENTER, WHERE THE MASSES CURVE TO EXPRESS A RECESSED ENTRANCE. (ROMER COLLECTION, MIAMI-DADE PUBLIC LIBRARY)

THE STERLING BUILDING ON LINCOLN ROAD WAS REMODELLED IN 1941 BY V. H. NELLENBOGEN. THE FACADE IS BROKEN INTO A SERIES OF HORIZONTAL BANDS; FROM TOP TO BOTTOM, A PARAPET WITH INLAID BLUE GLAZED TILES, A ROW OF WINDOWS, A CONTINUOUS BAND OF GLASS BLOCKS, AND THE COMMERCIAL WINDOWS ON THE GROUND FLOOR, JUST BELOW THE PROJECTING FLAT CANOPY. ▲

LINCOLN ROAD SCENE. TALL BUILDING WAS CARL FISHER'S OFFICES. (ROMER COLLECTION, MIAMI-DADE LIBRARY) ◄

162

GAS STATIONS

THIS FLAGLER STREET GAS STATION HAS A STRONG STREAMLINE DESIGN, BASED ON THE TRIANGULAR SITE IT OCCUPIES. IT WAS BUILT IN 1941.

GAS STATION ON CORAL WAY, BUILT IN 1938 BY LESTER AVERY AND CURTIS HALEY, AFTER A PROTOTYPE STATION DESIGN BY RUSSELL PANCOAST. THE DESIGN COMBINES A MEDITERRANEAN ROOF WITH ART DECO FEATURES.

FROM THE SAME PROTOTYPE AS THE CORAL WAY STATION, THIS STATION STOOD ON 5TH STREET ON MIAMI BEACH (SPILLIS, CANDELA AND PARTNERS)

ART DECO/STREAMLINE HOUSE ON ALTON ROAD, BUILT IN 1938.

ENTRANCE DETAIL OF CARVED KEY-STONE BAS-RELIEF.

RESIDENTIAL DESIGNS

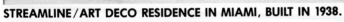

STREAMLINE/ART DECO RESIDENCE IN MIAMI, BUILT IN 1938.

FINE EXAMPLE OF STREAMLINE ARCHITECTURE IN A PRIVATE RESIDENCE, DESIGNED BY HENRY HOHAUSER IN 1938.

THE MIAMI BEACH POST OFFICE (HOWARD L. CHENEY, 1938) HAS THE MASSING CHARACTERISTIC OF STREAMLINE ARCHITECTURE, BUT IN CLOSER DETAIL IT HAS MEDITERRANEAN TILE ROOFS AND A ROMAN INSPIRED ENTRANCE ROTUNDA, WITH A SHALLOW DOME AND W.P.A. MURALS.

DEPRESSION MODERNE ARCHITECTURE— SOBERING TIMES

The New Deal programs that gave work to thousands of unemployed across the country produced a well defined art form that only recently has become recognized and appreciated. Under the Public Works Admin-

istration a new building vocabulary emerged, still based on the Moderne forms of rounded corners and Streamlined designs, but in a more sober tone. This became manifest in the incorporation of more traditional elements and classical features, reinterpreted in the Moderne idiom. In the Miami Beach Post Office a Roman inspired rotunda with a shallow dome gives the building a definite association

THE SCULPTURE, BY JON KELLER, DEPICTS THE STRENGTH AND ANGULARITY THAT CHARACTERIZES THE WORK OF DEPRESSION MODERNE ARTISTS.

THE CORAL GABLES POLICE AND FIRE STATION (PHINEAS PAIST AND HAROLD STEWARD) IS DESIGNED IN A MEDITER-RANEAN IDIOM AND FACED IN KEYSTONE, BUT DECORA-TION IS SPARSE AND SIMPLE, HIGHLIGHTED BY THE TOWER AND THE SCULPTED BUSTS OF FIREMEN.

with classical architecture. The Coral Gables Police and Fire Station retains the strong Spanish influence, but the design is considerably more reserved than the earlier Mediterranean buildings of Coral Gables. The most significant decorative elements are the carved busts of firemen over the garage doors of the fire station. The expression and the profound angularity of the faces is typical of the Works Progress Administration's art form, intent on depicting the hard working American putting the country on its way back to economic prosperity.

A similar sobering influence was visible in private buildings, as the new idiom spread through the architecture of the late 1930s. The Alfred I. Dupont Building is one of Miami's most outstanding works of Depression Moderne architecture. The elegant stone facing on the exterior and the exquisite materials and craftsmanship of the interior demonstrate that luxury and fine quality had not gone out of style, they were just displayed in less flamboyant fashion than during the previous decade.

Although the Dupont building was a private project, in its ornamental elements it reflects the style established by the government buildings of the era. Their designs displayed an appropriate seriousness in view of the mass hardship and suffering inflicted by the country's economic picture. That austerity, however, was lightened and made hopeful by the application of the WPA art works whose themes consciously emphasized a national pride and strength of character. In addition to employing out of work artists, the project served its purpose well by addressing a dejected national psyche that needed to be reminded of the fundamental vitality of the country.

THE ALFRED I. DUPONT BUILDING, BY JACKSONVILLE ARCHITECTS MARSH AND SAXELBYE, GAVE THE SITE OF THE OLD HALCYON HOTEL A WHOLE NEW LOOK IN 1938. IN TYPICAL DEPRESSION MODERNE FASHION, THE DESIGN USES A RESTRAINED ART DECO VOCABULARY IN A CLASSICAL THREE PART COMPOSITION. THE BRONZE BAS-RELIEFS AND HAND-PAINTED WOODS OF THE SECOND STORY LOBBY GIVE THE BUILDING ONE OF THE MOST SPECTACULAR INTERIORS IN DOWNTOWN MIAMI. (ROMER COLLECTION, MIAMI-DADE PUBLIC LIBRARY)

GREYNOLDS PARK, BUILT AS A PROJECT OF THE CIVILIAN CONSERVATION CORPS, WAS COMPLETED IN 1939. VIEW OF THE BOATHOUSE.

BISCAYNE PARK VILLAGE HALL WAS BUILT AS A LOG CABIN IN 1933 BY THE WORKS PROGRESS ADMINISTRATION.

EPILOGUE

The historical events from World War II to the Cuban immigration have been as formative an influence as the arrival of the F.E.C. Railroad was in 1896. However, the perspective that is necessary for the historian to assess the relevance of this recent history is only acquired with time. This is especially true in evaluating how the character of an era relates to architectural expression. Art Deco for example, was not recognized as nearly so comprehensive a style as it was, until the late 1960s, when Bevis Hillier and the Minneapolis Institute of the Arts mounted the first major exhibition on the subject in this country since its initial popularity. Certainly there have been more recent design trends just as pervasive as Art Deco here in the 1930s or Mediterranean in the 1920s. To attempt to evaluate their significance at this point in time would be premature, but the importance of some historical events is obvious, regardless of how their effects may be interpreted in the future.

With the decline of the real estate boom, and the Depression, Miami and its environs regain something of the small-town character it lost during the 1920s. That atmosphere was not destined to last for very long. A revival in the number of tourists and new residents coming south to Florida was occurring before World War II engulfed the nation.

War was a circumstance difficult to reconcile with the sun, sea, and parties. After an initial spate of enlistment and anticipation, Miami settled back into business as usual and the regular winter season picked up, prompting local newspapers to question the propriety of tuxedoes, cocktail parties and suntans when young men were dying to preserve the noble cause of liberty.[1] The realization of war came soon enough when the tanker *Pan Mas-*

168

SOLDIERS DRILLING ON MIAMI BEACH DURING WORLD WAR II. (HISTORICAL ASSOCIATION OF SOUTHERN FLORIDA)

sachusetts was sunk off the Florida coast by a German submarine.[2] Several dozen tankers were attacked in the Florida waters in the early years of the war and rumors of German spies and secret refueling bases in Miami often circulated.

By the end of 1942, well over one hundred Miami Beach hotels were being used as barracks to house enlisted men and officers in training.[3] The Miami Beach Golf Course was leased by the Officer Candidate School as a drill ground and the beaches were soon filled with soldiers practicing maneuvers. Many foreign soldiers trained here as well. The University of Miami was training British soldiers in navigation. The Submarine Chaser Training Center was attended by Russian soldiers who stayed in hotels along Biscayne Boulevard. Military personnel from Norway, France, Cuba, Chile, and Uruguay were being schooled in one field or another in the Miami area.[4]

As the war proceeded, wounded soldiers were flown directly to Miami hospitals. The Coral Gables Biltmore Hotel was converted to a veteran's hospital as were others on Miami Beach. Many of Miami's buildings were converted to war time uses. The Roo-

sevelt Hotel downtown became the Lindsey Hopkins Vocational School to teach mechanical trainees war time skills. Part of the Dupont Building in Miami was taken over by the U.S. naval command. The Air Force made use of several of the local air fields and two POW camps were opened in south Dade County.[5] On Miami Beach, the South Beach Pier became a serviceman's club staffed by local volunteers. Other recreational facilities were opened and operated by concerned citizens, including one in Overtown for black soldiers who were not allowed in the white clubs.

When the war finally ended, the growth of Miami did not exactly take up where it had left off. Many veterans and their relatives who came to the area in connection with wartime activities came back to settle and Miami was back on its boom and bust cycle. Although the rapid change brought about by sporadic development was a familiar phenomenon to Dade Countians in the twentieth century, that pattern did not hold true for the residents of Colored Town who struggled disproportionately for every slight mark of progress. Segregation laws in Miami had eased little.

Finally Overtown, formerly Colored Town and later known as Culmer after Father

John Culmer, experienced its own economic boom during the post-war resurgence. Black performers such as Billie Holliday, Lena Horne, Louis Armstrong, Nat "King" Cole, Ella Fitzgerald, and the Ink Spots, who were suddenly popular attractions in Miami Beach clubs and hotels, were still not welcome as guests in those places. As a result, they stayed in Overtown with friends or in hotels.[6] The Mary Elizabeth Hotel, which had opened on Second Avenue in 1918, was later followed by the Sir John and the Lord Calvert. Second Avenue soon became known as "Little Broadway"

BILLIE HOLIDAY AT GEORGETTE'S TEA ROOM IN LIBERTY CITY.

because of the nightclubs where world famous entertainers performed in their off hours. In the words of popular composer Fats Waller, "The joint was jumpin.'" The commercial district was anyway. Much of the surrounding population still lived in substandard conditions. As segregation laws eased in the next decades, a wider spectrum of employment and educational opportunities became available, but integration also encouraged white-owned businesses to compete for black dollars and struck a serious blow to the Overtown business district.

POSTERS FOR THE KNIGHT BEAT CLUB OF THE SIR JOHN HOTEL. (THE BLACK ARCHIVES)

THE CARVER HOTEL WAS AMONG THE MOST POPULAR NIGHT SPOTS IN OVERTOWN IN THE 1950s.

THE ZEBRA LOUNGE IN OVERTOWN.

171

Changes came rapidly to Dade County in the post war years. As the wilderness disappeared under encroaching development, interest grew in preserving and maintaining some of its features. In 1944, Congress authorized the transfer of 847,175 acres of Everglades to the National Park Service.[7] In 1947, the Rickenbacker Causeway was dedicated, providing access to the new Crandon Park on Key Biscayne.[8]

In Miami and Miami Beach significant development resumed after the war's end, but the reputation of the area was tarnished by the bad publicity the expansion of the illegal gambling industry attracted. In 1949, the Congressional Crime Committee, headed by Estes Kefauver, came to town to investigate the allegations of criminal activity. The committee's report was filled with statements of condemnation for local officials. Among many unflattering things it stated,

> ...criminals from all over the nation were able to act freely in the Miami area because the concentration of economic power they brought in from outside enabled them to control local government and corrupt substantial portions of the community.[9]

In the aftermath of the hearings, many gambling establishments closed their doors for good, particularly on Miami Beach where they were concentrated.

In spite of the seedy nature of that episode, many of the respectable citizens of the Beach still believed in the fantasy created by Carl Fisher. Hotels with names like the Marseilles, the Sorrento, the Monte Carlo, the Casablanca, Algiers, and Bombay continued to spring up on the waterfront, each eliciting some exotic daydream from their guests. The mobsters ousted from Miami by the Kefauver Commission moved on to Havana where they reinstituted the same system of corruption. Another episode in the evolution of Dade County had passed, leaving South Florida in the midst of the 1950s with the same concerns as the rest of the nation: Communism or McCarthyism, Korea, the advent of rock and roll, and an uneasy loss of individual identity as many families moved into planned suburbs with row upon row of identical housing and no way to tell if they were living in Iowa or California.

Technological advancements, the proliferation of, and improvements in communications and transportation also served to erase local identities. The more time that passed, the less Miami and all of Dade County thought and acted as an appendage isolated from the rest of the nation. International homogenization affected everything and was a trend led in many respects by the early twentieth century Modernist architects who believed the worldwide standardization of design principles would produce buildings for the modern age that were more aesthetically pleasing, symoblically appropriate and behaviorally effective.

While architects built, and their critics debated the gap between intellectual theory and real world application, larger numbers of people became interested in the preservation of vernacular forms of architecture. This was an important change in attitude for Dade County, particularly because it is a region that is largely dependent on the appeal of its local identity. When we try to visualize what elements combine to make up the character of the Miami area, both as it is and as we would like it to be, what comes to most people's minds are palm trees, the blue Atlantic, an international urban center of sophisticated highrises, the low-scale Art Deco hotels facing the beach, the two-story porch of a tropical Bahamian home, an eccentric building in oolitic limestone, and the breeze-filled courtyard of a Mediterranean house. Humanity's additions to the natural terrain of South Florida did not begin with Henry Flagler's railroad, nor does it end with the 1920s real estate boom, or the Cuban immigration. The wood and concrete manifestations of the continuing human effort in Dade County combine to contribute to a developing character that is vital to any city, and that cannot exist when people do not have a visible reference to their origins.

MIAMI SKYLINE IN 1910. (ROMER COLLECTION. MIAMI-DADE PUBLIC LIBRARY)

MIAMI SKYLINE IN 1935. (ROMER COLLECTION. MIAMI-DADE PUBLIC LIBRARY)

MIAMI SKYLINE 1989.

I. ARCHITECTURAL STYLES

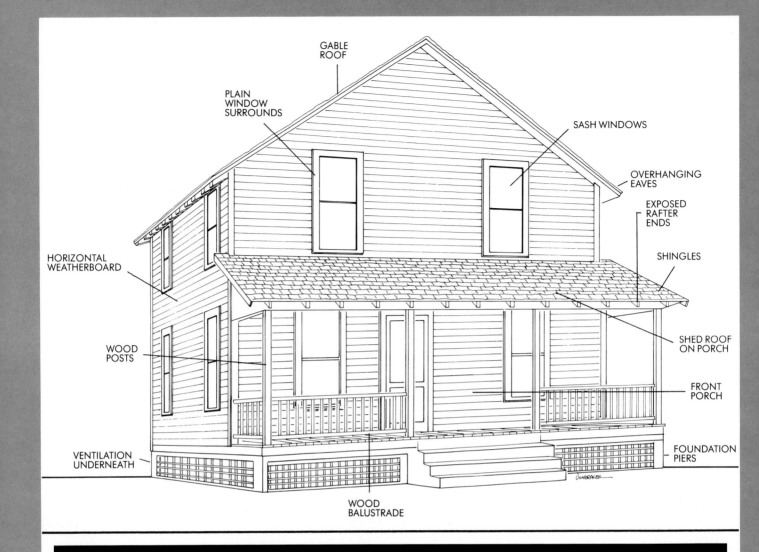

GABLE ROOF

PLAIN WINDOW SURROUNDS

SASH WINDOWS

OVERHANGING EAVES

EXPOSED RAFTER ENDS

SHINGLES

HORIZONTAL WEATHERBOARD

SHED ROOF ON PORCH

WOOD POSTS

FRONT PORCH

VENTILATION UNDERNEATH

FOUNDATION PIERS

WOOD BALUSTRADE

FRAME VERNACULAR

Frame vernacular refers to the common wood frame building vocabulary of South Florida. Construction is the product of the builder's experience, available resources and response to the local environment, not of stylistic or academic dictates. The typical frame vernacular building is rectangular in plan and mounted on masonry piers of Dade County pine and balloon frame construction. Buildings are one or two stories, with a one-story front porch and gable roofs. Two-story structures with gable or hip roofs steep enough to accommodate an attic are generally of earlier construction between 1890 and 1920, whereas frame vernacular roofs of the 1920s and later have lower pitched gables, and hip roofs are rare. Overhanging eaves are an important environmental consideration. Roof overhangs are wider in the earlier buildings, sometimes resting on wood brackets, and rafter ends are left exposed. Wood shingles are used as a roof surfacing in the earlier buildings, but composition shingles in a variety of shapes and colors replaces wood as the most popular roofing material. Horizontal weatherboard siding and the more elaborate drop siding are the most widely used exterior wall surface materials. Vertical board and batten is used at times, especially in very early construction. Wood shingles in a variety of shapes are often seen in buildings prior to 1920, while asbestos shingles are more common to post-1930s construction or as resurfacing for older buildings. Stucco was used as exterior surfacing to create Spanish and Mission style effects during the 1920s and 30s, and as resurfacing in later years. Wood double-hung sash windows are typical, although many have been replaced since the 1940s by aluminum awning and jalousie windows. Decoration is sparse. Wall shingles, porch columns, roof brackets and oolitic limestone details on porches and chimneys are usually the only source of decoration.

The frame vernacular of the early South Dade houses reflects the open, rural character of the area at that time. These buildings are large in scale, their floor plans taking advantage of the availability of open land. Comfortable, well ventilated rooms, with tall ceilings and attics are common interior features. On the exterior the result is a series of large masses with multiple gable and hip roofs of generous pitch. The houses here have little or no decoration, but they are well built, strong and of a simple beauty that transcends time.

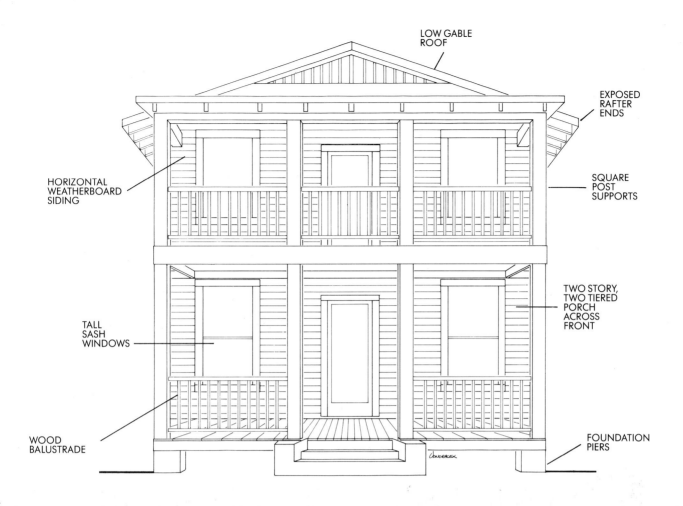

LOW GABLE
ROOF

EXPOSED
RAFTER
ENDS

HORIZONTAL
WEATHERBOARD
SIDING

SQUARE
POST
SUPPORTS

TALL
SASH
WINDOWS

TWO STORY,
TWO TIERED
PORCH
ACROSS
FRONT

WOOD
BALUSTRADE

FOUNDATION
PIERS

BAHAMIAN OR CONCH (1896 - 1920s)

Found mostly in the Culmer-Overtown area of Miami and in the Charles Avenue area of Coconut Grove, this architecture was brought in by black Bahamians who came to build a new city and a new home. Buildings in the early black communities of Miami are typical "Conch" houses, the work of shipbuilders turned carpenters in the Bahamas and Key West. Buildings have a two story rectangular mass, with broad gable or low hip roofs. Their construction in Miami is balloon frame wood, rather than the original cross-braced system of heavy timbers, based on shipbuilding techniques employed by the Conch builders. Structures are raised off the ground on wood posts or masonry piers, allowing air circulation underneath the house. Exterior surfaces are of horizontal weatherboards and windows are double-hung sash type. The most salient feature of these buildings is the balustraded porch across the front, sometimes wrapping around the sides, on both stories.

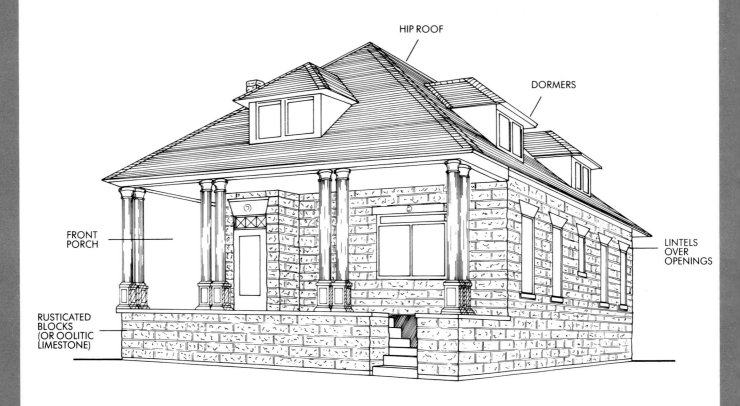

HIP ROOF

DORMERS

FRONT
PORCH

RUSTICATED
BLOCKS
(OR OOLITIC
LIMESTONE)

LINTELS
OVER
OPENINGS

MASONRY VERNACULAR

Three main types of masonry structures date back to the early days of Dade County: hollow clay tile, cement block and oolitic limestone buildings. Brick was never quite popular as a local building material, mostly due to the scarcity of clay in the area. Hollow clay tile or terra cotta tile, however, was often used up to the 1920s, especially in larger construction, such as commercial and public buildings. Its virtue lies in its light weight compared to cement blocks, but the latter could be easily manufactured locally from materials indigenous to this area. Soon after, another building material became popular in the Miami area. Rusticated cement blocks could be used in construction without the need of other surface finishes. These blocks which may appear as stone to the untrained eye are made by pouring the cement mixture into metal molds, hand-beaten to produce their rough-cut stone look. Rusticated blocks were popular prior to 1920 and are still seen in many older houses, especially in the area now known as Little Havana. These early buildings are larger in scale than more recent constructions, their proportions are taller and so are their gable and hip roofs. Except for the material, these buildings are very similar to the frame vernacular of the same period.

Of all the masonry building materials employed in South Florida, oolitic limestone is the most typical in the area and the most unique to the rest of the country. Commonly believed to be coral rock, oolitic limestone is actually limestone with some coral and other sealife formations, disintegrated through thousands of years. Small egg-like animals, known as oolites, which lodge themselves inside the coral and then explode, give the stone its porous texture. The stone is soft and sandy in color when first quarried, soon turning a gray shade. Oolitic limestone is generally used uncut and unfinished, in rubble form. This stone, used in Dade County since the mid-nineteenth century, may be used as structural or as facing material, and sometimes as decorative highlights. Oolitic limestone has been adapted to practically all building forms found in this area, from the early vernacular forms to the Spanish idiom of Mission and Mediterranean architecture, and especially in combination with wood in the construction of bungalows.

Keystone, which became very popular during the 30s and 40s, is closer to actual coral rock than oolitic limestone, as evidenced by the clearly visible shells and coral formations in the rock. This stone is quarried in the Florida Keys and is cut into large thin slabs, often dyed in shades of pink and green and used as surface veneer or decorative accents on buildings.

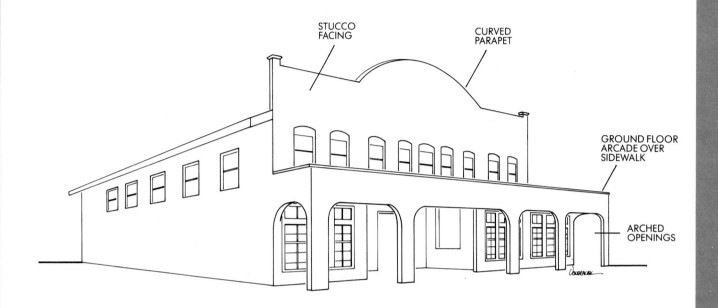

STUCCO
FACING

CURVED
PARAPET

GROUND FLOOR
ARCADE OVER
SIDEWALK

ARCHED
OPENINGS

COMMERCIAL MASONRY VERNACULAR

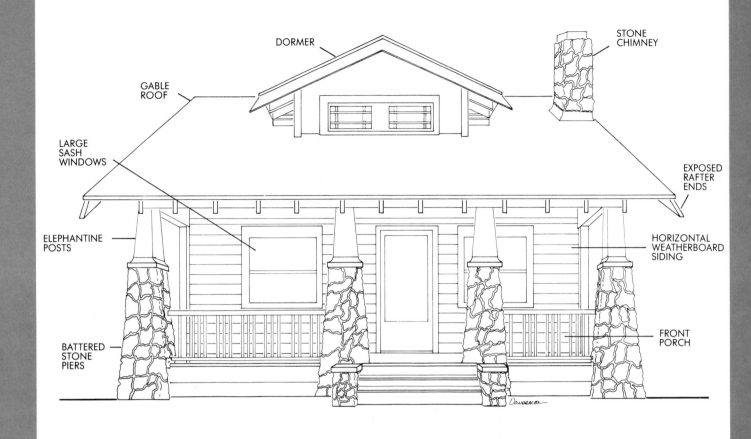

Labels (clockwise from top):
DORMER
STONE CHIMNEY
GABLE ROOF
EXPOSED RAFTER ENDS
LARGE SASH WINDOWS
HORIZONTAL WEATHERBOARD SIDING
ELEPHANTINE POSTS
FRONT PORCH
BATTERED STONE PIERS

BUNGALOWS (1910s – 1930s)

Bungalows are one of the most popular middle-class residential styles in Dade County and across the nation during the first three decades of the twentieth century. These houses were built primarily from mail-order, house plan catalogues published in southern California, where the style originated. Full sets of building plans could be purchased for as low as five dollars.

Typical bungalows are one or one and a half story houses, modest in size and luxury, but comfortable, simple and economic to build. Bungalows in South Florida are of wood frame construction, with porch railing walls and vertical supports, foundations and chimneys generally built of oolitic limestone. The building form is well suited to the local climate, with features such as broadly pitched gable roofs with wide, overhanging eaves, deep porches, large sash windows arranged in cross ventilation patterns and dormer windows or louvered vents in the attic space to facilitate upward air circulation. Exposed structural members and unfinished surfaces are part of the building's vocabulary. Horizontal weatherboards and wood shingles are the most commonly used materials for exterior surfaces. Porch supports are one of the major distinguishing features of a bungalow.

Broad masonry piers, generally tapering up, rise to about half the height of the porch. A wood post or a combination of smaller posts reach to support the roof beams. The most popular variety of these posts are called elephantine columns because of their broad, squatty appearance, reminiscent of elephant's feet. The variety of expression on these posts is as individual as the builders who created them.

There are several types of bungalows in the Miami area. The most commonly found has a gable roof, its ridge perpendicular to the street, and a front porch with separate gable, slightly off-center. Others have the broadside of the gable parallel to the street and a dormer piercing the roof plane. The largest, most elaborate models are the Airplane or Belvedere bungalows, built with a central two story mass, smaller in area than the first floor plan.

Bungalows still contribute significantly to the cohesive urban fabric in the areas of Edgewater and what is now known as Little Havana, especially the Lawrence Estates Park and Riverview subdivisions.

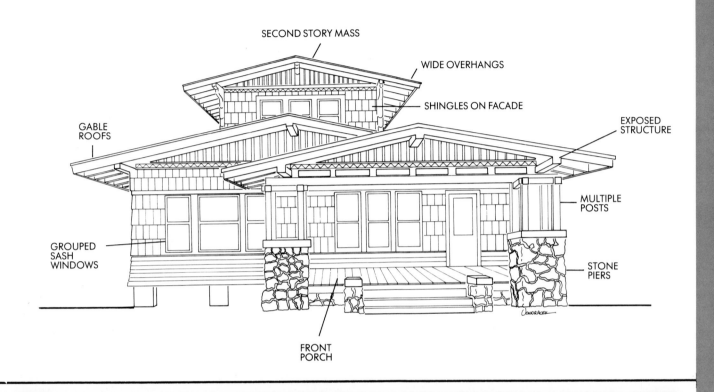

SECOND STORY MASS

WIDE OVERHANGS

SHINGLES ON FACADE

GABLE ROOFS

EXPOSED STRUCTURE

MULTIPLE POSTS

GROUPED SASH WINDOWS

STONE PIERS

FRONT PORCH

BELVEDERE BUNGALOWS

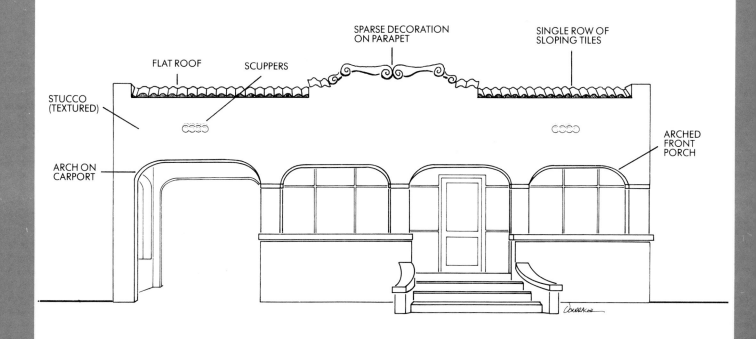

STUCCO (TEXTURED)

FLAT ROOF

SCUPPERS

SPARSE DECORATION ON PARAPET

SINGLE ROW OF SLOPING TILES

ARCH ON CARPORT

ARCHED FRONT PORCH

MISSION (1910 - 1930s)

Inspired by the early Spanish mission churches in California, these buildings are simple in design and details. Surfaces are stuccoed, sometimes roughly textured. Flat roofs are hidden behind flat or curved parapets. The same parapet lines are often repeated over the front porch. Parapets may be topped with a simple stucco molding, or with a single row of sloping Mission tiles. Secondary roofs are sloped, covered with Mission tiles. Cylindrical tiles, or scuppers, grouped in different patterns pierce the parapet, letting rain water drain off the flat roofs. Arched openings are common but not the rule. Windows may be sash or casement type. An arch motif on the facade openings or on the front porch sometimes extends over the carport or garage entrance to one side of the main building mass. Applied decoration is kept to a minimum.

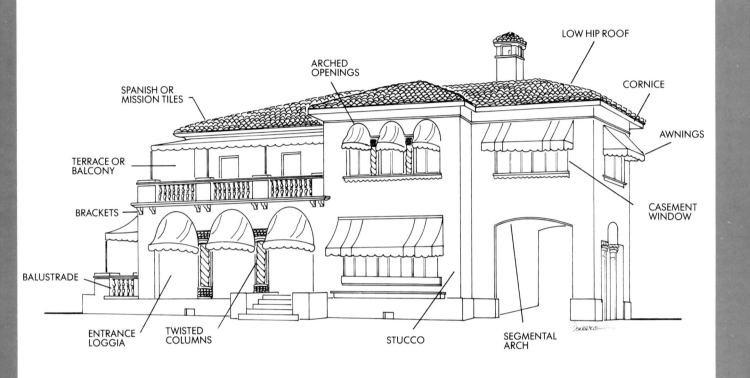

SPANISH OR
MISSION TILES

ARCHED
OPENINGS

LOW HIP ROOF

CORNICE

AWNINGS

TERRACE OR
BALCONY

BRACKETS

CASEMENT
WINDOW

BALUSTRADE

ENTRANCE
LOGGIA

TWISTED
COLUMNS

STUCCO

SEGMENTAL
ARCH

MEDITERRANEAN REVIVAL (1917 - 1930s)

Mediterranean Revival architecture is an elaboration on the themes established during the first two decades of the twentieth century by the Mission and Spanish Colonial Revival styles. Although strongly influenced by Spanish architecture, the derivation here is more directly from European, rather than Spanish-American models. As the name indicates, the style is the product of the variety of architectural expression along the Mediterranean coast. Italian, Moorish themes from southern Spain and North Africa, and even French details are the sources of inspiration for the Mediterranean Revival.

Applied decoration is generously used, usually concentrated around doorways, windows, balconies and cornices. Stucco walls, red tile roofs, wrought iron grilles and railings, wood brackets and balconies, applied oolitic limestone and terra cotta ornaments and glazed ceramic tiles are the materials most often used. Parapets, straight or decorative, twisted columns, pediments and other classically derived details are frequently used, but the elaborate stucco Churrigueresque decoration of Spanish Baroque derivation, is the favorite theme. Patios, courtyards, balconies and loggias replace the front porch. Arches are one of the most widely used features, coming in a variety of shapes, with semi-circular, segmental, flat, pointed and Moorish elaborations, among the most popular. Casement windows are the most commonly used type. Articulation of wall massing and of roof lines is one of the trademarks of the style. Wall surfaces may be especially treated to achieve an aged, weathered effect. Mediterranean architecture works best in large scale buildings, where elaborate detailing can be fully realized, but many buildings have successfully used the style in a small scale.

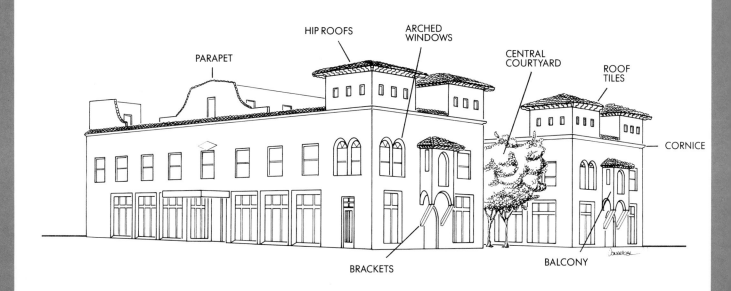

PARAPET

HIP ROOFS

ARCHED WINDOWS

CENTRAL COURTYARD

ROOF TILES

CORNICE

BRACKETS

BALCONY

COMMERCIAL MEDITERRANEAN

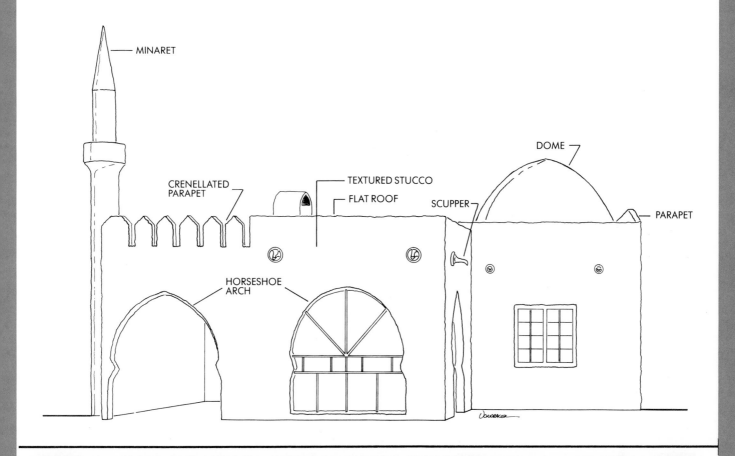

MINARET

CRENELLATED
PARAPET

TEXTURED STUCCO

FLAT ROOF

DOME

SCUPPER

PARAPET

HORSESHOE
ARCH

MOORISH (1925 - 1930s)

The Moorish architecture of Opa-locka is more of a design theme than a style. It is inspired by the **Tales from the Arabian Nights** and it belongs more to the world of fantasy than to any real architectural style. Islamic architecture is the basis for this building form. Domes, minarets, arches in pointed, horseshoe, and scalloped shapes, and crenellated parapets are among the salient features of Moorish architecture. Multicolored glazed tiles, stucco crescent moons, stars and other Islamic symbols, and cracked stucco are among the special effects used in these buildings. The richness of decorative elements that form part of the Moorish vocabulary are best expressed in the larger scale projects. Domes, minarets and large arches seem out of proportion with the small, modest residential designs that were built in Opa-locka. Still, it is partly this awkwardness that makes this one of the most unique local building styles in South Florida.

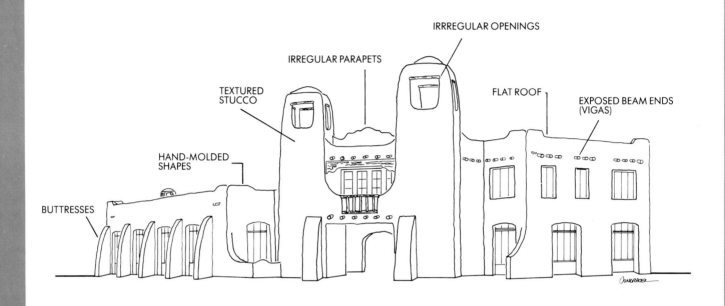

IRRREGULAR OPENINGS

IRREGULAR PARAPETS

TEXTURED
STUCCO

FLAT ROOF

EXPOSED BEAM ENDS
(VIGAS)

HAND-MOLDED
SHAPES

BUTTRESSES

PUEBLO (1926 - 1930s)

Originating in Arizona and New Mexico, the Pueblo style is based on the adobe houses of the Southwest American Indians. The crude hand molded forms of the original Pueblo construction, made of sun dried mud, are expressed through stuccoed concrete block or wood frame building techniques. The rough, hand-shaped surfaces are bumpy and irregular; lines are rarely straight and corners are soft and rounded. Roofs are flat with parapets of irregular contours. Wood beam ends pierce the parapets, although these are usually applied decoration and not actual, exposed structural members. Thick walls may taper up, and openings are small and sometimes irregular in shape. Buildings are generally of small scale, and applied decoration is seldom used. Features of Mission architecture may be added without major conflict, due to the common roots of both styles. Pueblo architecture is found in greatest concentration in Miami Springs.

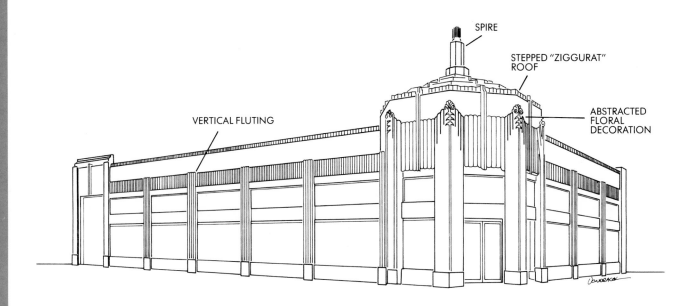

VERTICAL FLUTING

SPIRE

STEPPED "ZIGGURAT" ROOF

ABSTRACTED FLORAL DECORATION

ART DECO (1929 - 1940)

The terms Art Deco and Moderne are generally used to describe a number of artistic movements that spread through the country during the twenties and thirties. The major currents of these movements are known as Art Deco or Zig Zag Moderne, Streamline and W.P.A. or Depression Moderne. The Art Deco architecture generally associated with Miami Beach is a local adaptation, which combines Streamline massing with Art Deco applied details based on tropical symbols.

Art Deco first came to light in America after the Paris Exposition of 1925, where the style was featured as a reconciliation between the decorative arts and the advancements in industry and technology. Art Deco is a relaxing form of the hardline architecture, devoid of any ornament, which later became known as the International Style. It offered a new language for applied decoration, based on abstracted organic forms and geometric

patterns, executed in the latest materials and methods of construction available. Forms are angular, and facades often step back, especially in taller buildings. Decorative elements range from industrial symbols to Egyptian, Mayan and American Indian themes. Building forms and decoration generally have a vertical orientation.

In South Florida, especially in Miami Beach, nautical and tropical motifs are the main source of artistic inspiration. Palm trees, flamingoes, pelicans, the moon and the ocean are among the favorite decorative themes, expressed in bas-relief stucco panels, etched glass and murals.

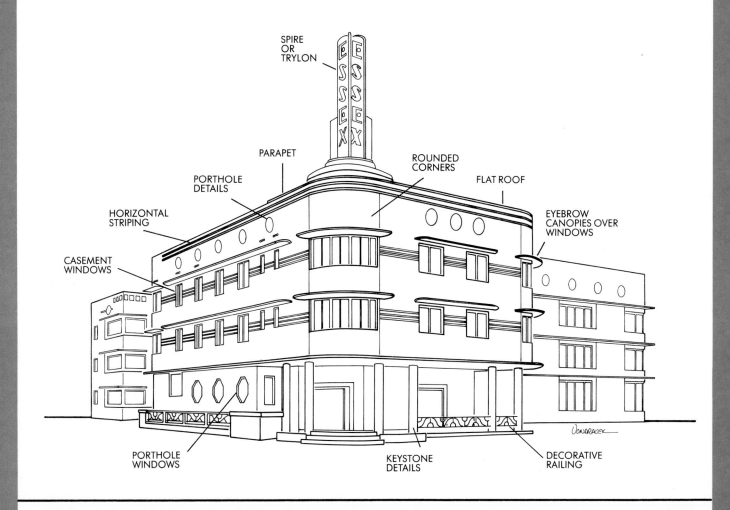

SPIRE
OR
TRYLON

ESSEXX

PARAPET

ROUNDED
CORNERS

FLAT ROOF

PORTHOLE
DETAILS

EYEBROW
CANOPIES OVER
WINDOWS

HORIZONTAL
STRIPING

CASEMENT
WINDOWS

PORTHOLE
WINDOWS

KEYSTONE
DETAILS

DECORATIVE
RAILING

STREAMLINE MODERNE

Streamline Moderne is another movement aimed to bring American architecture closer to the mainstream of the International Style. The term "streamline" refers to the shape that facilitates the rapid displacement of a body through air or liquid. As speed and travel were among the growing influences of society in the 1930s, designers depicted the laws of aerodynamics in their brand of architecture. Building forms are inspired by automobiles, trains, ocean liners and airplanes. Building massing in abstract, simplified forms, devoid of most applied decoration is the main vehicle for the Streamline Moderne. The angularity of Art Deco is replaced by soft forms and rounded corners. Horizontal compositions, banding of windows, racing stripes and flat roofs with parapets are among the major features of this architectural movement. New materials such as vitrolite, glass blocks, chrome, stainlesss steel and terrazo, as well as neon and indirect lighting, are all integral elements of the Streamline Moderne.

A major feature of these buildings in Miami and Miami Beach is the cantilevered slabs which serve as canopies or "eyebrows" over the windows, reducing the penetration angle of the sun. Front porches and courtyards are other local environmental design considerations. Porthole windows, pipe railings, sun decks and flagpoles are some of the ocean liner symbols widely employed. Art Deco bas-relief panels depicting tropical scenes are used as applied ornamentation to produce the unique combination of styles typical of Miami Beach architecture in the 1930s.

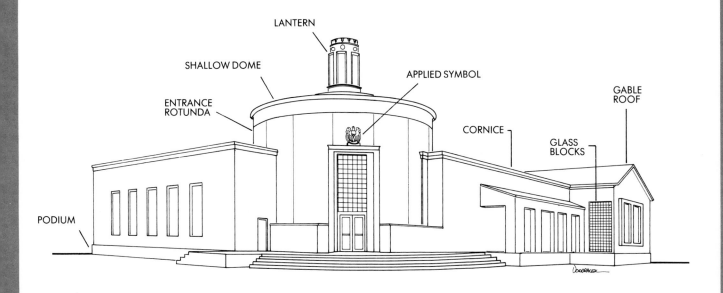

LANTERN

SHALLOW DOME

ENTRANCE
ROTUNDA

APPLIED SYMBOL

GABLE
ROOF

CORNICE

GLASS
BLOCKS

PODIUM

DEPRESSION MODERNE

In the midst of the Great Depression the United States government started a series of programs aimed at giving jobs to the nation's thousands of unemployed. The Public Works Administration (P.W.A.) commissioned the construction of new roads, government buildings, and other public improvements. The Works Progress Administration (W.P.A.) created work for artists, commissioning murals, sculpture and other embellishments for public buildings. The architecture these programs produced has the distinctive traits of the Streamline Moderne, but there is a return to more conservative, traditional vocabulary, befitting the governmental nature of these works. Classical elements are thus reintroduced, replacing the more playful forms and details of earlier years with decoration used primarily as a vehicle for political and social commentary. The style extended beyond government projects, and many fine examples of Depression Moderne architecture were built by the private sector.

RENDERING OF THE GOVERNOR HOTEL BY HENRY HOHAUSER. (ROMER COLLECTION, MIAMI-DADE PUBLIC LIBRARY)

ANIS, ALBERT

Prolific in the Art Deco/Streamline styles in Miami Beach

Whitelaw Hotel (1936) 808 Collins Avenue
Bancroft Hotel (1939) 1501 Collins Avenue
Poinciana Hotel (1939) 1555 Collins Avenue
Berkeley Shore Hotel (1940) 1610 Collins Avenue
Normandy Theater (1947) 7401 Collins Avenue
Barnett Bank (1940) 420 Lincoln Road
Waldorf Towers Hotel (1937) 860 Ocean Drive
Tyler Apartments (1940) 430 Twenty-first Street

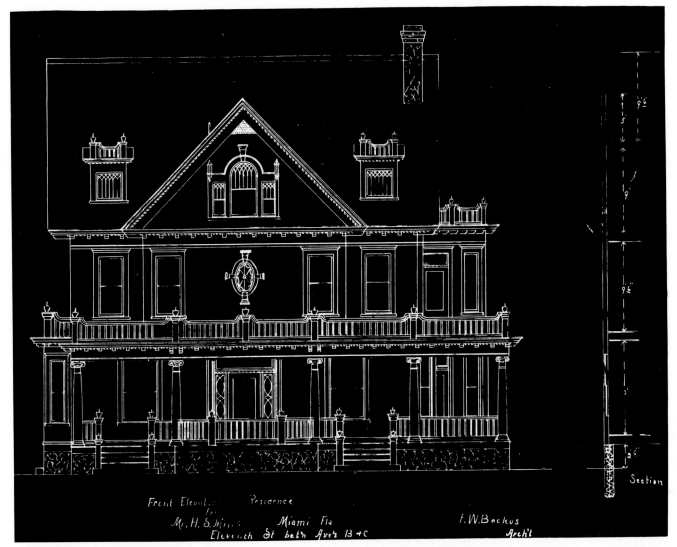

BLUEPRINT OF A VICTORIAN STYLED HOUSE DESIGNED BY ARCHITECT F.W. BACKUS FOR A LOCATION ON N.E. 1ST STREET NEAR BISCAYNE BAY.   (MARIA T. TEMKIN)

BACKUS, FREDERICK W.

Advertisement in the 1904 Miami City Directory lists "Artificial stone" or rusticated blocks as his speciality; did work in a Queen Anne fashion in the early days of Miami.

A.O. Bliss residence (demolished)
Charles C. Brickell residence (demolished)
William M. Burdine residence (demolished)
Mrs. E.S. Huddlestone residence (demolished)

191

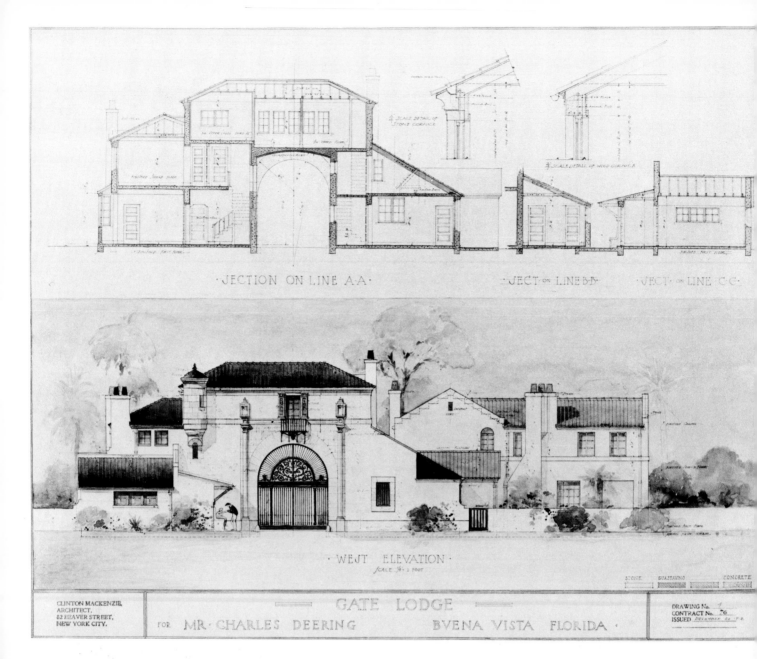

·JECTION ON LINE A·A·   ·JECT ON LINE B·B·   ·JECT ON LINE C·C·

·WEST ELEVATION·
SCALE ¾= 1 FOOT

CLINTON MACKENZIE,
ARCHITECT,
52 BEAVER STREET,
NEW YORK CITY.

GATE LODGE

FOR MR · CHARLES DEERING   BVENA VISTA FLORIDA ·

DRAWING No.
CONTRACT No.
ISSUED

BROWN, A. TEN EYCK

Architect from Atlanta, Georgia. Best known for his courthouse designs in Athens, Atlanta and Albany, Georgia and New Orleans.

> Colisseum (1925-27) 1500 Douglas Road
> Dade County Courthouse (1926-29) 73 West Flagler Street
> (August Geiger, associate architect)

BROWN, WILLIAM FRANCIS

Born in 1886, came to Miami from London in 1922. Most of his work is in the Spanish Mediterranean style.

> Biscayne Collins Hotel (1925) 135 Biscayne Street
> Ambassador Hotel (1925) 227 Michigan Avenue
> Dan Hardie residence (1924) Palm Island
> Boulevard Hotel (1925) (demolished)

BUTTERWORTH, S.D.

        Floridian Hotel (Biscaya Hotel, 1925) 540 West Avenue

CHALFIN, PAUL

Associate architect for Vizcaya, responsible for interiors and furnishings.

CHENEY, HOWARD L.

        Miami Beach Post Office (1937) 1300 Washington Avenue

DE GARMO, WALTER C.

A native of Illinois, he came to Miami in 1904. Studied at the University of Pennsylvania. Worked in New York with John Russell Pope before moving to Miami. Designed many of the early public buildings in Miami, Miami Beach and Coral Gables.

        Coral Gables Bank and Post Office (1924) Alhambra Circle
        J.C. Penny residence (1924) Belle Island.
        McAllister Hotel (1916) 10 Biscayne Boulevard
        Coconut Grove Housekeeper's Club addition (1921)
        Hugh Matheson residence (1925) Coconut Grove
        St. Teresa School (with Phineas Paist, 1924) Coral Gables
        Miami Beach Community Church (1921) 500 Lincoln Road
        Highleyman residence (1918) 1402 South Bayshore Drive
        Coral Gables Administration Building (1924) (demolished)
        Ogden residence. Lemon City (demolished)
        Miami Central School (demolished)
        Miami City Hall (1907) West Flagler Street (demolished)
        Miami Fire Station #1 (1907) West Flagler Street (demolished)

        Collaborated on: Colonnade Building
                        Douglas Entrance

DIXON, L. MURRAY

Prolific in the Miami Beach Art Deco/Streamline styles.

        Tiffany Hotel (1939) 801 Collins Avenue
        Tudor Hotel (1939) 1111 Collins Avenue
        Palmer House Hotel (1939) 1119 Collins Avenue
        Marlin Hotel (1939) 1200 Collins Avenue
        Senator/Nash Hotel (1939) 1201 Collins Avenue
        Haddon Hall Hotel (1941) 1500 Collins Avenue
        Ritz Plaza Hotel (1940) 1701 Collins Avenue
        Raleigh Hotel (1940) 1777 Collins Avenue
        Victor Hotel (1937) 1144 Ocean Drive
        The Tides Hotel (1936) 1220 Ocean Drive
        Adams Hotel (1938) 2030 Park Avenue

EBERSON & EBERSON

Chicago firm, known for their atmospheric theater designs around the country.
        Gusman Hall (Olympia Theater, 1925) 174 East Flagler Street

FINK, DENMAN

Native of Springdale, Pennsylvania, he came to Miami in 1924 to work with his nephew, George Merrick. A painter, he studied at the Boston Museum of Art. Did portraits, magazine illustrations and murals. Art instructor at the University of Miami for twenty-five years, until his death in 1956.
        Master Plan for Coral Gables
        Mural for Federal Courthouse (1940) 300 N.E. 1st Avenue
        Collaborated on numerous public and private projects in Coral Gables.

FINK, H. GEORGE

Came to Miami in 1904 from Pennsylvania. Worked for Carl Fisher in Miami Beach from 1915 to 1921. Became associated with George Merrick, his cousin, in the development of Coral Gables in 1921. Designed many of the early houses along Coral Way. Received an honorary citation from King Alfonso XIII for his Spanish work in America.

> 814 Coral Way
> 920 Coral Way
> 1119 Coral Way
> 1141 Coral Way
> 1217 Coral Way
> 1254 Coral Way
> 1203 North Greenway Drive
> 902 South Greenway Drive
> 932 South Greenway Drive
> 1100 South Greenway Drive

FRANCE, ROY F.

Moved to Miami in 1932 from Chicago. Worked mostly in the Art Deco/Streamline style, popular in Miami Beach.

> St. Moritz Hotel (1939) 1565 Collins Avenue
> Sands Hotel (1939) 1601 Collins Avenue
> National Hotel (1940) 1677 Collins Avenue
> Versailles Hotel (1940) 3425 Collins Avenue
> Cavalier Hotel (1936) 1320 Collins Avenue

BLUEPRINT OF AUGUST GEIGER'S DESIGN FOR THE BULMER APARTMENTS, BUILT BY THE BRICKELL FAMILY ON EIGHTH STREET AND BRICKELL AVENUE, IN 1918 AND DEMOLISHED IN 1978. (HISTORICAL ASSOCIATION OF SOUTHERN FLORIDA)

GEIGER, AUGUST C.

Born in 1888, came to Miami in 1905 from New Haven, Connecticut. Architect for Dade County School Board and for Carl Fisher.

> First Church of Christ Scientist (1924) 1836 Biscayne Boulevard
> Neva King Cooper School (Homestead Public School, 1914)
> Carl Fisher residence (1920) North Bay Road
> Miami Women's Club (1925) 1737 North Bayshore Drive
> Washington Avenue Community Center (Miami Beach Municipal Golf Course, 1915) 2100 Washington Avenue
> Associate architect for Dade County Courthouse (1925)
> Miami City Hospital. "The Alamo." (1915) Jackson Memorial Hospital

HAHN, F.W.

One of the earliest architects in Miami. Ad in the 1904 Miami City Directory reads: "Do not get a Northern architect to build a Southern home."

HALL, KINGSTON

1535 Meridian Avenue (1935)
1545 Meridian Avenue (1935)
Blackstone Hotel (1929) 800 Washington Avenue

HAMPTON, MARTIN LUTHER

Designed mostly in a Spanish style.

> Variety Hotel (1922) 1700 Alton Road
> Hampton Court (1924) 2800 Collins Avenue
> Miami Beach City Hall (1927) 1130 Washington Avenue
> Congress Building (1923) 111 N.E 2nd Avenue

HAMPTON & EHMAN

Most work in a Spanish idiom.

> 3224, 3227, 3300 Biscayne Boulevard (1925)
> Langford Building (1925) 121 S.E. 1st Street

HENDERSON, T. HUNTER

Miami Beach Art Deco/Streamline architect.

> David Alan Store (1929) 744 Lincoln Road
> S.H. Kress Building (1935) 1201 Washington Avenue
> McArthur Hotel (1930) 701-745 Fifth Street

HOFFMAN, F. BURRALL, JR.

Architect for Vizcaya, the Deering Estate. Studied at Harvard and L'Ecole des Beaux Arts in Paris. Worked in New York with Carrere and Hastings, architects for the Ponce de Leon Hotel in St. Augustine.

HOHAUSER, HENRY

Born in 1896, came to Miami in 1932. His firm designed over three hundred buildings in the area. One of the leading architects of the Art Deco/Streamline style in Miami Beach.

> Essex House Hotel (1938) 1001 Collins Avenue
> Shepley Hotel (1938) 1340 Collins Avenue
> Commodore Hotel (1939) 1360 Collins Avenue
> Warsaw Ballroom (1940) 1450 Collins Avenue
> New Yorker Hotel (1940) 1611 Collins Avenue
> Neron Hotel (1940) 1110 Drexel Avenue
> Century Hotel (1939) 140 Ocean Drive
> Edison Hotel (1935) 960 Ocean Drive
> Cardozo Hotel (1939) 1300 Ocean Drive
> Beth Jacob Social Hall (1936) 301 Washington Avenue
> Governor Hotel (1939) 435 Twenty-first Street

KAMPER, LOUIS

Originally from Detroit, Michigan.

> Huntington Building (1925) 168 S.E. 1st Street
> Lindsey Hopkins (Roosevelt Hotel, 1925) 1410 N.E. 2nd Avenue

KIEHNEL AND ELLIOTT

Pittsburgh firm, formed in 1906. First commission in Miami in 1917. In 1920 opened an office in Miami with Richard Kiehnel in charge, John M. Elliott in charge of Pittsburgh office. Richard Kiehnel was born in Germany in 1870. Studied at the University of Breslau, Germany and the Ecole Nationale des Beaux Arts, Paris. His work was the major force in the introduction of Mediterranean Revival architecture in Miami. Editor of *Florida Architecture and Allied Arts* magazine 1935-1942.

> Coral Gables Congregational Church (1923) 3010 De Soto Boulevard.
> Players State Theater (Coconut Grove Playhouse, 1925) 3500 Main Highway
> El Jardin (Carrollton School) (1917) 3747 Main Highway
> Coral Gables Elementary School (1926) 105 Minorca Avenue
> Scottish Rite Temple (1922) 303 N.W. North River Drive
> Carlyle Hotel (1941) 1250 Ocean Drive
> Miami Senior High School. (1927) 2450 S.W. 1 Street

John B. Orr residence (1926) Palm Island
Seybold Building (1925) 36 N.E. 1st Street
Miami Senior High School (1927) 2400 S.W. 1st Street
King Cole Hotel (1925) (demolished)

LAMB, THOMAS W.

Best known for his theater designs, having built over three hundred theaters.

Lincoln Theater (1935) 555 Lincoln Road.
Cinema Theater (interior, 1938) 1201-1259 Washington Avenue
Cameo Theater (1938) 1445 Washington Avenue

LAPIDUS, MORRIS

Born in Russia in 1902. Studied at New York University and Columbia School of Architecture.

Fontainebleau Hotel (1953) 4441 Collins Avenue
Eden Roc Hotel (1955) 4525 Collins Avenue
Lincoln Road Pedestrian mall

LEWIS, ALEXANDER D.

Braman Cadillac Building (1927) 2044 Biscayne Boulevard
Firestone Tire and Rubber Co. (1929) 1200 Flagler Street

MANLEY, MARION

First known woman architect in Miami. Studied at the University of Illinois, came to Miami in 1917. Worked with Walter De Garmo and Robert Law Weed.

University of Miami dormitories
Dooly Building. University of Miami (with Robert L. Weed)
Residential designs
Collaborator in Federal Courthouse. 1931. 300 N.E. 1st Avenue

MARSH & SAXELBYE

Architectural firm from Jacksonville, Florida.

Alfred I. DuPont Building (1937) 169 East Flagler Street

MALONEY, HENRY J.

Edward Hotel (1935) 953 Collins Avenue
Waves Hotel (1934) 1060 Ocean Drive

MULLER, BERNHARDT

New York architect. Designed mostly in Tudor and English cottage styles. Commissioned by Glenn Curtiss to design Opa-locka based on an "Arabian Nights" theme. Designed most of the early buildings in Opa-locka.

Seaboard Coastline Train Station (1926) 490 Ali Baba Avenue
Opa-locka Hotel (Hurt Building, 1926) 432 Opa-locka Boulevard
Opa-locka City Hall (Administration Building, 1926) 777 Sharazad Avenue

MUNDY, HASTINGS

Coconut Grove Elementary School (1912) 3351 Matilda Street
Old Homestead City Hall (1917) 43 North Krome Avenue
Dade County Agricultural School (Miami Edison, 1931) 6101 N.W. 2nd Avenue
Robert E. Lee Junior High School (1924) 3100 N.W. 5th Avenue
Trinity Episcopal Cathedral (1924) 464 N.E. 16th Street

MURPHY, HENRY K.

Expert in Chinese architecture. Graduated from Yale in 1899. Designed the University of Yale in China. Designed the Chinese Village in Coral Gables in 1926. Appointed architectural advisor to the Chinese government in 1928.

NELLENBOGEN, V.H.

Prolific in the Miami Beach Art Deco/Streamline styles.

Franklin Hotel (1934) 860 Collins Avenue
Primrose Hotel (1935) 1120 Collins Avenue
Alamac Hotel (1934) 1300 Collins Avenue
Sterling Building remodelling (1940) 927 Lincoln Road
Savoy Plaza (1935) 425 Ocean Drive

NIMMONS, CARR & WRIGHT

Architectural firm from Chicago, Illinois.

Sears, Roebuck & Co. (1929) 1300 Biscayne Boulevard

PAIST, PHINEAS E.

Graduated from the Dextrell Institute of the Pennsylvania Academy of Fine Arts. Paist had worked on several major projects in Philadelphia and as associate architect on the Villa Vizcaya before moving to Miami in 1924. He was named supervising architect for Coral Gables in 1925.

Colonnade Building (1925) 133-169 Miracle Mile
Boake Building (1926) 2701 Ponce de Leon Boulevard
Charade Restaurant (Granada Shops, 1925) 2900 Ponce de Leon Boulevard
San Sebastian Apartments (University of Miami Building, 1925) 333 University Drive
U.S. Post Office and Courthouse (with Harold Steward, 1931) 300 N.E. 1st Avenue
Charles Deering Mansion. (1922) Old Cutler Road and 167 Street

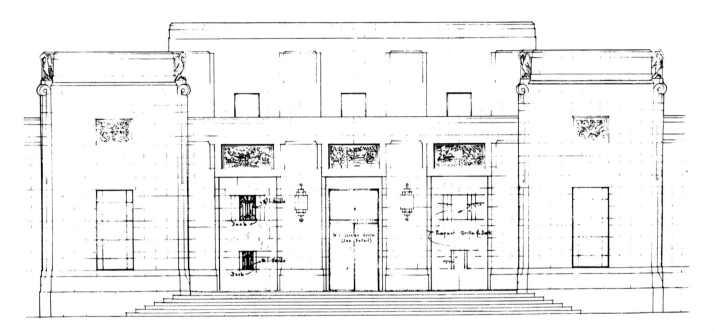

· EAST · ELEVATION ·
· Scale ⅜"=1'0" ·

DETAIL OF FRONT ELEVATION FOR THE COLLINS LIBRARY, NOW THE BASS MUSEUM ON MIAMI BEACH, DESIGNED BY RUSSELL PANCOAST IN 1929. (FERENDINO, GRAFTON, SPILLIS & CANDELA)

PANCOAST, RUSSELL THORN

Born in Merchantville, New Jersey. A grandson of Miami Beach pioneer John A. Collins, Pancoast came to Miami in 1913. Studied architecture at Cornell University. Founded Pancoast, Ferendino, Grafton & Skeels, architects and engineers.

Peter Miller Hotel (1936) 1900 Collins Avunue
Miami Beach Surf Club (1929) 9011 Collins Avenue
Miami Beach Public Library (Bass Museum of Art, 1930) 2100 Park Avenue
Collins residence. 5011 Pine Tree Drive

PFEIFFER & O'REILLY

George L. Pfeiffer was born in Germany in 1861 and came to Miami in the 1890s. Organized the Florida Chapter of the American Institute of Architects and served as officer in several other organizations. Gerald J. O'Reilly was born in Reading, Pennsylvania in 1896, and moved to Miami at the age of eight. Studied architecture at the Massachusetts Institute of Technology. Worked on writing the Miami Building Code in 1922.

Leonard Hotel (1925) 54 Ocean Drive
Hahn Building 140 N.E. 1st Avenue
Dade Federal Building (1925) 120 N.E. 1st Street
Lindsey Hopkins Vocational School (Roosevelt Hotel, 1925) 1410 N.E. 2nd Avenue

POLEVITZKY, IGOR

Born in Russia in 1912. Studied at the University of Pennsylvania. Moved to Miami in 1934.
> Albion Hotel (1939) 1650 James Avenue
> Shelborne Hotel. Miami Beach

PRICE & MCLANAHAN

Architectural firm from Philadelphia. Designed the Flamingo Hotel in 1921 for Carl Fisher.

ROBERTSON, E.L.

Came to Miami in 1919 after studying in New York City. Originally from Mobile, Alabama.
> Texaco Station. 540 Biscayne Boulevard
> Burdine's remodelling and additions (1039) 22 East Flagler Street
> Sabra Restaurant (1934) 605 Washington Avenue
> Friedman's Bakery (1934) 685 Washington Avenue

SCHULTZE AND WEAVER

Prominent New York firm. Collaborated on design of Grand Central Station. Designers of Waldorf-Astoria, Los Angeles Biltmore, Havana Biltmore hotels, among others.
> Daily News/Freedom Tower (1925) 600 Biscayne Boulevard
> Miami Biltmore Hotel (1926) 1200 Anastasia. Coral Gables
> Ingraham Building (1927) 25 S.E. 2 Street

SKISLEWICZ, ANTON

> Breakwater Hotel (1939) 940 Ocean Drive
> Plymouth Hotel (1940) 2035 Park Avenue

WEED, ROBERT LAW

Born in Sewickley, Pennsylvania in 1897, studied at Carnegie Institute, and moved to Miami in 1919. Started his career designing mansions in Palm Beach Miami Beach.
> Boulevard Shops (Mahi Shrine Temple, 1930) 1401 Biscayne Boulevard
> General Electric Model Home (1935) La Gorce Drive
> Burdine's. 1675 Meridian Avenue
> Florida Power and Light Building (Ryan Motors Showroom, 1925) 400 S.W. 2nd Avenue
> Miami Shores Elementary School (with Robertson & Patterson, 1930) 10351 N.E. 5th Avenue
> Florida Model Home (1933) Chicago World's Fair

WENDEROTH, OSCAR

Amerifirst Fedeal (U.S. Post Office, 1913) 100 N.E. 1st Avenue

WYETH, MARION SYMS

> Dutch South African Village (1925) Le Jeune Road

On the following pages are listed some of Dade County's more historically and architecturally significant structures. The buildings were selected from the results of Metro-Dade County's comprehensive Historic Survey which compiled information on more than 6,000 historical, architecturally important buildings. They are selected on variety and by region so anyone wishing to discover the historic resources of their neighborhood may begin here.

DOWNTOWN MIAMI

SITE ADDRESS	SITE NAME	SIGNIFICANCE*	DATE
1737 N. Bayshore Drive	Miami Women's Club	August Geiger, architect, formerly Flagler Library, National Register site	1925
1852 N. Bayshore Drive	Villa Chioca		1916
600 Biscayne Blvd.	News/Freedom Tower	Schultze & Weaver, architects, National Register site	1925
1300 Biscayne Blvd.	Sears Roebuck	Earliest Art Deco in Miami	1929
1401 Biscayne Blvd.	Boulevard Shops/Shrine Building	Robert L. Weed, architect, formerly Mahi Shrine Temple, early Art Deco style	1930
1836 Biscayne Blvd.	First Church of Christ Scientist	August Geiger, architect	1925
1845 Biscayne Blvd.	Mediterranean style		1926
3224, 3300 Biscayne Blvd.		Two building group in Mediterranean style	1925
1500 Brickell Avenue	Petit Douy	Martin Hampton, architect, replica of French medieval chateau	1931
22 E. Flagler Street	Burdines	First department store in downtown, remodelled in 1936	
23 E. Flagler Street	McCrory's		1906, 1937
44 E. Flagler Street	Woolworth		1903
51 E. Flagler Street	J. Byron's	Old Red Cross Pharmacy	1906
169 E. Flagler Street	Dupont Building	Depression Moderne style. National Register.	1938
174 E. Flagler Street	Gusman Cultural Center	Originally the Olympia Theatre, vaudeville attrac- ions, atmosphere theatre. National Register	1925
73 W. Flagler Street	Dade County Courthouse	A. Ten Eyck Brown & Geiger, architects. National Register	1926
30 N. Miami Avenue		Ground floor arcade on commercial building.	ca. 1913
200 S. Miami Avenue	Downtown Center	Depression Moderne style, old Goodwill industries building, originally MIAMI HERALD building	1941
1000 S. Miami Avenue	Fire Station #4	Mediterranean style. National Register	1922
1150 S. Miami Avenue	Burkhart House	Multi-colored tile details	1937
100 N.E. 1st Avenue	Amerifirst Savings	Old Post Office	1912
117 N.E. 1st Avenue	Capital Building	Only Second Empire style mansard roof in Miami	1926
300 N.E. 1st Avenue	U.S. Post Office and Courthouse	Paist & Steward, architects. National Register	1931
500 N.E. 1st Avenue	Central Baptist Church	Classical, Palladian style. National Register	1927
1221, 1227 N.E. 1st Avenue	Anderson Hotel Annex	National Register	
1227 N.E. 1st Court	Anderson Hotel	National Register	
36 N.E. 1st Street	Seybold Building	Kiehnel & Elliott, architects	1921-1925
120 N.E. 1st Street	Dade Federal Building	Pfeiffer & O'Reilly, architects. National Register	1925
168 S.E. 1st Street	Huntington Building	Sculpture on building parapet. National Register	1925
138 N.E. 2nd Avenue		Second story arcade	

*Indicates architect, style, history or National Register status.

DOWNTOWN MIAMI

SITE ADDRESS	SITE NAME	SIGNIFICANCE*	DATE
901 N.E. 2nd Avenue		Formerly Burdine & Quarterman, finely crafted Venetian Gothic detailing, now removed	1925
25 S.E. 2nd Avenue	Ingraham Building	Schultze & Weaver, architects, Italian Renaissance. National Register	1927
118 N.E. 2nd Street	Gesu Church	National Register site	1922
431 N.W. 3rd Street	Temple Court Apartments		
471 N.W. 3rd Street	Scottish Rite Temple	Kiehnel & Elliott, architects, Egyptian-inspired features showing early ArtDeco influences	1922
1800 block N.E. 4th Avenue		Residential group converted to commercial use.	1920s
2927 N.E. 4th Avenue		Central bay window	1917
328 N.W. 4th Avenue			
428 N.W. 4th Street 436, 444 N.W. 4th Street 452 N.W. 4th Street		Lummus Park Neighborhood	ca. 1920's
49 N.W. 5th Street	Salvation Army	Robert A. Taylor, architect, Venetian Gothic influence	1925
668 N.W. 5th Street	Valiant Auto Body Shop	Mediterranean design. National Register	
28 S.E. 6th Street			
190 S.E. 12 Terrace	Dade Heritage Trust Headquarters	Frame vernacular with classical details, Dr. Jackson's Office. National Register	1905
84 S.W. 13th Street		Oolitic limestone house	1922
139 S.E. 15th Road			
153 S.E. 16th Road			
464 N.E. 16th Street	Trinity Episcopal Church	H.H. Mundy, architect, Neo-Romanesque style. National Register site	1924
235 N.E. 17th Street	Orange Bowl Corp.	Mediterranean adaptive re-use	1924
263 N.E. 18th Street			
43 S.W. 21st Road			
411 N.E. 21st Street		Eastwood Estate	1918
51 S.W. 22nd Road		Mediterranean style	1925
421 N.E. 22nd Street		Belvedere bungalow with Oriental features	1916
261 N.E. 23rd Street	First Evangelical Church	Neo-Gothic	1925
319 N.E. 23rd Street		Neo-Classical Revival with Spanish style roof	1922
320 N.E. 23rd Street			1918
402 N.E. 23rd Street		Belvedere bungalow	1917
329 N.E. 28th Street			
455 N.E. 28th Street		Bayfront estate	1921
416 N.E. 34th Street		Bungalow	1922
332 N.E. 36th Street			1918
400 N.E. 36th Street			
PARKS:	Bayfront Park		
	Brickell Park	Donated by the Brickell family to the city of Miami	
	Fort Dallas Park	Flagler Cottage	
	Lummus Park	English slave quarters, Wagner House, oldest structures in Miami	1825 1858
	Simpson Park	Last remaining portion of Brickell hammock	

*Indicates architect, style, history or National Register status.

SITE ADDRESS	SITE NAME	SIGNIFICANCE*	DATE
1400 N.W. 4th Street	Orange Bowl/Tatum Field		1928-1930
1057 W. Flagler Street	Luby Chevrolet		1921-1925
1200 W. Flagler Street	Firestone Station		1928-1930
1240 W. Flagler Street	Gulf Service Station	Streamline style	1941
1349 W. Flagler Street	Plummer Funeral Home	Formerly J.R. Tatum's home	1915-1918
2987 W. Flagler Street	St. Michael's Rectory	Fine masonry vernacular, formerly the Brigham estate	1916
104, 109, 118 S.W. S. River Drive, 428, 438 S.W. 1st Street		South River Drive Historic District. National Register	1914-1918
553 N.W. 1st Street			pre-1914
667 N.W. 1st Street			1919
1519, 1529, 1535 N.W. 1st Street		Belvedere bungalow	1915-1918
2450 S.W. 1st Street	Miami Senior High School and Gymnasium	Kiehnel & Elliott, architects	1927
742 N.W. 2nd Street		Frame vernacular, B.B. Tatum's Residence	1910-1913
1617, 1627 N.W. 2nd Street 138 N.W. 16th Avenue		Belvedere bungalows	post 1920
600 and 700 blocks S.W. 2nd Street and even side of 100 and 200 blocks of S.W. 7th Avenue	Bungalows		1914-1925
2401 S.W. 3rd Avenue (Coral Way)	St. Sophia Greek Orthodox Church		1947-1953
2625 S.W. 3rd Avenue (Coral Way)	Beth David Synagogue		1947-1953
660 S.W. 3rd Street	Ada Merritt Jr. High		1923
111 S.W. 5th Avenue	Warner Place	Neo-Classical style, first florist in Miami. National Register	ca. 1912
862 S.W. 6th Street	Riverside Apartments		1925-1927
2264 S.W. 6th Street		Brick bungalow	ca. 1920
2534 S.W. 6th Street		Octagonal turret	1925-1936
136 N.W. 7th Avenue		Rusticated blocks and shingles	1916
240 S.W. 7th Avenue		Rusticated blocks	1914-1918
2200 N.W. 7th Street		Oolitic limestone, McKenzie Residence, early stone mason in Miami	ca. 1913
227 N.W. 8th Avenue		Hip roof, frame vernacular	1914-1918
218 S.W. 8th Avenue		Oolitic limestone	1914-1918
104 S.W. 9th Street			ca. 1914
120 S.W. 9th Street			1910-1915

*Indicates architect, style, history or National Register status.

SITE ADDRESS	SITE NAME	SIGNIFICANCE*	DATE
128 S.W. 9th Street			ca. 1913
1600 block of S.W. 9th Street			1920S
1900 block of S.W. 9th Street		Mission style	1920S
2300 block of S.W. 9th Street		Mission style	1920
1500 block of S.W. 10th Street			
1601 S.W. 10th Street		Masonry vernacular	1925-1936
2100 block of S.W. 10th Street			1920S
545 S.W. 11th Avenue		Rusticated blocks, corner entrance	pre-1915
1400 block of S.W. 11th Street			1920S
1411 S.W. 11th Street	St. Peter and Paul Eastern Orthodox Church	John B. Reilly Residence, first mayor of Miami	ca. 1924
1600 block of S.W. 11th Street		Mission style	1920S
1601 S.W. 11th Street		Mission style	1920S
1621 S.W. 11th Street		Mediterranean style	1924
1799 S.W. 11th Street		Mission style	pre-1925
1800 S.W. 11th Street		Mediterranean style	1926
1400 block of S.W. 11th Terrace		Mission style	1920S
1700 block of S.W. 11th Terrace		Mission style	1920S
1700, 1800 blocks of S.W. 12th Street (South Shenandoah area)			1920S
1200 block of S.W. 13th Avenue		Bungalows	1921-1925
1604 S.W. 14th Street		Mediterranean style	ca. 1925
124 N.W. 15th Avenue	Biscayne Bay Masonic Lodge	Egyptian Revival details	1928-1930
1621, 1622, 1628, 1630, 1634, 1661, 1670, 1671, 1677 S.W. 15th Street		Mission style	1920S
2434 S.W. 15th Street		Frame vernacular	pre-1925
41 N.W. 16th Avenue		Belvedere bungalow	ca. 1920S
138 N.W. 16th Avenue		Belvedere bungalow	ca. 1920S
1400, 1500 blocks of S.W. 16th Street		Mission style	1920S
2300 Block of S.W. 16th Terrace		Mission style	ca. 1930
1950 S.W. 19th Street	Shenandoah Jr. High School		1940
1000 block of S.W. 20th Avenue		Mission style	ca. 1920S
2900 block of S.W. 21st Street		Mission style	

*Indicates architect, style, history or National Register status.

202

SITE ADDRESS	SITE NAME	SIGNIFICANCE*	DATE
1700 S.W. 22nd Street (Coral Way)	Gulf Station	Russell Pancoast, architect, Art Deco/Mediterranean	1938
1760, 1768, 1776, 1790 S.W. 23rd Terrace		Mission style	1920S
2653 S.W. 24th Terrace		Mission style	ca. 1920
900 S.W. 26th Road	St. Peter and Paul Church		1936-1940
PARKS: 2301 S.W. 13th Street 1415 S.W. 32nd Avenue 2755 S.W. 37th Avenue 3260 S.W. 8th Street	Bryan Park Coral Gate Park Douglas Park Woodlawn Park Cemetery, Chapel and Mausoleum Complex		1927 1951 1937 1913 1928

CITY OF MIAMI NEIGHBORHOODS: Culmer-Overtown

SITE ADDRESS	SITE NAME	SIGNIFICANCE*	DATE
1213 N.W. 1st Place		Bahamian wood frame	1910
1233 N.W. 1st Place		Bahamian wood frame	1918-1925
1301 N.W. 1st Place	New Hope Primitive Baptist Church		1940
1311 N.W. 1st Place			ca. 1925-1936
819 N.W. 2nd Avenue	Lyric Theatre	Masonry vernacular with parapet detail. National Register site.	1910-1914
1415 N.W. 2nd Avenue	Trinity Wesleyan Methodist Church		1918
1445 N.W. 2nd Avenue			1920s
1328 N.W. 3rd Avenue	St. John the Baptist Church		1940
1750 N.W. 3rd Avenue	St. Agnes Episcopal Church		1921-1925
245 N.W. 8th Street	Bethel A.M.E. Church		1927-1943
227 N.W. 9th Street	J. & S. Building	Fine masonry vernacular commercial building. Formerly the Cola-Nip Bottling Company. National Register site	1925
250 N.W. 9th Street	D.A. Dorsey House	Frame vernacular, former home of D.A. Dorsey, Black pioneer businessman. National Register site	1910
301 N.W. 9th Street	Mt. Zion Baptist Church	National Register	1928
229 N.W. 12th Street		Fine frame vernacular, Bragg House, early builder in area	1914
232 N.W. 17th Street		Fine frame vernacular	1918-1921

*Indicates architect, style, history or National Register status.

SITE ADDRESS	SITE NAME	SIGNIFICANCE*	DATE
North-N.W. 67th Street East-N.W. 12th Avenue South-N.W. 62nd Street West-N.W. 15th Avenue	Liberty Square	First public housing project in Miami, P.W.A.	1937

CITY OF MIAMI NEIGHBORHOODS: Highland Park, Allapattah, And Surrounding Area

947 N.W. North River Drive		Fine masonry vernacular	1921-1925
1401 N.W. North River Drive		Fine bungalow	pre-1921
1500 N.W. North River Drive		Fine masonry vernacular	1921
3001 N.W. 2nd Avenue	Buena Vista Elementary School		1918-1921
3001 N.W. 2nd Avenue	Northeast building, Buena Vista Elementary School		1914-1918
N.W. 7th Avenue and 7th Street	Bridge		1918
3220 N.W. 7th Avenue		Masonry vernacular, Cellon Residence, early grove owner	1908
804 N.W. 7th Street Road		Outstanding frame vernacular	1921-1925
1133 N.W. 8th Street		Unusual frame vernacular	1920
1010 N.W. 9th Court		Fine Masonry Vernacular	1925
1017 N.W. 9th Court		Fine Mediterranean	1925
870 N.W. 11th Street	The Hindu Temple	Classical and Middle Eastern details, patterned after a movie set built on same site	1920
801 N.W. 11th Street			1915
1475 N.W. 12th Avenue	Halissee Hall	Outstanding oolitic limestone vernacular with classical details, Sewell House, early mayor of Miami, National Register site	1912
1611 N.W. 12th Avenue	The Alamo	August Geiger, architect, first Jackson Memorial Hospital building, National Register site	1915-1918
803 N.W. 12th Street		Frame vernacular	1915
813 N.W. 12th Street		Frame vernacular	1915
1433 N.W. 13th Terrace		Oolitic limestone Vernacular	1921-1925
1110 N.W. 19th Avenue		Frame vernacular, Coppinger Home, moved from Musa Isle.	1919
3616 N.W. 20th Avenue		Unusual masonry vernacular	1925
3650 N.W. 20th Avenue		Oolitic limestone vernacular	1925
50 N.W. 26th Street		Oolitic limestone vernacular	1925-1936
1491 N.W. 26th Street		Unusual masonry with Russian Byzantine detail	1925-1936
1503 N.W. 26th Street		Fine Mediterranean	1925-1928
252 N.W. 29 Street		Fine masonry vernacular	ca. 1921

*Indicates architect, style, history or National Register status.

CITY OF MIAMI NEIGHBORHOODS: Highland Park, Allapattah, And Surrounding Area

SITE ADDRESS	SITE NAME	SIGNIFICANCE*	DATE
701 N.W. 36th Street	Firestation #4 Tower, Miami Fire College		1925-1936
PARK: N.W. South River Drive and N.W. 17th Avenue	E.G. Sewell Park		1964

CITY OF MIAMI NEIGHBORHOODS: Lemon City, Buena Vista, Little River, Morningside

SITE ADDRESS	SITE NAME	SIGNIFICANCE*	DATE
5925 N. Bayshore Drive		Fine Mediterranean	1926
5945 N. Bayshore Drive			1925
5051 Biscayne Blvd.	Women's Care Center		1925
5811 N. Miami Avenue	Villa Paula	Cuban style with Neo-Classical details, originally Cuban Consulate	ca. 1927
3800 N.E. 2nd Avenue		Masonry vernacular commercial building	1926
4000 N.E. 2nd Avenue	Pallant Building	Old Buena Vista Post Office	1925
6041, 6045 N.E. 2nd Avenue	DuPuis Medical Office and Drugstore	Masonry vernacular	1902
6311-6514 N.E. 2nd Avenue	Lemon City Methodist Church	Frame vernacular, stuccoed, congregation dates from 1893	1904
6101 N.W. 2nd Avenue	Miami Edison Middle School	Masonry vernacular. National Register	1928
6101 N.W. 2nd Avenue	Miami Edison Auditorium	National Register	1931
6101 N.W. 2nd Avenue	Miami Edison Gymnasium	National Register	1928
3902 N.W. 3rd Avenue		Fine bungalow	1925
5454 N.E. 4th Avenue		Frame vernacular, stuccoed, moved from original site, Stearn Residence.	1913
6620 N.E. 5th Avenue	Morningside Elementary School	Kiehnel & Elliott, architects, Mediterranean	
3838 N.E. 6th Avenue		Fine masonry vernacular, Dale Miller House	1916
5731 N.E. 6th Avenue		Mediterranean	1925
5925, 5928, 5929, 5940 N.E. 6th Court		Mediterranean	ca.-1925-1936
7101 N.E. 10th Avenue		Fine masonry vernacular	1924
447 N.E. 39th Street		Outstanding frame vernacular, Gaston Drake House	ca. 1918
452 N.E. 39th Street		Fine masonry vernacular	ca. 1918
191 N.E. 40th Street	Moore Furniture Company	Masonry vernacular	pre-1925
177 N.W. 51st Street		Outstanding bungalow/cottage	ca. 1925
467 N.E. 55th Terrace		Unusual masonry vernacular	1934
601 N.E. 56th Street		Outstanding Mediterranean	1925-1928
549 N.E. 59th Street		Mediterranean	ca. 1925
602 N.E. 59th Street		Oolitic limestone vernacular	1925-1934
592 N.E. 60th Street	The Cushman School	R.T. Pancoast, architect, Mediterranean	1925
240 N.E. 61st Street	Goode House	Fine frame vernacular, early Lemon City	ca. 1908
382 N.E. 61st Street	Mather House	Frame vernacular	pre-1925

*Indicates architect, style, history or National Register status.

SITE ADDRESS	SITE NAME	SIGNIFICANCE*	DATE
594 N.E. 61st Street	Thrift House	Frame vernacular, early Lemon City	1898-1900
668 N.E. 61st Street	Filer/Hewitt House	Frame vernacular, altered, early Lemon City	ca. 1905
682 N.E. 63rd Street		Masonry vernacular, rusticated block with classical details	ca. 1920
661 N.E. 68th Street	The Green House	Frame vernacular with Neo-classical details,	ca. 1910
742 N.E. 68th Street	The Elmira Club	Outstanding frame vernacular, clubhouse for Elmira Subdivision	ca. 1909
285 N.E. 79th Street	Little River Hotel		1925
365 N.E. 82nd Terrace		Fine frame vernacular with bungalow details	1925
399 N.E. 79th Street		Greatly altered, formerly pioneer A. J. Huskey store	1899
701 N.E. 81st Street		Krames Residence	1924-1929
261 N.E. 82nd Street	Jesse Spivey Residence	Masonry vernacular, Home of Little River pioneer	1925
365 N.E. 82nd Terrace		Fine frame-vernacular with bungalow details	1925
399 N.E. 82nd Terrace		Frame vernacular, altered	1900
986 N.E. 84th Street		Outstanding frame vernacular with bungalow details	pre-1925
N.E. 85th Street Near 10th Avenue	Arthur M. Griffing house	Fine masonry vernacular,	ca. 1904
301 N.E. 86th Street		Fine English cottage style	1925
PARKS:	Legion Park Morningside Park Soar Park	Formerly William Ogden estate (ca. 1912)	1965 1935 1954

COCONUT GROVE

SITE ADDRESS	SITE NAME	SIGNIFICANCE*	DATE
3561 Avocado Avenue		Masonry vernacular with classical details	ca. 1937
3564 Avocado Avenue		Masonry vernacular cottage	ca. 1936
North Bay Homes Drive		Fine example of masonry vernacular residences-most notable, 3598 (Bay Rock) and 3611	ca. 1909-1920
1641 S. Bayshore Drive		Fine masonry vernacular	1925-1936
1650 S. Bayshore Drive		Fine Mediterranean	1923
1665 S. Bayshore Drive		George L. Pfeiffer, architect, unique limestone vernacular	pre-1918
1702 S. Bayshore Drive		Walter De Garmo, architect, outstanding frame vernacular	ca. 1916
1717 S. Bayshore Drive		Fine frame vernacular with classical details	ca. 1900
1855 S. Bayshore Drive		Outstanding Mediterranean	1921-1925

*Indicates architect, style, history or National Register status.

SITE ADDRESS	SITE NAME	SIGNIFICANCE*	DATE
1871 S. Bayshore Drive		Outstanding Mediterranean	1925
2035 S. Bayshore Drive (moved back on lot to Tigertail)	Ransom/Everglades Middle School-Headmaster's House	Outstanding bungalow, Brisbane House	ca. 1903
2131 S. Bayshore Drive		Outstanding Neo-classical, built by John T. Peacock of Coconut Grove Pioneer family	ca. 1900
2143 S. Bayshore Drive		Fine masonry vernacular	pre-1921
2167 S. Bayshore Drive		Outstanding Mediterranean	post 1931
2484 S. Bayshore Drive	Coral Reef Yacht Club	Outstanding Mediterranean	ca. 1923
2485 S. Bayshore Drive			1914-1917
2521 S. Bayshore Drive	Trapp House	Wood frame	ca.-1890
2985 S. Bayshore Drive	Women's Club of Coconut Grove	Walter De Garmo, architect, Housekeeper's Club, National Register Site	1921
1700 S. Bayshore Lane		Outstanding Mediterranean	1936
1900 S. Bayshore Lane			1925-1930
Bayview Road		Subdivided by the Sunshine Fruit Co. in 1912, many fine examples of early residential styles, particularly 3609, 3612 (H. de B. Justison House), 3659 (former Miss Harris School), and 3672 (R.M. Price Home)	1912-1920
3635 Bougainvillea Road	El Dorado	Fine masonry vernacular, formerly guest house and restaurant	ca. 1922
3007 Brickell Avenue			ca. 1935
3029 Brickell Avenue		V.H. Nellenbogen, architect, outstanding Mediterranean	ca. 1931
3031 Brickell Avenue		Fine masonry vernacular	ca. 1918
3115 Brickell Avenue	Villa Serena	William Jennings Bryan House	1911-1915
3149 Brickell Avenue		Fine masonry vernacular	1918
3231 Calusa Street	Rock Reef	Walter De Garmo, architect, fine Mediterranean	ca. 1922
Charles Avenue		Black pioneer settlement in Coconut Grove, Bahamian architecture, particularly noteworthy are 3241, 3242 (E.W.F. Stirrup House), 3298 (Mariah Brown House), and 3420	ca. 1889-1920s
3429 Devon Road	First Coconut Grove School House	National Register site	1894
3429 Devon Road	Plymouth Congregation Church	Spanish Colonial Style, National Register site	1916-1917
3432 Devon Road		Fine masonry vernacular	1915-1923
Dinner Key	U.S. Naval Air Station, Merrill Stevens Yachts		ca. 1919 ca. 1930-1938
Douglas Road (between 3700 and 4200 blocks)		Many outstanding vernacular examples from the teens and twenties, particularly noteworthy are 3700 (Crawford House), 3856 (Irving Thomas House), 3909 (De Garmo House), and 3985	ca. 1915-1925

*Indicates architect, style, history or National Register status.

SITE ADDRESS	SITE NAME	SIGNIFICANCE*	DATE
3814 El Prado Blvd.		Fine Mediterranean	pre-1925
3987 El Prado Blvd.		Fine Mediterranean	1925
3058 Elizabeth Street		Fine frame vernacular	ca. 1920-1925
3224 Emathla Street		Outstanding Mediterranean	1925-1926
3232 Emathla Street		Fine frame vernacular	1925-1936
Espanola Drive		Several fine examples of Mediterranean and masonry vernacular residences	mid-1920s
1747 Espanola Drive		Masonry vernacular, cottage design	1926
3939 Hardie Road		Fine, unusual frame vernacular, former Biscayne Bay Yacht Club, moved in 1925	1901
3481 Hibiscus Street	Christ Espiscopal Church	Church was founded ca. 1901 by the black community, Rev. Theodore Gibson, former city commissioner, was minister	1920
3670 Hibiscus Street		Kiehnel and Elliott, architects, outstanding Mediterranean with Moorish details	1923
3074 Kirk Street		Fine early frame vernacular	1925-1929
3650 Klebba Drive	Hugh Matheson House	Outstanding Mediterranean	1925-1929
2237 Lincoln Avenue		Fine frame vernacular	1924
2538 Lincoln Avenue			ca. 1900
2621 Lincoln Avenue		Altered masonry vernacular, second Coconut Grove School-house, replaced in 1911 by current elementary school	1894
3400 Main Highway	Coconut Grove Bank Building/ The Sunshine Building	Walter De Garmo, architect. Built by the Sunshine Fruit Company	ca. 1920
3432 Main Highway		Walter De Garmo, architect	ca. 1920
3434 Main Highway		Walter De Garmo, architect. Outstanding Mediterranean, original Coconut Grove Bank, in 1963 became John Lilly Research Institute	ca. 1920
3436-3448 Main Highway	Peacock Plaza and Anthony Arcade	Outstanding Mediterranean	1925-1928
3439 Main Highway	St. Stephen's Church	Fine mission religious style	1912
3484 Main Highway	Angela's Cafe	Fine frame vernacular, built by Commodore Ralph Munroe as caretaker's cottage	1895-1898
3485 Main Highway	The Barnacle	Ralph Munroe House, pioneer and one of the founders of present Coconut Grove, National Register site	1891
3500 Main Highway	The Coconut Grove Playhouse	Kiehnel and Elliott, architect	1926
3540 Main Highway	Taurus Steak House	Built by Ralph Munroe and son, Wirth, for daughter, Patty, operated as the Tea Chest	1919
3551 Main Highway		Richard Kiehnel, architect, outstanding masonry vernacular, Kirk Munroe House, pioneer and author of boy's books	1926-1930
3575 Main Highway	Pagoda, Ransom/ Everglades School	Greene and Wicks, architects, outstanding frame verna-cular, early Ransom School building, National Register site	1902

*Indicates architect, style, history or National Register status.

SITE ADDRESS	SITE NAME	SIGNIFICANCE*	DATE
3592 Main Highway	Ransom/Everglades School	Built by Paul Ransom as a gatehouse for Adirondack Florida School	1898
3713 Main Highway	Bryan Memorial United Methodist Church	Outstanding example of religious architecture with Byzantine features, built as memorial to William Jennings Bryan on land donated by him	1925-1926
3715 Main Highway	The Anchorage/Marymount	Fine masonry vernacular, bought by William Jennings Bryan in 1919	ca. 1908
3734 Main Highway	Cherokee Lodge	Kiehnel & Elliott, architects, outstanding masonry vernacular with English cottage features	1917
3747 Main Highway	Carrollton School/El Jardin	Kiehnel and Elliott, architects, outstanding Mediterranean, built for John Bindley, President of Pittsburgh Steel Company, National Register site	1918
3939 Main Highway	Vanguard School	Formerly Gulliver School, and Sunshine Inn Restaurant	ca. 1913
3940 Main Highway		Originally frame vernacular, altered to fine mission style residence in the 1920s, Sunshine Fruit Co. Guest House	1909
Matheson Avenue		Several fine examples of Mediterranean and masonry vernacular, particularly 3618, 3753, 3782 and 3813	1920s
3551 Matilda Street	Coconut Grove Elementary School		1911-1921
2875 McFarlane Road		Eva Munroe Grave Site, old Coconut Grove Library	1901 Orig. 1963 New
2893 McFarlane Road	Peacock House	Fine frame vernacular, built by Albert Peacock, grandson of Coconut Grove pioneers	ca. 1910
3251 S. Miami Avenue	Villa Vizcaya and Gardens	F. Burrall Hoffman, Paul Chalfin and Diego Suarez architects, National Register site	1914-1917
Micanopy Avenue		Several fine examples of frame vernacular, particularly 1765, 1779, 1794	early 1900s
The Moorings		Several fine examples of of Mediterranean architecture, particularly 3435 N. Mooring Way and 3465, 3500, 3505, and 3574 S. Mooring Way	1920s
3500 Pan American Drive	Miami City Hall	Pan American Seaplane Base and Terminal, National Register site	1931
3641 Park Lane	John Gifford House	Fine frame vernacular	ca. 1900
3777 Pine Avenue		Outstanding masonry vernacular	1920
Poinciana Avenue		Several fine examples of various vernacular styles, unusual structure at 3605 is the tower from the Irving Thomas estate, ca. 1912	teens and 1920s
3410 Poinciana Avenue	Four Way Lodge	Outstanding masonry vernacular, William Matheson House	ca. 1911
Royal Palm Avenue		Many fine examples of various vernacular styles, particularly 3537, 3564, 3608, 3610, 3613, 3649, 3685	teens and 1920s
Steward Avenue		Several fine examples of vernacular styles, including the Marjory Stoneman Douglas House, George Hyde, architect	
Thomas Avenue		Several fine examples of frame vernacular, particularly 3521, 3523, 3566 and 3649 built by E.W.F. Stirrup ca. 1920, and 3672	
1710 Tigertail Avenue		Fine masonry vernacular	1921-1925
1946 Tigertail Avenue		Outstanding masonry vernacular	ca. 1925
3456 William Avenue		Fine frame vernacular with Bahamian influence	ca. 1925

*Indicates architect, style, history or National Register status.

COCONUT GROVE

SITE ADDRESS	SITE NAME	SIGNIFICANCE*	DATE
3845 Wood Avenue		Outstanding Mission	1927-1928
2951 S.W. 27th Avenue	Alfred Browning Parker Office	Gifford House	ca. 1900
50 S.W. 32nd Road	Vizcaya Farm Buildings	F. Burrall Hoffman, architect	ca. 1914
Parks	Charlotte Jane Memorial Park Annex Peacock Park Silver Bluff Silver Bluff Alice C. Wainwright Park	Former site of the Peacock Inn	

CORAL GABLES

SITE ADDRESS	SITE NAME	SIGNIFICANCE*	DATE
Intersection of Alhambra Circle, Greenway Court, and Ferdinand Street	Coral Gables Water Tower		1926
Intersection of Alhambra Circle, Madeira Avenue, and Douglas Road	Commercial Entrance	Denman Fink, designer	1924
800 Douglas Road, Intersection of Douglas Road and Tamiami Trail	Douglas Entrance	Walter DeGarmo, Phineas Paist, Denman Fink, architects, National Register site	1925-1927
Intersection of Country Club Prado and Tamiami Trail	El Prado Entrance	Denman Fink, designer	1927
Intersection of Granada Boulevard and Tamiami Trail	Granada Entrance	Denman Fink, designer	1925
Intersection of Alhambra Circle and Granada Boulevard	Alhambra Plaza	Denman Fink, designer	1925
Coral Way at intersection of S. Greenway Drive, DeSoto Blvd. and Anderson Road	Balboa Plaza	Denman Fink, designer	1925
Coral Way at intersection of Columbus Blvd., and Indian Mound Trail	Columbus Plaza	Denman Fink, designer	1925
Intersection of Sevilla Avenue, Granada Blvd. and De Soto Blvd.	De Soto Plaza	Denman Fink, designer	1925
Intersection of Granada Blvd. and Alhambra Circle	Granada Plaza	Denman Fink, designer	1925
Intersection of Coral Way and Le Jeune Road	Le Jeune Plaza	Denman Fink, designer	1925
Coral Way at Granada Blvd.	Ponce de Leon Plaza	Denman Fink, designer	1925
Intersection of Coral Way, Segovia Street and N. Greenway Drive	Segovia Plaza	Denman Fink, designer	1925
Intersection of Sunset Drive and Erwin Road	Pinewood/Cocoplum Cemetery		1855
Intersection of S.W. 57th Avenue and 34th Street	Coral Gables Wayside Park	National Register site	1926

*Indicates architect, style, history or National Register status.

SITE ADDRESS	SITE NAME	SIGNIFICANCE*	DATE
116 Alhambra Circle	Hotel La Palma	George Fink, architect	1924
303 Alhambra Circle	American Legion Hall	Old City Hall (until 1927)	1922
817 Alhambra Circle			1925
907 Alhambra Circle			1929
2715 Alhambra Circle		Outstanding Mediterranean	1926
3417 Alhambra Circle	Home of John Murrel	A.L. Klingbeil, architect, home of first president of Coral Gables Chamber of Commerce	1925
760 Anastasia Avenue	Denman Fink's Residence		1938
803, 907, 911 Anastasia Avenue			1925
1200 Anastasia Avenue	Miami-Biltmore Hotel	Schultze & Weaver, architects, National Register site	1925
1212 Anastasia Avenue	Metropolitan Museum and Art Center	National Register site	1925
1233 Anastasia Avenue			1925
1270 Anastasia Avenue	Little Flower Rectory and Church	G.M. Barry and F.O. Kay of Chicago, architects	1927
410 Andalusia Avenue	First Church of Christ Scientist		1934
1000 Augusto Street	Ponce de Leon Junior High School	George Fink, architect	1925
405 Biltmore Way	City Hall	National Register site	1927
2416 Columbus Blvd.			1922
2709 Columbus Blvd.		Oolitic limestone vernacular, George Fink, architect, Stokes Residence	1925
536 Coral Way	Coral Gables Methodist Church	Paist and Stewart, architects	1933-1960
809, 825 Coral Way			1922
814, 832, 900 Coral Way		Oolitic rock vernacular, George Fink, architect	1922-1930
840 Coral Way	Maxwell Residence	John and Coulton Skinner, architects	1926
907 Coral Way	Coral Gables House	The Merrick House, masonry vernacular with limestone and classical details, National Register site	1906
920 Coral Way	Briggs/Haddock House	George Fink, architect, oolitic rock vernacular, one of the first houses built by Coral Gables Corp.,	1915
937 Coral Way	Cleys House	Oolitic limestone vernacular, built by George Merrick for his new bride, Eunice Merrick	1916
1001, 1041, 1119 Coral Way		Oolitic limestone vernacular	1921-1938
1032 Coral Way	Kreidt Residence	Oolitic limestone vernacular, originally built as one of the houses in the Merrick family estate.	1913
1044 Coral Way		Oolitic limestone vernacular, built by the Merrick family	1910
1141 Coral Way		George Fink, architect, built for E. Dammers, the first mayor of Coral Gables	1924
1217 Coral Way		Oolitic limestone vernacular, George Fink, architect, built by the Coral Gables Corporation	1922
1232, 1248, 1264 Coral Way			1925-1931
1235, 1251 Coral Way			ca. 1927-1932

*Indicates architect, style, history or National Register status.

SITE ADDRESS	SITE NAME	SIGNIFICANCE*	DATE
1254 Coral Way	Casa Azul	Limestone vernacular, H. George Fink's House	1925
1215, 1402 Country Club Prado Street			1924
1800 Country Club Prado Street			1925
2604 De Soto Blvd.			1922
2616 De Soto Blvd. 2615 Granada Blvd.			1922
2701 De Soto Blvd.	Venetian Pool and Casino	Denman Fink, Phineas Paist, architects. National Register site	1924
3010 De Soto Blvd.	Coral Gables Congregational Church	Kiehnel and Elliott, architects, National Register site	1923
1500 Douglas Road	Coliseum		1925
200 Edgewater Drive	Java Head Estate	Fine example of Art Deco, James Smith, architect, Charles Baker, original owner	1936
1217 Granada Blvd.			1929
1710, 1818, 2114, 2214 Granada Blvd.			
1920 Granada Blvd.		Limestone vernacular, formerly Country Club, Apts., Granada Manor Hospital	1922
3800 Granada Blvd.			1925
3903 Granada Blvd.			1922
238 Grand Avenue	George Washington Carver School		1925
611, 623, 625, 641, 665 N. Greenway Drive			1924-1939
709 N. Greenway Drive	Dorn Residence		1926
717 N. Greenway Drive			1927
725, 737, 751, 803 N. Greenway Drive			1922
741 N. Greenway Drive		Anthony de H. Zinc, architect, Montanus Residence, former mayor of Coral Gables	1929
997 N. Greenway Drive	Coral Gables Country Club	Oolitic limestone vernacular	1922
1115, 1135 N. Greenway Drive			1923-1927
1203 N. Greenway Drive	Humphreys/Maxwell Residence		1923
1217, 1225, 1303, 1327, 1402, 2010, 2022, 2200 N. Greenway Drive			1924
1006, 1012 S. Greenway Drive			1922-1926
1100 S. Greenway Drive			1925
1110, 1126 S. Greenway Drive			1922

*Indicates architect, style, history or National Register status.

SITE ADDRESS	SITE NAME	SIGNIFICANCE*	DATE
1234, 1242, 1260 S. Greenway Drive			1922
501, 517, 541 Hardee Road	French Country Village	Edgar Albright, architect	1925
6612, 6700, 6704, 6710 Le Jeune Road, 6705 San Vincente Street	Dutch South African Village		1925
1104 Malaga Avenue			1922
6810 Maynada Street	Lang Adams House	Frame vernacular	1899
105 Minorca Avenue	Coral Gables Elementary School	Kiehnel and Elliott, architects. National Register site	1926
133-169 Miracle Mile	Colonnade Building	Phineas Paist, architect	1925
432 Navarre Avenue			1922-1925
9610 Old Cutler Road	Matheson Hammock	Limestone vernacular, structures built by the PWA	
10091 Old Cutler Road	Fairchild Tropical Gardens		1939
1001 E. Ponce De Leon Blvd.	Coral Gables Women's Club	Oolitic limestone	1937
2100 Ponce De Leon Blvd.			1933
2506 Ponce De Leon Blvd.	University Professional Building	George Fink, architect and original owner	1925
2701 Ponce De Leon Blvd.			1926
158 S. Prospect Drive			1925
5125, 5129, 5133 Riviera Drive, 5100 Menendez Avenue, 5112 Castania Avenue, 5104, 5108 Maggiore Avenue, 5100 Sansovino	Chinese Village	Henry K. Murphy, architect	1926
6312 Riviera Drive	Coral Cove		1937
111 Salamanca Avenue			1925
2325 Salzedo Street (285 Aragon Avenue)	Old Police and Fire Station		1938
4409, 4515, 4520 Santa Maria Avenue, 4620 Mendavia Avenue	Colonial Village		1925
620 Santa Maria Street			1925
1375 Sunset Drive	Cocoplum Women's Club		1926
2800 Toledo Street	Venetia Apartments		1926
333 University Drive	San Sebastian Apts.	Originally University of Miami building	1925
4419 University Drive	Telfair Knight		1926
404, 406, 408, 409, 413, 416, Vizcaya Avenue, 3621 Le Jeune Road	French Provincial Village	John & Coulton Skinner, architects	1926-1927

*Indicates architect, style, history or National Register status.

SITE ADDRESS	SITE NAME	SIGNIFICANCE	DATE
15779 W. Dixie Highway	People's Gas System	Brick vernacular	1920s
16711 W. Dixie Highway	Spanish Monastery	National Register site originally built in Spain.	1141 const. 1952 reconst.
17530 W. Dixie Highway	Greynolds Park		ca. 1933
N.E. 172nd Street and 24th Avenue	Fulford-by-the-Sea Monument		1925

North Miami

SITE ADDRESS	SITE NAME	SIGNIFICANCE	DATE
11900 N.E. 16th Avenue		Frame vernacular, altered Burr House, Arch Creek pioneer	1907
2601 N.W. 119th Street	Westview Country Club	Mediterranean	1925
715 N.E. 125th Street	Old City Hall		ca. 1925
1200 N.E. 125th Street	William Jennings Bryan Elementary School	Fine Mediterranean, E.L. Robertson, architect	1930
Parks	Zapota Park	Formerly Palmango Estate	

Miami Shores**

SITE ADDRESS	SITE NAME	SIGNIFICANCE	DATE
257 N.E. 91st Street		National Register site	1925
353 N.E. 91st Street		National Register site	1925
357 N.E. 92 Street		National Register site	1925
477 N.E. 92 Street		National Register site	1925
379, 384, 436 N.E. 94th Street		National Register site	1925
431 N.E. 94th Street		First house built in the Miami Shores Subdivision	1924
145 N.E. 95th Street		National Register site	1925
940 N.E. 95th Street			1925
989 N.E. 95th Street			1925
1000 N.E. 95th Street			1925
107 N.E. 96th Street		National Register site	1925
262 N.E. 96th Street		Kiehnel & Elliott, architects, owned by Roy C. Wright, developer of Miami Shores	1928
284, 287, 540, 577 N.E. 96th Street		National Register site	1925- 1928
361 N.E. 97th Street		National Register site	1925
273 N.E. 98th Street		National Register site	1925
276 N.E. 98th Street		National Register site	1925
253, 260, 269, 310, 389 N.E. 99th Street			ca. 1920
121 N.E. 100 Street		National Register site	1925
553, 561 N.E. 101 Street		National Register site	1925
1291 N.E. 102 Street		National Register site	1925
10108 N.E. 1 Avenue		National Register site	1925

*Indicates architect, style, history or National Register status.

Miami Shores

9823 N.E. 4th Avenue	Miami Shores Community Church	Old pump house	ca. 1925
10351 N.E. 5th Avenue	Miami Shores Elementary School	Fine Art Deco	ca. 1929
421 Grand Concourse Boulevard	Grand Concourse Apartments	National Register site	1925

Biscayne Park

640 N.E. 114th Street	Village Hall and Police Station	Unusual log-construction	1933

El Portal

N.E. 85th Street and 4th Avenue	El Portal Burial Mound	Archaeological site	
301 N.E. 86th Street	Sherwood Forest House		1925
6 N.E. 89th Street		Frame vernacular, restored, built by Charles Finch	ca. 1910

THE CURTISS-BRIGHT DEVELOPMENTS: Hialeah

2 Circle Drive (Deer Park area)		Mission style, home of Harry Howell, associate of Curtiss & Bright	pre-1926
Miami River Canal and 1st Street (Hialeah Drive)	Swing Bridge, Hialeah-Miami Springs	First bridge connecting east and west banks of Miami River in the Hialeah area	1923
Miami River Canal and 1st Avenue	Vertical Light Bridge, Hialeah-Miami Springs	Originally crossed Miami River at N.W. 36th Street, moved in 1954	1927
45 Olive Drive (Deer Park area)		Mission style, home of James Bright, developer of Hialeah	1921
932 Palm Avenue	Airline Hotel (Hialeah Apartment Hotel)	One of the earliest extant buildings in Hialeah	1924
216 Pen-na-na Drive (Deer Park area)		Mission style, home of Carl Adams, friend of Curtiss & Bright	pre-1926
Seaboard Coastline Railroad and S.E. 10th Court	Hialeah Passenger Station	Spanish Colonial Revival style	1926
201 To-To-Lo-Chee Drive (Deer Park area)	Snyder Residence	Frame vernacular, classical details	pre-1926
700 W. 2nd Avenue (Okeechobee Road)	City of Miami Water Plant	Fine Mission style, oolitic limestone construction	1924
E. 4th Avenue	Hialeah Race Track (Miami Jockey Club)	Originally contained the first greyhound track in the U.S., a jai-alai fronton and an amusement park, National Register site	1925-1950s
265 E. 5th Street	South Hialeah Elementary School	Spanish styled, De Garmo, architect	1923

*Indicates architect, style, history or National Register status.

Opa-locka**

SITE ADDRESS	SITE NAME	SIGNIFICANCE*	DATE
490 Ali Baba Avenue	Opa-locka Railroad Station	National Register	1926
940 Caliph Street	First Baptist Church	Bernhardt Muller, architect, Egyptian revival style. Built as a bank. National Register	1926
401 Dunad Avenue		Bernhardt Muller, architect. National Register site	1926
811 Dunad Avenue		Bernhardt Muller, architect. National Register site	1926
1035 Dunad Avenue		Bernhardt Muller, architect. National Register site	1926
1141 Jann Avenue		Bernhardt Muller, architect. National Register site	1926
432 Opa-locka Blvd.	Opa-locka Hotel	Bernhardt Muller, architect National Register site.	1926
1110 Peri Street		Bernhardt Muller, architect. National Register site	1926
1156 Peri Street		Bernhardt Muller, architect. National Register site	1926
111 Perviz Avenue		Bernhardt Muller, architect. National Register site	1926
1210-1212 Sesame Street		Bernhardt Muller, architect. National Register site	1926
1214-1216 Sesame Street		Bernhardt Muller, architect. National Register site	1926
613 Sharar Avenue		Bernhardt Muller, architect. National Register site	1926
721 Sharar Avenue		Bernhardt Muller, architect. National Register site	1926
915 Sharar Avenue		Bernhardt Muller, architect. National Register site	1926
1011 Sharar Avenue		Bernhardt Muller, architect. National Register site	1926
777 Sharazad Blvd.	City Hall	Bernhardt Muller, architect National Register site	1926
826 Superior Street		Bernhardt Muller, architect. National Register site	1926
951 Superior Street		Bernhardt Muller, architect. National Register site	1926

**All significant buildings in Opa-locka are Moorish style, unless otherwise indicated

Miami Springs

SITE ADDRESS	SITE NAME	SIGNIFICANCE*	DATE
200 Azure Street	Osceola Apartment Hotel	Pueblo style. National Register site	1925
Canal Street	Miami Springs Bridge		ca. 1930
45 Curtiss Parkway		Pueblo style. National Register site	1925
201 Curtiss Parkway	Fair Havens Retirement Home	Pueblo style, Battle Creek Hotel	ca. 1925
85 Deer Run	The Alamo	Pueblo style. National Register site	1925
500 Deer Run	Curtiss Home	Pueblo style, Curtiss Residence	1925

*Indicates architect, style, history or National Register status.

Miami Springs

SITE ADDRESS	SITE NAME	SIGNIFICANCE*	DATE
281 Glendale Drive		Hunting Lodge and Skeet Club	1924
31 Hunting Lodge Court		Pueblo style, "Mama Lua's" Residence. National Register site	1925
27 Hunting Lodge Drive			1920s
150 Hunting Lodge Drive		Pueblo style. National Register site	1925
424 Hunting Lodge Drive		Pueblo style. National Register site	1925
851 Hunting Lodge Drive		Pueblo style. National Register site	1925

MIAMI BEACH: Art Deco District**

SITE ADDRESS	SITE NAME	SIGNIFICANCE*	DATE
1569 Alton Road	Firestone	Zurwelle & Whitaker, architects	1939
227 Biscayne Street	Joe's Stone Crabs		1921
801 Collins Avenue	Tiffany Hotel	L.M. Dixon, architect	1939
860 Collins Avenue	Franklin Hotel	V.H. Nellenbogen, architect	1934
904 Collins Avenue			1918-1920
953 Collins Avenue	Edward Hotel	Henry J. Maloney, architect	1935
1001 Collins Avenue	Essex House	Henry Hohauser, architect	1938
1111 Collins Avenue	Tudor Hotel	L.M. Dixon, architect	1939
1119 Collins Avenue	Palmer House	L.M. Dixon, architect	1939
1120 Collins Avenue	Primrose Hotel	V.H. Nellenbogen, architect	1935
1200 Collins Avenue	Marlin Hotel	L.M. Dixon, architect	1939
1300 Collins Avenue	The Alamac Hotel	V.H. Nellenbogen, architect	1934
1340 Collins Avenue	Shepley Hotel		1938
1360 Collins Avenue	Commodore Hotel	Henry Hohauser, architect	1939
1450 Collins Avenue	Warsaw Ballroom	Henry Hohauser, architect	1940
1500 Collins Avenue	Haddon Hall	L.M. Dixon, architect	1941
1501 Collins Avenue	Bancroft	Albert Anis, architect	1939
1565 Collins Avenue	St. Moritz	Roy France, architect	1939
1601 Collins Avenue	Sands	Roy France, architect	1939
1610 Collins Avenue	Berkeley Shore Hotel- Apartments	Albert Anis, architect	1940
1677 Collins Avenue	National	Roy France, architect	1940
1685 Collins Avenue	Delano	Swartburg, architect	1947
1701 Collins Avenue	Ritz Plaza	L.M. Dixon, architect	1940
1900 Collins Avenue	Peter Miller	Russell Pancoast, architect	1936
1920 Collins Avenue	Greystone	Henry Hohauser, architect	1939
2001 Collins Avenue	Coronet Retirement Residence	Henry Hohauser, architect	1936
2100 Collins Avenue	Bass Museum of Art	Russell Pancoast, architect, formerly Miami Beach Public Library	1930

*Indicates architect, style, history or National Register status.

MIAMI BEACH: Art Deco District**

SITE ADDRESS	SITE NAME	SIGNIFICANCE*	DATE
1424 Drexel Avenue	Ida M. Fisher School	August Geiger, architect, Mediterranean style	1936
Espanola Way		Taylor, architect, developed by N.B.T. Roney as the "Spanish Village", an artist colony	1925
1350, 1352, 1354 Euclid Avenue, 700 14th Street	Claire Apartments	Henry Hohauser, architect	1938
1650 James Avenue	Albion	Polevitsky & Russell, architects	1939
621 Lenox Avenue			1920
1538 Lenox Avenue	S. Bell Telephone Company	Alger, architect	1926
1630 Lenox Avenue	Chase Federal Office Building	August Geiger, architect	1947
1901-1907 Liberty Avenue	Santa Barbara Hotel Apartments	Russell Pancoast, architect	1934
420 Lincoln Road	Barnett Bank	Albert Anis, architect	1940
500 Lincoln Road	Miami Beach Community Church (United Church of Christ)	Walter De Garmo, architect, Mediterranean style	1921
555 Lincoln Road	Lincoln Cinema	Robert E. Collins and T.W. Lamb, architects	1935
605 Lincoln Road		Robert E. Collins, architect	1935-1937
744 Lincoln Road	David Alan	T.H. Henderson, architect	1929
910 Lincoln Road	Anglo-American Credit	Walter De Garmo, architect	1929
927 Lincoln Road	Sterling Building	Alexander Lewis, architect	1941
311-313 Meridian Avenue			1918
752-760 Meridian Avenue	Palm Gardens Apartments	H.H. Mundy, architect	1923
1507-1509 Meridian Avenue		H.J. Maloney, architect	1929
1521-1523 Meridian Avenue	James Apartments	Henry Hohauser, architect	1939
1525 Meridian Avenue		L.M. Dixon, architect	1939
1535, 1537, 1539 Meridian Avenue	Meridian Avenue Condominium	Kingston Hall, architect	1935
1545 Meridian Avenue		Kingston Hall, architect	1935
1551-1553 Meridian Avenue		Henry Hohauser, architect	1936
1557-1559 Meridian	Aldon Apartments	Henry Hohauser, architect	1936
227 Michigan Avenue	Ambassador Hotel	W.F. Brown, architect	1925
551, 557, 559 Michigan Avenue		Nolan, architect	1940
54 Ocean Drive	Hotel Leonard	Pfeiffer & O'Riley, architects	1925
112 Ocean Drive	Star Hotel	First hotel on Miami Beach	1914
140 Ocean Drive	Century Hotel	Henry Hohauser, architect	1939
425 Ocean Drive	Savoy Plaza Hotel	V.H. Nellenbogen, architect	1935

*Indicates architect, style, history or National Register status.
**Miami Beach's Art Deco District is on the National Register of Historic Places. This list roughly follows its boundaries, but includes some buildidngs that are stylistically compatible, south of the official district.

SITE ADDRESS	SITE NAME	SIGNIFICANCE*	DATE
918 Ocean Drive	Locust Apartments		1926
940 Ocean Drive	Breakwater	Skislewicz, architect	1939
960 Ocean Drive	Edison Hotel	Henry Hohauser, architect	1935
1114-1116 Ocean Drive	Amsterdam Palace Apartment-Hotel	LaPointe, architect, Mediterranean style	1930
1144 Ocean Drive	Victor	L.M. Dixon, architect	1937
1220 Ocean Drive	The Tides	L.M. Dixon, architect	1936
1244 Ocean Drive	Leslie Hotel	Albert Anis, architect	1937
1250 Ocean Drive	Carlyle	Kiehnel & Elliot, architects	1941
1300 Ocean Drive	Cardozo Hotel	Henry Hohauser, architect	1939
1320 Ocean Drive	Cavalier	Roy France, architect	1936
2030 Park Avenue	Adams	L.M. Dixon, architect	1938
2035 Park Avenue	Plymouth Hotel	Skislewicz, architect	1940
301 Washington Avenue	Beth Jacobs Congregation Hall	Henry Hohauser, architect, National Register site	1936
311 Washington Avenue	Social Hall	Rose, architect	1928
605-613 Washington Avenue		E.L. Robertson, architect	1934
685 Washington Avenue		E.L. Robertson, architect	1934
800 Washington Avenue	Blackstone	Masonry vernacular with Mediterranean details, first Jewish hotel on Miami Beach	1929
1001 Washington Avenue	Washington Storage	Robertson and Patterson, architects	1927
1130 Washington Avenue	Old Miami Beach City Hall	M.L. Hampton, architect Mediterranean style	1927
1201-1259 Washington Avenue	S.H. Kress Company	T.H. Henderson, architect	1935
1300 Washington Avenue	Miami Beach Post Office	Cheney, architect, Depression Moderne style	1937
1420 Washington Avenue	Leroy D. Fienberg Elementary School	Mission style	1920
1445 Washington Avenue	Cameo Theater	Robert E. Collins, architect	1938
1701 Washington Avenue	Temple Emanu-El	Charles Greco and Anis, architects	1947
2100 Washington Avenue	Miami Beach Community Center	August Geiger, architect	1937
701-745 5th Street	Hotel McArthur	T.H. Henderson, architect	1930
805 5th Street	Old Western Union Office	Walter De Garmo, architect	1925
1125-1131 5th Street		Masonry vernacular, altered, old Post Office	1920
999 11th Street	Flamingo Park		1921
736 13th Street	Parkway Apartments	Henry Hohauser, architect	1936
529-535 15th Street	Cameo	Henry Hohauser, architect	1939
850 15th Street	Wasserman's Apartments	L.M. Dixon, architect	1939

*Indicates architect, style, history or National Register status.

MIAMI BEACH: Art Deco District**

SITE ADDRESS	SITE NAME	SIGNIFICANCE*	DATE
318 20th Street	Collins Plaza	Henry Hohauser, architect	1936
337 20th Street	Riviera Plaza	R.A, Preas, architect	1924
435 21st Street	Governor	Henry Hohauser, architect	1939
309 23rd Street	Palm Court		1923
Ocean Drive from 6th Street to 14th Place	Lummus Park		1915

MIAMI BEACH: North Of The National Register District

SITE ADDRESS	SITE NAME	SIGNIFICANCE*	DATE
411, 417, 422, 437, 441, 524, 532, 548, 555 Arthur Godfrey Road		Martin L. Hampton, architect	1934-1936
711 Arthur Godfrey Road	North Beach Elementary School	August Geiger, architect, Mediterranean style	1936
5000 block of N. Bay Road		August Geiger, architect, Neo-classical style, Carl Fisher Residence	1925
2800 Collins Avenue	Hampton Court Apartments	Martin L. Hampton, architect	1924
3425 Collins Avenue	Versailles Hotel	Roy France, architect	1941
3720 Collins Avenue	Croydon Arms Hotel		1930s
3925 Collins Avenue	Cadillac Hotel	Melvin Grossman, architect	1956
4300 Collins Avenue	International Hotel	Roy F. France, architect	1936
4441 Collins Avenue	Fontainbleau Hilton	Morris Lapidus, architect, Resort modern	1953
4525 Collins Avenue	Eden Roc	Morris Lapidus, architect, Resort modern	1955
5937 Collins Avenue	Bath Club	Robert A. Taylor, architect, Mediterranean style	1927
9011 Collins Avenue	Surf Club	Russell T. Pancoast, architect, Mediterranean style	1929-1930
3707 Garden Avenue	St. Patrick's Church	Gerald Barry, architect, Mediterranean style	1928
Palm Avenue, Palm Island	Dan Hardie Residence Villa Encantada	William F. Brown, architect, Mediterranean style	1924
Palm Avenue, Palm Island	John B. Orr Residence	Kiehnel & Elliot, architect, Mediterranean style	1926
Palm Avenue, Palm Island	Capone House	Mediterranean style	1922
E. Star Island Drive, Star Island	John Levi Residence	John N. Bullen, architect, Mediterranean style	1935
E. Star Island Drive, Star Island	Col. Green Residence/ Star Island Yacht Club	Mediterranean style	1920
250 W. 63rd Street	St. Francis Hospital	August Geiger, architect, Mediterranean originally, greatly altered.	1924

*Indicates architect, style, history or National Register status.

SITE ADDRESS	SITE NAME	SIGNIFICANCE*	DATE
5900, 5904 S. Dixie Highway, 5900 Sunset Drive	Dorn Building	Commercial Mediterranean	1924-1925
Old Cutler Road	Historic Highway		late 1800s
7400 Ponce de Leon Road	Stonegate	Unusual oolitic limestone vernacular	1923-1927
5190 Sunset Drive	The Teacherage	Wood frame	1911
	Sunset Elementary School, main building	Mediterranean	1915
5530 Sunset Drive	Tropical Audubon Society	Robert Finch Smith, architect, fine frame vernacular	1932
6130 Sunset Drive	Sylva Martin Center	Oolitic limestone vernacular	1934
6491 Sunset Drive	George Orr House	Limestone vernacular	1936
7425 Sunset Drive	Fairholm	Masonry vernacular	1914
7460 S.W. 47th Avenue	Wheeler House	Fine frame vernacular	1914
7850 S.W. 47th Avenue	The Erwin Home	Frame vernacular, altered, originally the Adam Richard's Homestead House	ca. 1890
7310 S.W. 47th Court	Cornell Home	Built in Georgia and moved to Miami in the 1950s	
8251 S.W. 52nd Avenue	Hervey Allen Studio	Oolitic limestone vernacular, Hervey Allen was the author of "Anthony Adverse," National Register site	mid 1930s
6461 S.W. 59th Place	St. John's A.M.E. Church	Fine masonry vernacular, built on land donated by Black pioneer, Marshall Williamson	1916
6500 S.W. 60th Avenue		Marshal Williamson's Home, Black pioneer	ca. 1912
4700 S.W. 74th Street		Fine frame vernacular, moved to this location ca. 1940	1910
5340 S.W. 80th Street		Robert Frost's winter home	1940

SITE ADDRESS	SITE NAME	SIGNIFICANCE*	DATE
24101 S. Dixie Highway			ca. 1905
10400 Old Cutler Road	Maude Black House	Wood frame, built by Cutler pioneer, Charles Seibold	ca. 1891
13601 Old Cutler Road	Subtropical Horticultural Research Station		1923
Old Cutler Road and S.W. 167th Street	Deering Estate	Wood frame, the former Richmond Inn	1900
Old Cutler Road and S.W. 167th Street	Deering Estate	Outstanding Mediterranean Charles Deering house, National Register	1922

*Indicates architect, style, history or National Register status.

SITE ADDRESS	SITE NAME	SIGNIFICANCE*	DATE
6040 S.W. 86th Street		Former Kendall F.E.C. Station, moved and converted to a residence	ca. 1907
6355 S.W. 133rd Drive	Devonwood	English Tudor style	1926
26055 S.W. 134th Avenue		Log cabin style ca. 1914	
21690 S.W. 137th Avenue		Preston Lee House, former County Commissioner	1910
22400 S.W. 147th Avenue (Old Dixie Highway)	Cauley Square	Limestone and masonry vernacular commercial building	1920
26549 S.W. 147th Avenue (Old Dixie Highway)		Fine oolitic limestone vernacular from early Naranja	ca. 1912
28655 S.W. 157th Avenue	Coral Castle	Unusual limestone sculpture garden by Edward Leedskalnin. National Register	1921-1930s
24375 S.W. 162nd Avenue (Farmlife Road)		William Anderson Home	1900
25755 S.W. 162nd Avenue (Farmlife Road)			ca. 1914
24800 S.W. 187th Avenue	Redland Methodist Church		1914
24801 S.W. 187th Avenue	Fruit and Spice Park	Redland School House	1907
17201 S.W. 216th Street		Mohn House	1912
13550 S.W. 218th Street		Mobley House	1910
13301 S.W. 232nd Street (Silver Palm Drive)			ca. 1913
15655 S.W. 232nd Street (Silver Palm Drive)		Silver Palm School House, National Register	1904
15700 S.W. 232nd Street	Anderson's Corner	Old general store, National Register site	1911
1-36 S.W. 137th Avenue		Frame vernacular worker cottages from the former Drake Lumber Company	ca. 1904
15750 S.W. 232nd Street		Former Lowry Anderson Blacksmith Shop	ca. 1912
16525 S.W. 232nd Street (Silver Palm Drive)		Charles Graham House	ca. 1908
13425 S.W. 248th Street		Former Drake Commissary	ca. 1912
16475 S.W. 248th Street			1916
18240 S.W. 248th Street			1907
19701 S.W. 248th Street			1907
20740 S.W. 248th Street			1920s
18725 S.W. 256th Street	Bodil Kosel Lowe House		1902
19470 S.W. 264th Street			ca. 1915
13317 S.W. 266th Street			1913

*Indicates architect, style, history or National Register status.

Homestead

SITE ADDRESS	SITE NAME	SIGNIFICANCE*	DATE
17390 S.W. Avocado Drive	Tropical Palm Lodge	Fine frame vernacular	1912
17900 S.W. Avocado Drive		Lily Lawrence Bow Home	1908
5 S. Flagler Avenue	Redland Hotel	Fine frame vernacular	ca. 1913
55 S. Flagler Avenue	Landmark Hotel	Fine masonry vernacular	1916(?)
61 N.E. King's Highway			1920s
2-6 N. Krome Avenue	Synder's	Homestead Bank	1912
13 N. Krome Avenue	W.D. Horne Building		1921
43 N. Krome Avenue		Old Homestead City Hall	1917
240 N. Krome Avenue	First Baptist Church		1944
622 N. Krome Avenue	First United Methodist Church		1949
909 N. Krome Avenue		Frank Skill Home	1925
970 N. Krome Avenue		Moffit Home	ca. 1915
304 S. Krome Avenue			1914
109 W. Mowry Street			1910
1014 N.E. 1st Avenue			1920s
212 N.W. 1st Avenue	Lily Lawrence Bow Library	Fine oolitic limestone vernacular	1939
520 N.W. 1st Avenue	Neva King Cooper Grade School	August Geiger, architect, fine Mission style. National Register site	1914
50, 58 S.W. 1st Street		Fine frame vernacular	1912
650 N.W. 2nd Avenue	Homestead Junior High School		1920s
122 N.W. 3rd Street		Livingston House	1909
77 N.W. 4th Street	"Bolt" House	Named because it was entirely assembled with nuts and bolts so it could be disassembled and moved	1906
225 S.E. 4th Street	Christian Science Church	Fine frame vernacular	1916
153 N.W. 6th Street		Neva King Cooper Home	1925
92 N.E. 10th Street		Outstanding belvedere bungalow	1925
51 N.W. 11th Street		Fine frame vernacular, T.A. Campbell Home	1912
25 N.E. 12th Street		W.D. Horne Home	1920
19905 S.W. 320th Street			ca. 1910

SOUTH DADE: Florida City

SITE ADDRESS	SITE NAME	SIGNIFICANCE*	DATE
824 Krome Avenue	Florida Pioneer Museum and Railroad Depot	Outstanding frame vernacular, typical of early F.E.C. architecture, National Register site	1904
400 W. Palm Drive	Florida City Hall	Originally constructed with funds raised by the Women's Industrial Society	1912
122 S.W. 3rd Avenue		Stiling House	ca. 1911

*Indicates architect, style, history or National Register status.

SOUTH DADE: Longview

SITE ADDRESS	SITE NAME	SIGNIFICANCE*	DATE
Northwest corner of Palm Drive and Tower Road		School House/Longview Clubhouse	1911

SOUTH DADE: Outlying Areas

SITE ADDRESS	SITE NAME	SIGNIFICANCE*	DATE
Key Biscayne	Calusa Playhouse	Frame vernacular, former worker cottage from the Matheson plantation	post 1909
Key Biscayne	Crandon Park	Donated by the Matheson family	1947
Key Biscayne	Cape Florida Lighthouse	Oldest structure in Dade County, National Register site	1825
Fisher Island	Vanderbilt Estate	Fine Mediterranean	ca. 1925
Route 27	Graham Estate	Fine oolitic limestone, built by Ernest Graham, former State Senator and father of the current U.S. Senator, Bob Graham	1924

*Indicates architect, style, history or National Register

List of Demolished Structures

The following structures, originally listed among the significant sites in this publication, have been demolished since the time the first edition was published.

DOWNTOWN MIAMI

SITE ADDRESS	SITE NAME	SIGNIFICANCE	DATE
1756 N. Bayshore Drive	Brown House	Oolitic limestone, oriental style roof. Partially demolished in an attempt to relocate it to Watson Island.	1916
1402 S. Bayshore Drive	Highleyman House	DeGarmo, architect, home of Developer of Point View area.	1911
10 Biscayne Blvd.	McAllister Hotel	DeGarmo, architect, early highrise hotel in downtown	1916
204 Biscayne Blvd.	Hotel Toledo	Profusion of bay windows	1910-1914
1824 Biscayne Blvd.		Mediterranean style	1924
2501 Biscayne Blvd.	Boulevard Christian Church	Mediterranean Style	1925
3227 Biscayne Blvd.		Two building group in Mediterranean style	1925
1528 Brickell Avenue			1924
1581 Brickell Avenue			1920
1597 Brickell Avenue.	Palm Court		1920
1617 Brickell Avenue			1937
1627 Brickell Avenue.	Dr. Jackson's home		1920
2127 Brickell Avenue	Cocoplovis		1920, 1933
303 E. Flagler Street		Elks Club	1910
S. Miami Avenue	South Miami Avenue Bridge		
133 N.W. 1st Avenue	Miami Hotel		1924
400 S.W. 1st Avenue	Florida East Coast Railway Freighthouse	One of a kind construction Brick-Industrial Design	1925
229 S.W. 1st Street	Villa Tanner	Rusticated block construction	1906-1914
505 N.E. 2nd Avenue			1909
400 S.W. 2nd Avenue	Florida Power and Light	Robert Law Weed, architect, formerly Ryan Motors showroom	1925
22 N.E. 5th Street	Chaille House	Frame vernacular	1905
14 S.E. 6th Street			1904-1906
24 S.E. 6th Street			1904-1906
38 S.E. 6th Street			1908
42 S.E. 6th Street			
64 N.E. 17th Street		Bungalow	1918

*Indicates architect, style, history or National Register status.

DOWNTOWN MIAMI

SITE ADDRESS	SITE NAME	SIGNIFICANCE	DATE
141 N.E. 24th Street			
401 N.E. 26th Terrace			
717 N.E. 27th Street		Neo-Classical Revival with rusticated blocks	1922
916 S.W. 1st Avenue			1915
940 S.W. 1st Avenue			1912-1913
526, 530, 545 N.W. 1st Street			1912-1917
1375 N.W. 1st Street		Belvedere bungalow	1915-1918

CITY OF MIAMI NEIGHBORHOODS: Little Havana

102 S.W. 6th Avenue			ca. 1914
128 N.W. 7th Avenue		Rusticated blocks and shingles	1916
1200 S.W. 27th Avenue	Lasalle School	Oolitic limestone, McAllister Residence	

CITY OF MIAMI NEIGHBORHOODS: Culmer-Overtown

1623 N.W. 1st Court		Bahamian wood frame	1915-1918
1121 N.W. 1st Place		Bahamian wood frame	1915-1918
1133 N.W. 1st Place		Bahamian wood frame	1910 1914
1229 N.W. 1st Place		Bahamian wood frame	1918-1925
1452 N.W. 1st Place		Fine Bahamian wood frame	1918-1921
642 N.W. 2nd Avenue	Mary Elizabeth Hotel		ca. 1918
932 N.W. 2nd Avenue	Hotel Dorsey		1920
1029-1031 N.W. 2nd Avenue		Altered masonry and frame drugstore, Dr. Frazier's House, one of the first Black doctors in Miami	1906
1937 N.W. 2nd Court		Bahamian wood frame	pre-1915
1100 N.W. 3rd Avenue		YWCA for Black women in 1925	1910-1914
1705 N.W. 3rd Avenue		Wood frame, gingerbread details, first blacksmith house	1918
1200 N.W. 6th Avenue	Booker T. Washington School	First Black High School in Miami	1925-27
219 N.W. 6th Street		Fine Bahamian wood frame	pre-1903
143 N.W. 7th Street		Fine Bahamian wood frame	pre-1903
257 N.W. 7th Street		Fine Mediterranean	ca. 1920
528 N.W. 8th Street			1914-1918

CITY OF MIAMI NEIGHBORHOODS Culmer-Overtown

SITE ADDRESS	SITE NAME	SIGNIFICANCE	DATE
255 N.W. 9th Street			ca. 1906
152 N.W. 10th Street		Bahamian wood frame	pre-1906
156,162 N.W. 10th Street		Bahamian wood frame	1910-19145
276 N.W. 10th Street or 947 N.W. 3rd Street		Bahamian wood frame commercial lbuilding	1914-1918

CITY OF MIAMI NEIGHBORHOODS: Highland Park, Allapatah and Surrounding Areas

SITE ADDRESS	SITE NAME	SIGNIFICANCE	DATE
301 N.W. 29th Street	Coca Cola building	Fine Mediterranean	1927

COCONUT GROVE

SITE ADDRESS	SITE NAME	SIGNIFICANCE	DATE
2485 South Bayshore Drive	Treasure Trove		1917-1919
3041 Grand Avenue	Blue Water Marine	Sanders Peacock Store	1908-1909
3554 Main Highway	Real Estate Office	Frame vernacular	ca. 1900

MIAMI BEACH: Art Deco District

SITE ADDRESS	SITE NAME	SIGNIFICANCE	DATE
1201 Collins Avenue	Senator Hotel	L.M. Dixon, Architect	1939
1110 Drexel Avenue	Neron Hotel	Henry Hohauser, architect	1940
56 Washington Avenue	David Court	Site where Miami Beach's first Jewish congregation gathered	1925
540 West Avenue	Biscaya Hotel/Old Floridian	S.D. Butterworth, architect, Mediterranean style	1925
1200 5th Street		Old Chamber of Commerce	1923

MIAMI BEACH: North of National Register District

SITE ADDRESS	SITE NAME	SIGNIFICANCE	DATE
400, 410 Arthur Godfrey Road	Sheridan Theatre	Martin L. Hampton, architect	1936
4390 Collins Avenue	Surrey Hotel		1942-1947

SOUTH DADE: South Miami Area

SITE ADDRESS	SITE NAME	SIGNIFICANCE	DATE
5750 S. Dixie Highway	Holsum Bakery	Commercial Mediterranean originally the Riviera Theatre	1925

THE RAILROAD TOWNS

SITE ADDRESS	SITE NAME	SIGNIFICANCE	DATE
9921 E. Indigo		Perrine Station Master's House built by the F.E.C.	ca. 1903

V. GLOSSARY

ADOBE. Sun-dried mud brick. Commonly used as a building material in Mexico and by Southwestern American Indians. The soft forms are a result of the hand-shaped mud plastering.

ARCADE. A row of arches carried on piers or columns either freestanding or attached to a wall.

BALLOON FRAME. A timber framing method of construction introduced in the mid-nineteenth century where slender vertical members (studs) are nailed at close intervals from the sill plate over the floor to the eave or top plate. Previous structural systems used heavier timbers joined and pegged together.

BALUSTRADE. A railing consisting of a series of short posts or pillars.

BAROQUE. A style of the seventeenth and eighteenth centuries evolved from the classical forms of the Renaissance, characterized by bold, elaborate scrolls, curves and ornamentation.

BAS RELIEF. Sculpture or carving with slight projection from the background.

BATTERED. Walls that slope inward toward the top.

BAUHAUS. German school of architecture established by Walter Gropius in 1919. Its philosophies were based on team work and the interdisciplinary study of the different branches of the arts and crafts working towards the goal of "the building of the future." The style is simple, abstracted forms, flat roofs, smooth surfaces, devoid of ornament.

BAY WINDOW.   A window in a wall that projects angularly from a main wall and from the ground up.

BEAUX ARTS.   Architectural style from the turn-of-the-century characterized by monumentality and classicism of strong French derivation.

BELVEDERE.   A tower or turret with openings all around.

BOARD AND BATTEN SIDING.   Building exterior surfacing consisting of vertical boards with the joints covered by narrow strips of wood or battens.

BRACKET.   Supporting member for the overhang of a roof, usually in the shape of an inverted L, a solid triangle or a triangular truss.

CANTILEVER.   A horizontal projection from a wall or frame supported without external bracing thus appearing self-supported.

CAPITAL.   The head of a column or pilaster.

CASEMENT.   Windows with wood or metal frames hinged on the sides, so they open horizontally like a door.

CHICAGO SCHOOL.   Group of Chicago architects in the late 1800s specializing in the Commercial Style of architecture, most notably the development of the skyscraper.

CHURRIGURESQUE.   A type of Baroque characterized by lavish and over-decorated ornamentation. Typical of Spanish and South American architecture.

COLONNADE.   A row of columns carrying arches or flat entablatures.

COLUMN.   Upright structural member, circular in plan.

COMMERCIAL STYLE.   Early high rise architecture typical of Chicago in the last two decades of the nineteenth century. A steel skeleton reduces the wall to a direct expression of the structural system and allows larger window surfaces than possible until then. Louis Sullivan was one of the leading architects of the style.

CONCH ARCHITECTURE.   Building type popular in the Bahamas and Key West in the nineteenth century. "Conch", a hard shelled mollusk found in Bahama and Florida waters, became the nickname for Key West natives descended from Bahamians.

COQUINA.   A stone native to North Florida composed of tightly compacted shells, used as a building material.

CORNICE.   The uppermost, projecting part of an entablature, or a feature resembling it.

CRENELLATION.   A parapet with alternating indentations and raised portions.

CUPOLA.   A small dome topping a roof or turret.

DORMER.   A window piercing a sloping roof.

EAVE.   The part of a roof plane that overhangs the wall.

ECOLE DES BEAUX ARTS.   French national school of fine arts in Paris from which the Neo-Classical architectural style of the same name was derived in the late nineteenth century.

ENGAGED COLUMN.   A column attached to a wall or pier.

ENGAGED SCULPTURE.   Sculpture attached to, or recessed into a wall or pier.

ENTABLATURE.   The upper part of an order, such as base, column, and entablature. The top, or entablature consists of architrave, frieze, and cornice.

FACADE.   A face of a building, usually the front.

FACING.   The finish applied to the surface of a building, such as wood, stucco, shingles or metal.

FENESTRATION.   The arrangement or placement of openings on a facade.

FINIALS.   Pointed ornament at the top of a spire, gable, parapet or other high point on a building.

FLARED EAVE.   Outward curve of a sloping roof overhang.

FLUTING.   Grooving as on a column or pilaster.

FRIEZE.   The middle division of an entablature, between the architrave and cornice, usually decorated. Also refers to the decorated band along the upper part of an interior wall, immediately below the cornice.

GABLE.   Roof with two sloping planes.

GALLERY.   A roofed passageway projecting from an exterior wall, usually connecting interior spaces at either end.

GINGERBREAD.   Pierced, curvilinear wood ornaments cut with a jigsaw or scroll saw, located under the roof's eaves so as to hide the structural members. A decorative bargeboard, typical of Victorian Gothic buildings.

HIP.   A roof with slopes on all four sides.

INTERNATIONAL STYLE.   Term coined in the United States during the 1930s to collectively describe the variety of modern European movements based on abstracted, cubic and planar geometries, smooth surfaces with flat roofs and devoid of any surface decoration.

JOISTS.   Horizontal timbers laid parallel to each other, usually resting on beams and supporting roof or floor boarding.

LOGGIA.   A gallery or shallow porch, usually open on one or more sides.

MANNERISM.   Sixteenth century style based on a reinterpretation of the Renaissance classicism, through the use of the same decorative elements in deliberate opposition to their original meaning or context. Giulio Romano was one of the leading architects of the movement.

MANSARD ROOF.   Roof with double slopes on each of its planes, the lower being steeper than the upper slope. The top floor of the building is within the roof, which is pierced by dormer windows.

MINARET.   A tall, slender tower with a projecting top used in Moslem religion to call the faithful to prayer at the mosque, to which the minaret is attached or nearby.

MORTISE AND TENON JOINT.   The connection of two structural timbers, one cut out as a socket to receive the projection of the other member. System of wood joinery predominantly used prior to the use of nailing and bolting connections in balloon framing.

OOLITIC LIMESTONE.   A granular calcium carbonate stone of coarse texture commonly found in South Florida. Its color is a light buff when quarried and it weathers to a gray shade.

PALMETTO THATCH.   Covering of dried palmetto fronds densely layered over a sloping roof.

PARAPET. The vertical extension of an exterior wall past the roof line. The low wall over a flat roof, usually pierced by drains to let water off the roof.

PIAZZA. Public square or plaza. A front courtyard. Another name for a loggia or gallery.

PILASTER. A flat, projecting representation of a column, usually attached to a wall.

PITCH. The steepness of a roof slope.

PORCH. A covered entrance to a building.

PORTICO. A small porch usually supported on columns, serving as entrance to a building.

QUEEN ANNE. A style of architecture during the late 1800s consisting of irregular massing and plan and a variety of colors and textures combined in one building.

RAFTER. One of the sloping structural roof timbers that establish the pitch.

RENAISSANCE. Architectural style originating in fifteenth century Italy based on the revival of ancient Roman principles of construction and decoration. Scale, proportion, symmetry and harmony are among its major features.

RIDGE. The horizontal line resulting from the intersection of two sloping roof planes at the top.

ROCOCO. A late eighteenth century style derived from the late phases of the Baroque, using softer, more delicate forms and colors in its decoration.

RUSTICATED BLOCKS. Concrete blocks poured into molds to imitate stone.

RUSTICATION. Rough-surfaced finish on stones.

SASH. A window frame that opens by sliding up or down on vertical grooves running along the sides. Single and double hung sash are the most commonly found types.

SCUPPER. Tile drains, generally cylindrical, piercing a parapet to let water off a roof.

SECOND EMPIRE. An architectural style from the late 1800s characterized by tall mansard roofs with a curb around the top of the slopes.

SHOTGUN HOUSE. A building type one room across the front, with circulation through the rooms. Modest wood frame houses typical in the early Black community.

SPANDREL. The panel between two windows that are vertically aligned.

STUCCO. Plaster used for exterior walls.

TURRET. Small tower attached to the corner of a building and extending above it.

TRYLON. Tall, slender spire-like form, triangular in section, tapering toward the top. Describes one of the favorite features of the 1939 New York World's Fair.

VERANDA. A porch that wraps around two or more sides of a building.

VERNACULAR. The common vocabulary typical to a region. The architecture typical to an area, usually the product of builders rather than architects, and based on their previous experience and available resources, not on style or academics.

VICTORIAN ARCHITECTURE. General term that describes the many revivalist styles from the late nineteenth century.

WEATHERBOARDS. Horizontal overlapping boards, wedge-shaped in section, covering a wood frame structure.

FOOTNOTES

CHAPTER I

[1]U.S. Department of Commerce, Seventh Census of the United States, 1850, Dade County, Florida.

[2]A large portion of the eastern rim of the Everglades was drained to create more habitable land. The drainage program was begun in 1907 by Governor Napoleon Broward.

[3]Arva Moore Parks, "Where the River Found the Bay," Historical Study of the Granada Site, Miami, Florida. Unpublished report, July, 1979.

[4]Dr. Louise Hill, **Spanish Land Grants in Florida, Confirmed Claims,** Vol. I-V, (Tallahassee, Fla: State Library Board.)

[5]In 1828, a superior court was established at Key West to

adjudicate wrecks. It mandated the licensing of wreckers and their vessels. See Dorothy Dodd, "The Wrecking Business on the Florida Reefs: 1822-1860," **Florida Historical Quarterly,** April, 1944, p. 176.

[6]U.S. Department of the Interior, National Register of Historic Places Nomination Form, Prepared by Randy F. Nimnicht, February 24, 1971.

[7]John K. Mahon, **History of the Second Seminole War,** (Jacksonville, Florida: University of Florida Press, 1967), pp. 18-128.

[8]Glyndon G. Van Deusen, **The Jacksonian Era,** (New York: Harper & Row, 1959).

[9]Mahon, pp. 129-130.

[10]Hugo L. Black III, "Richard Fitzpatrick's South Florida: 1822-1840," Part II, **Tequesta,** No. XLI, 1981, p. 34.

[11]U.S. Congress, House, **Report of the Court of Claims,** H.R. 175, 35th Congress, First Session, 1858, pp. 14-15.

[12]Parks, pp. 84-86.

[13]The original boundaries of Dade County included what are today Broward and Palm Beach counties. See F.M. Hudson, "Beginnings in Dade County," **Tequesta,** Vol. 1, No. 3, July, 1943.

[14]Black, p. 39.

[15]Parks, p. 84.

[16]Ibid, p. 85.

[17] Ibid, pp. 35-36.

[18]Ibid, pp. 91-93.

[19]U.S. Department of Commerce, Seventh Census of the United States, 1850. Most of the remaining fled in 1849 when rumors of an impending Indian attack swept the county. See Oby J. Bonawit, **Miami, Florida, Early Families and Records,** (Miami, Florida: privately published, 1980), p. 8.

[20]Parks, p. 98.

[21]Hudson, p. 34.

[22]Parks, pp. 99-100.

[23]Mrs. A.C. Richards, "Reminiscences on the Early Days of Miami," **The Miami News,** Series beginning October 1, 1903; and Walter Keeler Scofield, "On Blockade Duty in Florida Waters," William J. Schellings, ed., **Tequesta,** Vol. XV, 1955.

[24]Richards, 1903; and Ralph Middleton Munroe and Vincent Gilpin, **The Commodore's Story,** (Norberth, Pennsylvania: Livingston Pub. Co., 1930), p. 94.

[25]Margot Ammidown, "The Wagner Family: Homesteading in Miami's Pioneer Era. 1855-1896," Unpublished research report for Dade Heritage Trust, 1981.

[26]Ibid.

[27]Ibid.

[28]See Arva Moore Parks, "Miami in 1876," **Tequesta,** Vol. XXXV, 1975, pp. 89-145; and Thelma Peters, **Biscayne Country: 1870-1926,** (Miami, Florida: Banyan Books, 1981). A particularly attention getting series publicizing Miami was published in **Harper's** at this time: J.B. Holder, "Along the Florida Reef," **Harper's New Monthly Magazine,** December, 1870 – May, 1871.

[29]"Abstract of Title to the James Hagan (Egan) Donation" Robbins, Graham, and Chillingsworth, Examining Counsel, July, 1897.

[30]Parks, "Where the River Found the Bay," p. 114.

[31]Arva Moore Parks, "Historical Study for the Barnacle," Bureau of Historic Sites and Properties, Division of Archives, History and Records Management: Miscellaneous Projects Report, No. 32, September, 1975, p. 11.

[32]Ibid, p. 15.

[33]Munroe and Gilpin, p. 115.

[34]Ibid, p. 110.

[35]Ibid, p. 113.

[36]Ibid, p. 170.

[37]Transcendentalism was a mid-nineteenth century American intellectual and literary movement which emphasized individualism, human brotherhood and an appreciation of nature. The movement was centered in New England, particularly in Concord, Massachusetts and was a reaction to the mass industrialization, pollution, and worker exploitation of the age.

[38]Parks, "Historic Study for the Barnacle."

[39]Many of Commodore Munroe's photographs can be seen in published form in: Arva Moore Parks, **The Forgotten Frontier,** (Miami, Florida: Banyan Books, 1977).

[40]Munroe and Gilpin, p. V.

[41]Parks, "Historical Study for the Barnacle," p. 40.

[42]Louise Davis, Kate Dean, and Lillian Mazon (daughters of E.W.F. Stirrup), Personal Interview (by Harvey and Mary Napier), Miami, Florida, May 29, 1973.

[43]Thelma Peters, **Lemon City: Pioneering on Biscayne Bay 1850-1925,** (Miami, Florida: Banyan Books, 1976), p. 21.

[44]Ibid, p. 23.

[45]Ibid, p. 64.

[46]Henry E. Perrine, **Some Eventful Years in Grandpa's Life,** (Buffalo, New York: E.H. Hutchinson Press, 1885).

[47]Letter, George M. Robbins to J.E. Ingraham, January 5, 1911, (William Keegin Papers, 1896-1911, Historical Association of Southern Florida). This document states that three squatters in the area were given deeds by the Perrines, J.A. Addison, C.M. Campbell, and William Fuzzard.

[48]Jean Taylor, "Cutler and Perrine Grant," Miami, Florida, Unpublished research report, 1981.

[49]E.V. Blackman, **Miami and Dade County, Florida,** Washington, D.C., 1921.

[50]Steve Trumbull, "Lighthouse Lore," **The Miami Herald,** p.G-1, March 25, 1956.

[51]Charles M. Brookfield, "Cape Florida Light," **Tequesta,** Miami, Florida, 1949, p. 6.

[52]Nimnicht, 1971.

[53]Arva Moore Parks, **Miami, The Magic City,** (Tulsa, Oklahoma: Continental Heritage Press, 1981) p. 29.

[54]Brookfield, p. 7.

[55]Parks, "Where the River Found the Bay," p. 88.

[56]Albert Manucy, "Some Military Affairs in Territorial Florida," **Florida Historical Quarterly,** XXV, October, 1946, pp. 20-21.

[57]Parks, "Where the River Found the Bay," p. 88.

[58]Ibid, p. 90.

[59]Ibid, p. 99.

[60]Ibid, p. 100.

[61]Ibid, p. 111.

[62]Ammidown, p. 62.

[63]Ibid, p. 115.

[64]Wayne Andrews, **Architecture, Ambition and Americans,** (New York: The Free Press, 1947), p. 149.

[65]A 1909 photograph shows the house prior to the addition of the ornamental shingles.

[66]See definition of Mission Style.

[67]Beverly Anderson was the property owner at the time.

[68]April 10, 1979.

[69]Maude Black, Personal Interview (by Arva Moore Parks), Miami, Florida, September 5, 1971.

[70]Munroe, p. 217.

[71]Parks, "Historical Study for the Barnacle," p. 14.

[72]Munroe, p. 217.

[73]Parks, "Historical Study for the Barnacle," p. 23.

[74]Ibid, pp. 24-29.

CHAPTER II

[1]"Abstract of Title to the Rebecca Hagan (Egan) Donation," Robbins, Graham, and Chillingsworth, Examining Council, January, 1907.

[2]James E. Ingraham, Address to the Miami Woman's Club, November 12, 1920, as reprinted in E.V. Blackman, **Miami and Dade County, Florida: Its Settlement, Progress, and Achievement,** (Washington, D.C.: Victor Rainbolt, 1921), pp. 53-54.

[3]Letter, Henry Flagler to Mrs. Julia Tuttle, St. Augustine, Florida, April 22, 1895, (Copy on file at the Historic Preservation Division, Butler House File, Dade County).

[4]Ibid.

[5]John Sewell, **Memoirs and History of Miami Florida,** (Miami, Florida: Franklin Press, 1933), pp. 9-10.

[6]Dade County, Florida, County Land Division Plat Book B, p. 41.

[7]Sewell, pp. 131-135.

[8]Sidney Walter Martin, **Florida's Flagler,** (Athens, Georgia: University of Georgia Press, 1949), p. 139.

[9]"Royal Palm Finished," **The Miami Metropolis,** January 15, 1897.

[10]"Cut Down Trousers Miami's First Depot," **The Miami Herald,** July 28, 1929.

[11]Wayne Andrews, **Architecture, Ambition and Americans,** (New York: The Free Press, 1947), pp. 197-198.

[12]Martin, p. 116.

[13]Ibid, p. 163.

[14]**The Miami Herald,** May 14, 1964, p. 2-E.

[15]Sewell, pp. 177-179.

[16]Blackman, p. 85.

[17]Valerie Lassman, "A History of a Residence of Early Miami," taken from Nathan Shappe's "Flagler's Undertakings in Miami in 1897," **Tequesta,** 1959.

[18]Martin, p. 163.

[19]**The Miami Metropolis,** (ads), May 15, 1896.

[20]Isador Cohen, **Historical Sketches and Sidelights of Miami,** (Miami, Florida: privately printed, 1925), p. 22.

[21]Ibid.

[22]Arva Moore Parks, **Miami: The Magic City,** (Tulsa, Oaklahoma: Continental Heritage Press, Inc.), p. 68.

[23]Ibid.

[24]Cohen, p. 24.

[25]Ibid.

[26]Parks, pp. 76-78.

[27]Cohen, p. 6.

[28]Dade County, Florida, County Recorder's Office, Deed Books P and Q.

[29]Cohen, p. 180.

[30]Kenneth de Garmo, Personal Interview (by Margot Ammidown and Ivan A. Rodriguez), Miami, Florida, January 27, 1982.

[31]Sewell, p. 28.

[32]Paul S. George, "Colored Town: Miami's Black Community, 1896-1930," **Florida Historical Quarterly,** April, 1978, pp. 432-447.

[33]"Time to Recall," **The Miami Herald,** December 27, 1964.

[34]Dorothy Fields, "Blacks Played Major Role in Building Miami," **The Miami Times,** July 1, 1976.

[35]Dorothy Fields, "Reflections on Black History: Miami's First Newspaper," **Update,** Vol. III, February, 1976.

[36]Romona Lown, "Meet Kelsey Pharr, Distinguished Miami Leader," **The Miami Times,** November 13, 1946.

[37]George, pp. 432-433.

[38]Miami, Florida, Black Archives Foundation, Inc., Black Photographic Archives and Oral History Collection of Pioneers in Dade County, Florida, Between 1896 and 1946, Portfolio #1, Archives #26.

[39]Garth Reeves and Dorothy Fields, "The Origin of the **Miami Times,"** **The Miami Herald,** June, 1978.

[40]Dorothy Fields, "Black Entertainment 1908-1919," **Update,** Vol. II, December, 1974.

[41]George, p. 441.

[42]Ibid.

[43]C.H. Ward, **The Lure of Southland,** (Harrisburg, Pa.: J. Horace McFarland Co.), 1915.

[44]Dade County, Florida, Historic Preservation Division, Bragg Residence File, 1978.

[45]Allan Reid Parrish, **Official Directory of Miami, Florida and Nearby Towns in Dade County, 1904,** (Reprinted, published by the Historical Association of Southern Florida, 1974.

[46]**Preservation Guidebook for the Old Section of the City of Key West,** (Key West, Florida: Old Island Restoration Commission, 1975).

[47]Sharon Wells and Lawson Little, **Portraits: Wooden Houses of Key West,** (Key West, Florida: Historic Key West Preservation Board, 1979).

[48]John Michael Vlach, "The Shotgun House: An African Architectural Legacy in the United States," **Journal of the Society of Architectural Historians,** New York, December, 1976, p. 293.

[49]Martin, pp. 202-227.

[50]Helen Muir, **Miami U.S.A.,** (New York: Henry Holt and Company, 1953), p. 59.

[51]Paul U. Tevis, "History of the City of South Miami," (Unpublished report for the City of South Miami), ca. 1966, pp. I-V.

[52]Adam G. Adams, "Some Pre-Boom Developers of Dade County," **Tequesta,** No. XVIII, 1957, pp. 31-46.

[53]Blackman, p. 12.

[54]Jean Taylor, Lecture Series (Unpublished papers on file at the Historical Association of Southern Florida), 1980.

[55]Jean Taylor, "Kendall and Westchester," (Unpublished paper on file at the Historical Association of Southern Florida), 1982.

[56]Plat Book B, p. 79.

[57] Jean Taylor, "Sawmills in South Dade," **Update**, June, 1976.

[58] Plat Book B, p. 144.

[59] Jean Taylor, Lecture Series, "Homestead," (Unpublished paper on file at the Historical Association of Southern Florida), June 19, 1980.

[60] Deed Abstracts, and Plat Book 5, p. 10.

[61] Jean Taylor, "Founding Florida City," **The Miami News**, April 6, 1971.

[62] George M. Chapin, "Official Souvenir, Key West Extension of the Florida East Coast Railway," (issued by the Oversea Railroad Extension Celebration Committee of Key West), (St. Augustine, Florida: The Record Co., ca. 1912.)

[63] Ibid..

CHAPTER III

[1] C.H. Ward, **The Lure of the Southland**, (Harrisburg, Pennsylvania: J. Horace McFarland Co., 1915).

[2] Ibid.

[3] Dade County, Florida, Land Division, Plat Books 2 and 3.

[4] Helen Muir, **Miami U.S.A.**, (New York: Henry Holt and Company, 1953).

[5] Dade County, Florida, Probate Office, Estate Proceedings, Mary Brickell File No. 1645.

[6] Plat Book B, p. 41.

[7] Carl J. Weinhardt, **Museum**, Volume 9, Number 1, May, 1977.

[8] John B. Bayley, "The Villa Vizcaya," **Classical America**, William A. Coles, 1973, p. 68.

[9] F. Burrall Hoffman, Jr. and Paul Chalfin, "Vizcaya, the Villa and Grounds," **The Architectural Review**, The Architectural Review Series, July, 1917, p. 122.

[10] The Palazzo del Te in Mantua, beginning in 1526, is a good example. From Christian Norberg-Schulz, **Meaning in Western Architecture**, (New York: Praeger Publishers, 1975), p. 265.

[11] Hoffman, Jr. and Chalfin, p. 122.

[12] Arva Moore Parks, "Historical Study for the Barnacle," Bureau of Historic Sites and Properties, Florida Division of Archives, History and Records Management, Miscellaneous Projects, Report No. 32, September, 1975.

[13] Plat Books.

[14] Ibid.

[15] Historical Association of Southern Florida, Miami, Florida, (clip file), "Miss Harris," 1914—ca. 1950.

[16] "Well Established Real Estate Firm Had a Novel Origin," **The Miami Metropolis**, March 3, 1923.

[17] Plat Books.

[18] Nixon Smiley, "Silver Bluff," **The Miami Herald**, June 3, 1962.

[19] J.E. Dovell, "The Everglades – Florida's Frontier," Economic Leaflets (5 and 6), April and May, 1947.

[20] John Griffin, Cultural Resource Management, "A History of Hialeah," unpublished report commissioned by the City of Hialeah, Florida, Community and Economic Development Division, September 30, 1979, p. 28.

[21] Jean Taylor, "Longview," unpublished report, Miami, Florida, 1982.

[22] U.S. Senate, "Everglades of Florida," Senate Document 89, 62nd Congress, 1st Session, Washington: Government Printing Office, 1911.

[23] Edward Ridolph, "The Street Railways of Miami," **Update**, June, 1974.

[24] Plat Book 2, p. 46.

[25] Plat Book 4, p. 45.

[26] Plat Book 5, p. 43.

[27] Plat Books 3 and 4.

[28] "Chronology of Early Development Patterns on Miami Beach up to 1930," prepared by Fifth Year students of the School of Engineering and Environmental Design, University of Miami, under the supervision of Professor Aristides J. Millas.

[29] Ibid.

[30] Plat Books.

[31] Ibid.

[32] "Chronology of Early Development Patterns on Miami Beach up to 1930."

[33] Ibid.

[34] Jane Fisher, **The Fabulous Hoosier**, (New York: Robert M. McBride & Co., 1947), pp. 1-9.

[35] E.W. Stilwell & Company, Los Angeles, California, **All American Homes**, Milwaukee, Wisconsin, C.N. Caspar Co., 1919.

[36] Charles E. White, Jr., **The Bungalow Book**, (New York: The MacMillan Company, 1923), p. 3.

[37] "Greene and Greene Revisited in L.A.," **Progressive Architecture**, April, 1977, p. 23.

CHAPTER IV

[1] For an excellent social history of the 1920s see : Frederick Lewis Allen, **Only Yesterday**, (New York: Harper & Row, 1931).

[2] Jane Fisher, **The Fabulous Hoosier**, (New York: Robert M. McBride & Co., 1947), pp. 1-9.

[3] Ibid.

[4] Polly Redford, **Billion Dollar Sandbar**, (New York: E.P. Dutton & Co., Inc., 1970), p. 130.

[5] Ibid, p. 76.

[6] Kenneth Ballinger, **Miami Millions**, (Miami, Florida: Franklin Press, 1936), p. 24.

[7] Ibid, and Charlton Tebeau, **A History of Florida**, (Coral Gables, Florida: University of Miami Press, 1971), pp. 377-392.

[8] Allen, p. 226.

[9] Ibid, p. 144.

[10] Ballinger, p. 5.

[11] Allen, p. 230.

[12] Thomas McMorrow, "Land of Promise," **The Saturday Evening Post**, March 6, 1926.

[13] Will Rogers, "Florida Versus California: A Debate Held Before the Prevaricator's Club of America," **The Saturday Evening Post**, May 29, 1926.

[14] Ida Tarbell, "Florida—And Then What?," **McCall's Magazine**, May, 1926.

[15] A.R. Pinci, "Salvaging Florida's Wrecked Boom," March 27, 1926.

[16] Tebeau, p. 387.

[17] Matlack Price, "The New Mediterranean Architectue of Florida," **The House Beautiful**, June, 1925, p. 665.

[18] **Chicago World's Columbian Exposition, Memorial Volume**, (Chicago: A.L. Stone Publishers, 1893), p. 97.

[19] The statement describes the architecture of Louis Gill, influential in the spread of the Mission style in San Diego, from "California Architecture Showing Moorish Feeling," **Touch-**

stone, Volume 8, January, 1921, p. 292.

[20]Renamed Neva King Cooper Elementary School.

[21]August Geiger, "The Model School Plan for Tropic Florida," **The Tropic Magazine,** June, 1914.

[22]The Miami Herald, on microfilm at the Florida Room, Miami-Dade Public Library, March 26, 1968.

[23]Rexford Newcomb, **Mediterranean Domestic Architecture in the United States,** (Cleveland, Ohio: J.H. Hansen, 1928), p. 2.

[24]Frank B. Shutts, editor, **Florida, the East Coast—Its Builders, Resources, Industries, Town and City Developments,** (Miami, Florida: The Miami Herald, 1925).

[25]Kiehnel and Elliott, Architects, (Miami, Florida: Miami Post Publishing Company, 1938).

[26]**Ibid.**

[27]U.S. Department of the Interior, National Register of Historic Places Nomination Form, Prepared by Mary K. Evans, 1973.

[28]Kiehnel and Elliott, Architects, 1938.

[29]For biographical information on George Merrick and Coral Gables see: Ballinger, 1936 and Charles E. Harner, **Florida's Promoters: The Men Who Made It Big,** (Tampa, Florida: Trend House, 1973), pp. 65-70, and Merrick Papers, Collections, Historical Museum of Southern Florida, Miami, Florida.

[30]Ballinger, p. 21.

[31]Shutts, p. 126, and Harner, pp. 67-68.

[32]Dade County, Florida, Historic Preservation Division, Colonnade Building File, 1978.

[33]Ibid.

[34]For biographical information on Glenn Curtiss see: Alden Hatch, **Glenn Curtiss: Pioneer of Naval Aviation,** (New York: Julian Messner, Inc., 1942).

[35]John Griffin, Cultural Resource Management, Inc., "A History of Hialeah," unpublished report commissioned by the City of Hialeah, Florida, Community Development Division, September 30, 1979, p. 42.

[36]Ibid, p. 33.

[37]Ibid, p. 28.

[38]Ibid.

[39]Ibid, p. 43.

[40]Ibid, p. 49.

[41]Ibid.

[42]Sources consulted for historical information on Miami Springs include:

Ruby Carson, "History of Miami Springs, Florida," (on file at the Miami Springs Woman's Club, unpublished), April, 1977.

"Country Club Estates, Miami, Florida, Showing Improvements and Industrial Developments in Progress in Vicinity," June, 1926, newspaper article reproduction, Miami Springs Public Library.

"How Miami Springs Started," **The Home News,** clippings, Historical Association of Southern Florida, April, 1964.

"Miami Springs Erects 74 New Homes as Building Continues," **Dade County Courier,** January 27, 1939.

J. Naiman, **Leaders and Pioneers of South Florida,** (Miami, Florida: Tropicana Publishers, 1945).

Nixon Smiley, "Miami Springs—From Sawgrass to City," **The Miami Herald,** December 9, 1968.

[43]Frank S. Fitzgerald Bush, **A Dream of Araby,** (Opa-locka, Florida: South Florida Archeological Museum, 1976), p. 1.

[44]Ibid, p. 2.

[45]Sources consulted for historical information on North Miami:

Vaughn Camp, "North Miami, 50 years of Challenge and Change," North Miami, Florida (project of North Miami's 50th Anniversary Committee), ca. 1976 (unpublished).

"Commemorative Book—City of North Miami 40th Anniversary," North Miami Chamber of Commerce, February, 1967.

Ed Long, "Ed Dougherty Incorporated Town on February 25, 1926," The Journal, February 25, 1976.

"Memoirs of C.G. Ihle," **Miami Shores Bulletin,** 1927.

North Miami, Florida, Master Plan for Town of North Miami, North Miami City Hall, 1925 to present (unpublished).

"Old Sites for Sore Eyes," **North Miami Journal,** February 10, 1966.

Thelma Peters, **Biscayne Country,** (Miami, Florida: Banyan Books, 1981).

Cheryl Rogers, Personal Interview (by Paul S. George), North Miami, Florida, August 7, 1980.

F. Page Wilson, "We Choose the Sub-Tropics," **Tequesta,** 1952.

[46]Ballinger, pp. 13-14.

[47]Peters, 1981.

[48]For further statistics on the South Florida real estate boom see Ballinger.

[49]Other sources consulted for information on Miami Shores:

"Artistic Ideals are Being Fulfilled in the Development of Miami Shores: Great Area," **Miami Daily News and Metropolis,** December 4, 1925.

"Miami Shores—America's Mediterranean—First Year of Development," **Miami Daily News and Metropolis,** December 4, 1925.

"Miami Shores Presents Wonderful Record, Sales Totals of Large Project Unprecedented," **Miami Daily News and Metropolis,** December 4, 1925.

Russell T. Pancoast, "Miami Architecture So Far," (published by the FAIA, ca. 1955).

Miami, Florida, Romer Photograph Collection, ca. 1910-1950, Miami-Dade Public Library, Florida Room.

Lawrence Thompson, "A Concrete Fantasy Come True," **The Miami Herald,** November 18, 1956.

Jeanne Wellenkamp, "Miami Shores Community Church Began in Pump House," **The North Dade Journal,** August 14, 1968.

[50]Peggy Newman Montague, "The Chaille Plan," **Update,** February, 1979.

[51]Ballinger, p. 7.

[52]Tebeau, pp. 385-386.

[53]Ballinger, pp. 6, 28.

[54]Ibid, p. 27.

[55]Ibid, p. 28.

[56]Ibid, p. 53 and Agnes Ash, "Mr. Rand's Grand Hotel That Never Was," **The Miami News,** August 29, 1965.

[57]"News of Interest to Builders," **Southern Construction Magazine,** July 11, 1925, p. 9.

[58]A. Ten Eyck Brown, "Designing and Planning of Courthouses," **The Architectural Forum,** June, 1927, pp. 513-520.

[59]"News Marks 60th Birthday While Building for Future," **The Miami News,** May 13, 1956.

[60]"Best in Architecture Demanded Here, New York Firm Enters Miami Building Field," **Miami Daily News**, July 26, 1925, and Leonard Schultze, Obituary, **Architectural Forum**, September, 1951.

[61]"News Tower Spanish Type Architecture," **Miami Daily News**, July 26, 1925.

[62]Ibid, also see description of El Jardin, this same chapter.

[63]"Nearly a Year to Bring Tile for Panel Use," **Miami Daily News**, July 26, 1925.

[64]Agnes Ash, "The Story of Biscayne Boulevard, As It Were," **The Miami News**, July 12, 1964. Also see Thompson, Ibid.

CHAPTER V

[1]Richard Shenkman and Kurt Reiger, **One-Night Stands with American History**, (New York: William Morrow & Co., Inc., 1980), p. 227.

[2]Charlton Tebeau, **A History of Florida**, (Coral Gables, Florida: University of Miami Press, 1971), p. 393.

[3]Ibid.

[4]**The Miami Herald**, (Microfilm, Miami-Dade Public Library), September 18, 1927.

[5]Ibid.

[6]Ibid, September 17, 1927.

[7]Ibid.

[8]Ibid, September 17 - November 11, 1927.

[9]Ibid, October 8, 1927.

[10]Dade County, Florida, Land Division, Plat Books 8-42.

[11]John A. Garraty, **The American Nation: A History of the United States Since 1865**, Vol. II, (New York: Harper & Row, 1975), p. 718.

[12]Ibid, p. 719.

[13]Dade County, Florida, Historic Preservation Division, Greynolds Park and Matheson Hammock Files.

[14]Dade County, Florida, Historic Preservation Division, Liberty Square, Miami Beach Post Office, Coral Gables Fire Station, and the Coral Gables Women's Club Files.

[15]Microfilm, September 17 - November 11, 1927.

[16]**Florida: A Guide to the Southernmost State**, compiled by the Federal Writer's Project of the WPA, (New York: Oxford University Press, 1939), p. 211.

[17]Stephen Harris, "Liberty Square Pointed Out as Good Precedent," **The Miami Herald**, December 12, 1942, and "Miami, Liberty Square, P.W.A. Housing Project," **The Architectural Forum**, May, 1937, pp. 422-423.

[18]Dade County, Florida, County Recorder's Office, Deed Abstracts.

[19]Jack Kofoed, **Moon Over Miami**, (New York: Random House, 1955), p. 56.

[20]John Griffin, Cultural Resource Management, Inc., "A History of Hialeah," unpublished report commissioned by the City of Hialeah, Florida, Community Development Division, September 30, 1979, p. 56.

[21]Ibid, p. 80.

[22]Tebeau, p. 396.

[23]Griffin, p. 80.

[24]Harold Mehling, **The Most of Everything**, (New York: Harcourt, Brace, 1960), p. 50.

[25]"Construction Totals $98,550,000," **The Beach Beacon**, (Progress Edition), 1937.

[26]Le Corbusier, **Towards A New Architecture**, translated from the French by Frederick Etchells, (New York: Praeger Publishers, 1927).

[27]Christian Norberg-Schultz, **Meaning in Western Architecture**, p. 366.

[28]Miami Beach, Florida, Florida Code Enforcement Construction Division, Building Permits, 1921 to present.

EPILOGUE

[1]Helen Muir, **Miami, U.S.A.**, (New York: Henry Holt & Co., 1953), p. 224.

[2]Ibid.

[3]Arva Moore Parks, **Miami: The Magic City**, (Tulsa, Oklahoma: Continental Heritage Press, 1981), p. 134.

[4]Muir, p. 230.

[5]Parks, p. 136.

[6]Dorothy Fields, "Reflections on Black History: The Season," **Update**, February, 1978.

[7]Charlton Tebeau, **Man in the Everglades**, (Coral Gables, Florida: University of Miami Press, 1968), p. 179.

[8]Jim Woodman, **Key Biscayne: The Romance of Cape Florida**, (Miami, Florida: privately printed, 1961), p. 64.

[9]U.S. Congress, Senate, Third Interim Report of the Special Committee to Investigate Organized Crime in Interstate Commerce, 81st Congress, Report No. 307, April, 1951.

BIBLIOGRAPHY

BOOKS:

Agey, Hoit. **Samuel Belcher.** Miami: Franklin Press, 1979.

Allen, Frederick Lewis. **Only Yesterday.** New York: Harper & Row, 1931.

Anderson, Edward C. **Florida Territory in 1844.** Stanley Hoole, editor. University of Alabama Press, 1977.

Andrews, Wayne. **Architecture, Ambition and Americans.** New York: The Free Press, 1947.

Ballinger, Kenneth. **Miami Millions.** Miami: Franklin Press, 1936.

Blackman, E.V. **Miami and Dade County, Florida: Its Settlement, Progress, and Achievement.** Washington, D.C.: Victor Rainbolt, 1921.

Bonawit, Oby J. **Miami, Florida, Early Families and Records.** Miami: privately published, 1980.

Brown, Curtis F. **Star-Spangled Kitsch.** New York: Universe Books, 1975.

Buker, George E. **Swamp Sailors.** Gainesville: University Presses of Florida, 1975.

Chicago World's Columbian Exposition, Memorial Volume. Chicago: A.L. Stone Publishers, 1893.

Cohen, Isador. **Historical Sketches and Sidelights of Miami.** Miami: privately printed, 1925.

Current, William R. and Karen Current. **Greene and Greene—Architetcts in the Residential Style.** Ft. Worth: 1974.

De Croix, F.W. **Historical, Industrial and Commercial Data of Miami and Fort Lauderdale, Florida.** St. Augustine: The Record Company.

Dickinson, Mary F. **The Early Days of Redland.** Federal Writers Program, 1937-1940.

DuPuis, Dr. John G. **History of Early Medicine; History of Early Public Schools; History of Early Agricultural Relations in Dade County.** Miami: privately printed, 1954.

E.W. Stillwell & Company. **All American Homes.** Milwaukee: C.N. Caspar Co., 1919.

Fisher, Jane. **The Fabulous Hoosier.** New York: Robert M. McBride & Co., 1947.

Fitzgerald-Bush, Frank S. **A Dream of Araby.** Opa-locka: South Florida Archeological Museum, 1976.

Florida Architecture and Allied Arts. Miami: The Miami Visitor Publishing Co., Inc., 1936.

Florida: A Guide to the Southernmost State. Compiled by the Federal Writer's Project of the WPA. New York: Oxford Press, 1939.

Garraty, John A. **The American Nation: A History of the United States Since 1865.** Vol. II. New York: Harper & Row, 1975.

Harner, Charles E. **Florida's Promoters: The Men Who Made It Big.** Tampa: Trend House, 1973.

Hatch, Alden. **Glenn Curtiss: Pioneer of Naval Aviation.** New York: Julian Messner, Inc., 1942.

Hill, Dr. Louise (editor). **Spanish Land Grants in Florida, Confirmed Claims,** Vol. I-V. Tallahassee: Historical Records Survey Division of Professional and Service Projects, Work Projects Administration, State Library Board.

Hohauser, Henry. **Selections From the Work of Henry Hohauser, Architect.**

Hollingsworth, Tracy. **History of Dade County, Florida.** Coral Gables: Glade House, 1949.

John, John E. **Florida During the Civil War.** Gainesville: University of Florida Presses, 1963.

Kent, Gertrude M. **The Coconut Grove School in Pioneer Days, 1887-1894.** Coral Gables: Parker Printing, 1972.

Kersey, Harry A., Jr. **Pelts, Plumes and Hides.** Gainesville: University Presses of Florida, 1975.

Kiehnel and Elliott, Architects. Miami: Miami Post Publishing Company, 1938.

Kofoed, Jack. **Moon Over Miami.** New York: Random House, 1955.

Le Corbusier. **Towards A New Architecture.** Translated from the French by Frederick Etchells. New York: Praeger Publishers, 1927.

Lummus, J.N. **The Miracle of Miami Beach.** Miami: Miami Post Publishing Company, 1940.

Mahon, John K. **History of the Second Seminole War.** Jacksonville: University of Florida Press, 1967.

Makison, Randall L. **A Guide to the Work of Greene and Greene.** Peregrine-Smith, Inc., 1974.

Martin, Sidney Walter. **Florida's Flagler.** Athens, Georgia: University of Georgia Press, 1949.

McCoy, Esther. **Five California Architects.** New York: Reinhold Publishing Company, 1960.

Mehling, Harold. **The Most of Everything.** New York: Harcourt, Brace, 1960.

Muir, Helen. **Miami, U.S.A..** New York: Henry Holt & Co., 1953.

Munroe, Ralph Middleton and Vincent Gilpin. **The Commodore's Story.** Norberth, Pennsylvania: Livingston Publishing Co., reprinted from 1930 edition, 1966.

Naiman, J. **Leaders and Pioneers of South Florida.** Miami: Tropicana Publishers, 1945.

Newcomb, Rexford. **Mediterranean Domestic Architecture in the United States.** Cleveland: J.H. Hansen, 1928.

Newest Facts About Coral Gables. Coral Gables: Parker Art Publishing, 1926.

Norberg-Schulz, Christian. **Meaning in Western Architecture.** New York: Praeger Publishers, 1975.

Parks, Arva Moore. **The Forgotten Frontier: Florida Through the Lens of Ralph Middleton Monroe.** Miami: Banyan Books, 1977.

Parks, Arva Moore. **Miami: The Magic City.** Tulsa: Continental Heritage Press, Inc., 1981.

Perrine, Henry E. **Some Eventful Years in Grandpa's Life.** Buffalo, New York: E.H. Hutchinson Press, 1885.

Peters, Thelma. **Biscayne Country: 1870-1926.** Miami: Banyan Books, 1981.

Peters, Thelma. **Lemon City: Pioneering on Biscayne Bay 1850-1925.** Miami: Banyan Books, 1976.

Preservation Guidebook for the Old Section of the City of Key West. Key West: Old Island Restoration Commission, 1975.

Rainbolt, Victor. **The Town That Climate Built.** Miami: Parker Art Printing.

Redford, Polly. **Billion Dollar Sandbar.** New York: E.P. Dutton & Co., Inc., 1970.

Reese, Joseph Hugh. **The History of Tamiami Trail.** Miami: Tamiami Trail Commissioners and the County Commissioners, 1928.

Rockwood, Caroline Washburn. **In Biscayne Bay.** New York: New Amsterdam Book Co., 1896.

Saylor, Henry H. **Bungalows.** New York: McBride, Winston & Co., 1911.

Scott, Walter Dill, and Robert B. Harshe. **Charles Deering: 1852-1927: An Appreciation Together With His Memoirs of William Deering and James Deering.** Boston: Privately printed, 1929.

Sewell, John. **Memoirs and History· of Miami, Florida.** Miami: Franklin Press, 1933.

Shenkman, Richard and Kurt Reiger. **One-Night Stands with American History.** New York: William Morrow & Co., Inc., 1980.

Shutts, Frank B. (editor). **Florida, the East Coast, Its Builders, Resources, Industries, Town and City Developments.** Miami: The Miami Herald, 1925.

Smiley, Nixon. **Yesterday's Miami.** Miami: Seaman, 1973.

Stearns, Frank F. **Along Greater Miami's Sun-Sea Area.** Miami: Privately printed, 1932.

Strand, Jonann. **A Greene and Greene Guide.** Pasadena: 1974.

Tebeau, Charlton. **A History of Florida.** Coral Gables: University of Miami Press, 1971.

Tebeau, Charlton. **Man in the Everglades.** Coral Gables: University of Miami Press, 1968.

Thompson, Arthur W. **Jacksonian Democracy on the Florida Frontier.** Gainesville: University of Florida Presses, 1961.

Trapp, Mrs. Harlan. **My Pioneer Reminiscences.** Privately printed, 1980.

Ward, C.H. **The Lure of the Southland: Miami and Miami Beach, Florida.** Harrisburg: J. Horace McFarland, Co., 1915.

Weigall, T.H. **Boom in Paradise.** New York: Alfred H. King, 1932.

Wells, Sharon and Lawson Little. **Portraits: Wooden Houses of Key West,** Key West: Historic Key West Preservation Board, 1979.

White, Charles E., Jr. **The Bungalow Book.** New York: McMillan Company, 1923.

Woodman, Jim. **Key Biscayne: The Romance of Cape Florida.** Miami: Privately printed, 1961

JOURNALS AND PERIODICALS:

Adams, Adam G. "Some Pre-Boom Developers of Dade County." **Tequesta,** 1957.

"Afro Agents Honored." **Miami Times,** February 22, 1947.

Alexander, Reverend Allen, (Obituary). **The Miami Herald,** August 8, 1969.

Allen, Ray. "I Remember Papa." **The Miamian,** September, 1970.

Anderson, Jack E. "Negro Schools Vie." **The Miami Herald,** January 29, 1949.

Anderson, William, (Obituary). **The Miami News,** February 18, 1961.

Andrews, J.S. "The Tropic Home: Belvederes." **The Tropic Magazine,** Autumn, 1916.

Andrews, Patricia. "At 88 the Doctor is Ill and Still Working." **The Miami Herald,** November 4, 1979.

The Architectural Forum. December, 1938.

Architectural League of Greater Miami. **Yearbook,** 1930.

American Architect and Architecture. November, 1936.

"Arrest of Caves." **Homestead Enterprise.** August 19, 1927.

"Artistic Ideals are Being Fulfilled in the Development of Miami Shores: Great Area." **Miami Daily News and Metropolis,** December 4, 1925.

Ash, Agnes. "Mr. Rand's Grand Hotel That Never Was." **The Miami News,** August 29, 1965.

Ash, Clarke. "Biscayne Park—A Community for Homeowners Only." **The Miami News,** July 26, 1959.

"Association Proposes to Keep High Standards." **Miami Riviera,** November 12, 1926.

Ayers, E.E. "Coconut Grove Business Development." **The Miami Tribune,** August 23, 1924.

Bayley, John B. "The Villa Vizcaya." **Classical America,** 1973.

"Beach Landmark Converted Into Stock Brokerage." **The Miami Herald,** August 15, 1965.

"Behind the Vulgarizing Bungalows." **Landscape Architecture,** May, 1976.

Bellamy, Jeannie. "25 Year Old Olympia Theatre Can Claim Firsts." **The Miami Herald,** 1950.

Bentley, George R. "Colonel Thompson's Tour of Tropical Florida." **Tequesta,** 1950.

"Best in Architecture Demanded Here, New York Firm Enters Miami Building Field." **Miami Daily News,** July 26, 1925.

Bethel, Walter, (Obituary). **The Miami Herald,** November 21, 1970.

Birnbaum, Jeff. "Tales of Little River Flow from Pioneer." **The Miami Herald,** May 4, 1970.

Black, Hugo L., II. "Richard Fitzpatrick's South Florida: 1822-1840." Part II, **Tequesta,** 1981.

Blanc, Giulio. "Paul Ransom's Dream." **The Catalyst,** September, 1978.

"Boulevard is Carl G. Fisher's Fifth Miami Beach Hotel." **The Miami Herald,** August 8, 1926.

"Brickell Home Down for Count." **The Miami Herald,** October 24, 1978.

"Bright Among Early Florida Developers." **The Dade County Courier,** January 27, 1939.

Brookfield, Charles M. "Cape Florida Light." **Tequesta,** 1949.

Brown, A. Ten Eyck. "Designing and Planning of Courthouses." **The Architectural Forum,** June, 1927.

Brown, Harlen. "Once Silver Palm School, Old Building Weathers Time." **News Leader,** February 4, 1975.

Buffington, Betsy. "Westview: Club-Fun — With Elegance." **The Miami Herald,** November 22, 1959.

Bush, Frank. "Opa-locka's Oldest Businessman." **Opa-locka Beat,** February, 1974.

Caffry, Charlotte. "Modest Amsterdam Palace Has Quite a Past." **Miami Beach Sun,** November 17, 1968.

"California Architecture Showing Moorish Feeling." **Touchstone,** Volume 8, January, 1921.

Carr, Robert S. "The Brickell Store and Seminole Indian Trade." **Florida Anthropologist,** December, 1981.

Carson, Ruby Leach. "Forty Years of Miami Beach." **Tequesta,** 1955.

Carson, Ruby Leach. "Miami: 1896-1900." **Tequesta, 1956.**

Cavendish, Hênry. "Romantic History of Hotel Halcyon Is Told as Landmark is Demolished." **The Miami Herald,** June 13, 1937.

"Chamber Honors Pioneers." **The Miami Herald,** July 19, 1979.

Conrad, Mary Douthit. "Homesteading in Florida During the 1890s." **Tequesta,** 1957.

"Construction Totals $ 98,550,000." **The Beach Beacon,** (Progress Edition), 1937.

Cotton, Jessie Hendry, (Obituary). **The Miami Herald,** August 18, 1957.

"Country Club Estates, Miami, Florida, Showing Improvements and Industrial Developments in Progress in Vicinity." (newspaper article reproduction), Miami Springs Public Library, June, 1926.

Cull, Betty. "Sunset School History Interwoven With Love of S. Miami District." **South Miami District Times,** February 7, 1957.

"Cut Down Trousers Miami's First Depot." **The Miami Herald,** July 28, 1929.

"The Depression Years Were Hard on Coral Gables." **The Miami Herald,** April 11, 1965.

"District History Told." **The Miami Herald,** June 27, 1926.

Dodd, Dorothy. "The Wrecking Business on the Florida Reefs: 1822-1860." **Florida Historical Quarterly,** April, 1944.

Dorn, Harold W. "Mango Growing Around Early Miami." **Tequesta,** 1956.

Dorn, J.K. "Recollections of Early Miami." **Tequesta,** 1949.

"Downtown Landmark Sold for $250,000." **The Miami Herald,** July 11, 1965.

Dunlop, Beth. "Opa-locka Was Araby in Mrs. Higgin's Day." **The Miami Herald,** May 4, 1977.

Emerson, Charles Stafford. "The Tropic Home." **The Tropic Magazine,** January, 1917.

Fabrico, Roberto. "New Vitality on Horizon for Little Havana." **The Miami Herald,** December 8, 1979.

"Father and Son Built Residence of Timber Found on Beach." **The Miami Herald,** July 25, 1943.

Faus, Joseph. "Lemon City: Miami's Predecessor." **Miami Daily News,** Septenber 19, 1948.

Fields, Dorothy. "Black Entertainment 1908-1919." **Update,** December, 1974.

Fields, Dorothy. "Blacks Played Major Role in Building Miami." **The Miami Times,** July 1, 1976.

Fields, Dorothy. "Liberty City: The Promised Land." **The Miami Times,** August 7, 1980.

Fields, Dorothy. "Reflections on Black History: Miami's First Newspaper." **Update,** February, 1976.

Fields, Dorothy. "Reflections on Black History: The Season." **Update,** February, 1978.

"First Train." **Opa-locka Times,** January 8, 1927.

Fitzpatrick, Richard H., (Obituary). **The Miami Herald,** December 31, 1960.

Fogerty, Fred. "City's Oldest Hotel Will Fall." **The Miami Herald,** May 16, 1968.

Forbes, Charles B. "Homes and Stores Tame Wilderness of 50 Years Ago." **Miami Daily News,** March 24, 1948.

Geiger, August. "The Model School Plan for Tropic Florida." **The Tropic Magazine,** June, 1914.

Geiger, August, (Obituary). **The Miami Herald,** March 26, 1968.

George, Paul S. "Colored Town: Miami's Black Community, 1896-1930." **Florida Historical Quarterly,** April, 1978.

"Gesu Church Historical Site." **The Miami Herald,** August 18, 1974.

Gondolier, Magazine of the Carl G. Fisher Hotels, first published January 6, 1926.

"Growing Bank Is Evidence of Gain in Town Business." **Miami Metropolis, March 3, 1923.**

Hampton, Dunn. "House Built to Last Centuries." **Update,** October, 1974.

Harris, Stephen. "Liberty Square Pointed Out as Good Precedent." **The Miami Herald,** December 12, 1942.

Hauser, Leo A. "Pioneer Reminiscence." **Update,** June, 1976.

Hitchcock, Edna B., (Obituary). **The Miami Herald,** September 13, 1979.

Hoffman, F. Burrall, Jr., and Paul Chalfin. "Vizcaya, the Villa and Grounds." **The Architectural Review,** The Architectural Review Series, July, 1917.

Holder, J.B. "Along the Florida Reef." **Harper's New Monthly Magazine,** December, 1870-May, 1871.

"Hotel Seminole," (advertisment). **Homestead Enterprises,** November 18, 1927.

"How Miami Springs Started." **The Home News,** (clippings), Historical Association of Southern Florida, April, 1964.

"H.U.D. to Restore 673 Homes Here." **The Miami Herald,** September 25, 1978.

Hudson, F.M. "Beginnings in Dade County." **Tequesta,** July, 1943.

Jacobs, Sam. "Miami River Park Means Disaster for Widow, Home." **The Miami Herald,** November 25, 1977.

Jeffries, Lillian, (Obituary). **The Miami Herald,** October 29, 1955.

Knight, Edwin. "Whatever Happened to Larkins, Fla.?." **The South Miami District Times,** October 25, 1956.

Kofoed, Jack. "Maude Brickell: Why the Change." **The Miami Herald,** (clippings).

Kofoed, William. "Wizard of Coral Castle." **Coronet,** February, 1958.

LaGorce, John Oliver. "Treasure House of the Gulf Stream." **National Geographic, January, 1921.**

Lassman, Valerie. "A History of a Residence of Early Miami." (taken from Nathan Shappe's "Flagler's Undertakings in Miami in 1897"), **Tequesta,** 1959.

Livingston, S.E. "How Homestead Got Its Name." **The Redlands District News,** December 5, 1947.

Long, Ed. "Ed Dougherty Incorporated Town on February 25, 1926." **The Journal,** February 25, 1976.

"A Look at Bakery History." **The Miami Herald,** September 2, 1973.

"Looking Back at Being Black." **The Miami Herald,** February 1, 1976.

Lown, Romana. "Meet Kelsey Pharr, Distinguished Miami Leader." **The Miami Times,** November 13, 1946.

Mahoney, Lawrence. "Cutler's Last Stand." **The Miami Herald,** January 30, 1972.

"Marshall Williamson Helped Found Church." **The Miami Herald,** June 8, 1972.

Mauncy, Albert. "Some Military Affairs in Territorial Florida." **Florida Historical Quarterly,** October, 1946.

McMorrow, Thomas. "Land of Promise." **The Saturday Evening Post,** March 6, 1926.

"Memoirs of C.G. Ihle." **Miami Shores Bulletin,** 1927.

Merrick, George E. "Pre-Flagler Influences on the Lower Florida East Coast." **Tequesta,** March, 1941.

The Miami Herald. (microfilm, Miami-Dade Public Library), 1927.

"Miami, Liberty Square, P.W.A. Housing Project." The Architectural Forum, May, 1937.

The Miami Metropolis. (ads), May 15, 1896.

"Miami Shores – America's Mediterranean – First Year of Development." Miami Daily News and Metropolis, December 4, 1925.

"Miami Shores Presents Wonderful Record, Sales Totals of Large Project Unprecedented." Miami Daily News and Metropolis, December 4, 1925.

"Miami's Silhouette Is Impressive Sight." The Miami Herald, June 28, 1935.

"Miami Springs Erects 74 New Homes as Building Continues." Dade County Courier, January 27, 1939.

Miller, Wilhelm. "A New Type of American Country Life." Country Life America, February, 1911.

Montague, Peggy Newman. "The Chaille Plan." Update, February, 1979.

"Mt. Zion Pastor's Half Century of Service." Miami Times, July 12, 1942.

Musselwhite, William, (Obituary). The Miami Daily News, January 4, 1957.

"Nearly a Year to Bring Tile for Panel Use." Miami Daily News, July 26, 1925.

"New Theater Named." The Miami Herald, September 9, 1925.

"News Marks 60th Birthday While Building for Future." The Miami News, May 13, 1956.

"News of Interest to Builders." Southern Construction Magazine, July 11, 1925.

"News Tower Spanish Type Architecture." Miami Daily News, July 26, 1925.

"Old Sites for Sore Eyes." North Miami Journal, February 10, 1966.

"Opa-locka Municipality Enters Second Year of Life." Opa-locka Times, February 23, 1927.

Pancoast, Russell T. "Miami Architecture So Far." FAIA, ca. 1955.

Parks, Arva Moore. "Miami in 1876." Tequesta, 1975.

Peters, Thelma. "From the Director's Desk." Update, June, 1974.

Peters, Thelma. "In the Days of the Two-Cent Stamp." Update, February, 1977.

Pinci, A.R. "Salvaging Florida's Wrecked Boom." The Magazine of Wall Street, March 27, 1926.

Price, Matlack. "The New Mediterranean Architecture of Florida." The House Beautiful, June, 1925.

Pritchard, Carleton. "Homestead Pioneer." The Miami Herald, July 14, 1925.

Ransom, Ruth Alice. "The History of the School." The History Log, June, 1928.

Reeves, Garth and Dorothy Fields. "The Origin of the Miami Times." The Miami Herald, June, 1978.

"Remembers Indians on Little River Streets, Says Miss Havenstreet." North Dade Journal, November 11, 1953.

Richards, Mrs. A.C. "Reminiscences on the Early Days of Miami." The Miami News, series beginning October 1, 1903.

Ridolph, Edward. "The Street Railways of Miami." Update, June, 1974.

Robinson, Nettie Bell Hurt. "My Neighbor Mister Frost." Update, December, 1976.

Rogers, Will. "Florida Versus California: A Debate Held Before the Prevaricator's Club of America." The Saturday Evening Post, May 29, 1926.

Rosner, George W. "Robert Frost and the University of Miami." Update, December, 1976.

"Royal Palm Finished." The Miami Metropolis, January 15, 1897.

Schultze, Leonard, (Obituary). Architectural Forum, September, 1951.

Scofield, Walter Keeler. "On Blockade Duty in Florida Waters." William J. Schellings, editor. Tequesta, 1955.

Scott, James E. "Miami's Liberty City Square Project." Crisis Magazine, March, 1942.

Sessa, F.B. "Miami on the Eve of the Boom: 1923." Tequesta, 1951.

Smiley, Nixon. "Florida City Once Called Second Eden." The Miami Herald, December 29, 1968.

Smiley, Nixon. "Miami Springs—From Sawgrass to City." The Miami Herald, December 9, 1968.

Smiley, Nixon. "Silver Bluff." The Miami Herald, June 3, 1962.

Smiley, Nixon. "Tiffany's Houses Odd—But Then So Was He." The Miami Herald, April 4, 1968.

Straight, William M. "James M. Jackson, Jr., Miami's First Physician." Journal of the Florida Medical Association, August, 1972.

Strul, Gene. "Perrine: Farming Not Tourist Is the Paying Crop Here." The Miami Daily News, July 20, 1947.

Swenson, Katherine. "Classic Antilla Hotel Sought by A.V. Davis." The Times, November 29, 1956.

Taylor, Jean. "Founding Florida City." The Miami News, April 6, 1971.

Taylor, Jean. "The Holsum Bakery Building." Update, December, 1977.

Taylor, Jean. "Sawmills in South Dade." Update, June, 1976.

Taylor, Jean. "South Dade's Black Pioneers." Update, June, 1976.

"Tea Chest Began as Castles in Air Some Years Ago." Miami Metropolis, March 3, 1923.

Thompson, Lawrence. "A Concrete Fantasy Come True." The Miami Herald, November 18, 1956.

"Three Cities Started by Glenn Curtiss." The Dade County Courier, January 27, 1939.

"Three Million Being Spent on Dade County Schools." The Miamian, August, 1925.

"Time to Recall." The Miami Herald, December 27, 1964.

Trumbull, Steve. "Lighthouse Lore." The Miami Herald, March 25, 1956.

Vlach, John Michael. "The Shotgun House: An African Architectural Legacy in the United States." Journal of the Society of Architectural Historians, December, 1976.

"W. A. Larkins, South Miami's Founder Dies." South Miami Times, January 1, 1946.

Weinhardt, Carl J. Museum, May, 1977.

"Well Established Real Estate Firm Had a Novel Origin." **The Miami Metropolis,** March 3, 1923.

Wellenkamp, Jean. "Miami Shores Community Church Began in Pump House." **The North Dade Journal,** August 14, 1968.

Wilson, F. Page. "We Choose the Sub-Tropics." **Tequesta,** 1952.

Yonge, P.K. "Lawrence Estate Is Placed on Market." **Florida Real Estate Journal and Industrial Record,** May, 1922.

UNPUBLISHED PAPERS, REPORTS, COLLECTIONS:

"Abstract of Title to the James Hagan (Egan) Donation," Robbins, Graham, and Chillingsworth, Examining Counsel, July, 1897.

"Abstract of Title to the Rebecca Hagan (Egan) Donation," Robbins, Graham, and Chillingsworth, Examining Counsel, January, 1907.

Allyn, Kenneth, "Memories of Miami and Coral Gables 1917 to 1924," Coral Gables Historical Preservation Archives, Coral Gables, Florida, February, 1974.

Ammidown, Margot, "The Wagner Family: Homesteading in Miami's Pioneer Era, 1855-1896," (research report), Dade Heritage Trust, Inc., Miami, Florida, 1981.

Black Archives Foundation, Inc., Miami, Florida, Black Photographic Archives and Oral History Collection of Pioneers in Dade County, Florida, Between 1896 and 1946, Portfolio #1, Archives #26.

Bow, R.L., "The Redlands District of Dade County, Florida," (compiled for W.D. Horne), Miami, Florida, July, 1914.

Burditt, A.K., Jr., P.K. Soderholm, D.H. Spalding, and R.J. Knight, Jr., "Seventy-five Years of USDA Research at Miami," (reprinted from Vol. 86 of the proceedings of the Florida State Horticultural Society), Miami, Florida, November 6-8, 1973.

Camp, Vaughn, "North Miami, 50 Years of Challenge and Change," (project of North Miami's 50th Anniversary Committee), North Miami, Florida, ca. 1976.

Cangahuala, Conrad, "First Federal Savings and Loan Association Building," (research paper), Miami, Florida, April, 1978.

Carson, Ruby, "History of Miami Springs, Florida," Miami Springs Woman's Club, Miami Springs, Florida, April, 1977.

Chapin, George M., "Official Souvenir, Key West Extension of the Florida East Coast Railway," (issued by the Oversea Railroad Extension Celebration Committee of Key West), St. Augustine, Florida: The Record Co., ca. 1912.

Cherry, Gwen, "The History of the Mary Elizabeth Hotel," Dade County Historic Preservation Division, Miami, Florida, October 11, 1978.

"Chronology of Early Development Patterns on Miami Beach Up to 1930," (prepared by Fifth Year students of the School of Engineering and Environmental Design, University of Miami, under the supervision of Professor Aristides J. Millas), Coral Gables, Florida, ca. 1975.

Coral Gables Historic Preservation Board Archives, Coral Gables, Florida, "History of the City of Coral Gables," 1965.

Coral Gables Historic Preservation Board Archives, Coral Gables, Florida, Landmark Site Worksheet.

Dade Heritage Trust, Inc., Miami, Florida, "Descriptions of Historic Waterfront Buildings and Sites," (Coconut Grove Historic Boat Tour), February, 1979.

Griffin, John, "A History of Hialeah," (commissioned by the City of Hialeah, Florida, Community Development, Division), Hialeah, Florida, September 30, 1979.

Historical Association of Southern Florida, Miami, Florida, Carl Graham Fisher Papers, 1874-1939.

Historical Association of Southern Florida, Miami, Florida, "Coconut Grove U.S.A. Centennial 1873-1973," ca. 1973.

Historical Association of Southern Florida, Miami, Florida, Willard Hubbell Scrapbook, 1926-1939.

Historical Association of Southern Florida, Miami, Florida, William Keegin Papers, 1896-1911.

Historical Association of Southern Florida, Miami, Florida, Larkin Pioneer Family Registration List, (pamphlet files), 1967.

Historical Association of Southern Florida, Miami, Florida, Matlock Photographic Collection.

Historical Association of Southern Florida, Miami, Florida, Merrick Papers.

Historical Association of Southern Florida, Miami, Florida, "Miss Harris," (clip file).

Historical Association of Southern Florida, Miami, Florida, Photographic Files, A-Z.

Hanshe, Robert B., and Daniel Cotton Rich, "Vizcaya, Dade County Art Museum," (handbook), Miami, Florida 1933.

Letter, Henry Flagler to Mrs. Julia Tuttle, St. Augustine, Florida, April 22, 1895, Historic Preservation Division, Miami, Florida.

Lily Lawrence Bow Library, Homestead, Florida, "Fourth Annual Commencement of the Homestead High School," May 20, 1920.

MacNeill, Mary S., "History of the First United Methodist Church of Homestead," Homestead, Florida, May, 1974.

Mesa, Carmen R., "The Biscaya and the Boulevard Hotel — Two That Are Still Standing," Dade County Historic Preservation Division, Miami, Florida, April 19, 1978.

Metro Planning Department, Miami, Florida, "A Tale of Two Cities 1914-1968, Homestead-Florida City," July, 1980.

Miami-Dade Public Library, Florida Room, Miami, Florida, Dade County Pioneers, (microfilm reel #72).

Miami-Dade Public Library, Florida Room, Miami, Florida, Romer Photograph Collection, ca. 1910-1950.

Miami-Dade Public Library, Florida Room, Miami, Florida, Agnew Welsh Scrapbook, Vol. IV.

North Miami Chamber of Commerce, North Miami, Florida, "Commemorative Book — City of North Miami 40th Anniversary," February, 1967.

North Miami City Hall, North Miami, Florida, Master Plan for Town of North Miami, 1925 to present.

Opa-locka Historical Society Driving Survey Report, Opa-locka, Florida, 1979.

Parks, Arva Moore, "Historical Study for the Barnacle," (Miscellaneous Projects Report, No. 32), Bureau of Historic Sites and Properties, Division of Archives, History and Records Management, Tallahassee, Florida, September, 1975.

Parks, Arva Moore, "The History of Coconut Grove, Florida 1825-1925," (M.A. Thesis, University of Miami), Coral Gables, Florida, June, 1971.

Parks, Arva Moore, "Where the River Found the Bay," (historical study of the Granada Site), Miami, Florida, July, 1979.

Ransom-Everglades School, Coconut Grove, Florida, Carle Lawyer Parsons Scrapbook, Winter, 1917.

Taylor, Jean, "Cutler and Perrine Grant," (research report), Historical Association of Southern Florida, Miami, Florida, 1981.

Taylor, Jean, "A Historic Tour of South Florida," (pamphlet), Historical Association of Southern Florida, Miami, Florida, 1980.

Taylor, Jean, "Kendall and Westchester," (research report), Historical Association of Southern Florida, Miami, Florida, 1982.

Taylor, Jean, Lecture Series, Historical Association of Southern Florida, Miami, Florida, 1980.

Taylor, Jean, "Longview," (research report), Historical Association of Southern Florida, Miami, Florida, 1982.

Taylor, Jean, Personal Collection of Materials Relating to South Dade Railroad Towns, Cutler Ridge, Florida, 1980.

Tevis, Paul U., "History of the City of South Miami," (commissioned by the City Council of South Miami), South Miami, Florida, 1971.

INTERVIEWS:

Adney, J., Personal Interview (by Margot Ammidown), Miami, January 29, 1981.

Allen, Eugenia Dillon, Personal Interview (by Margot Ammidown and Dan Elswick), Miami, August 8, 1979.

Armbrister, Esther Mae, Personal Interview (by Karen DeGannes And John E. Hunter), Miami, March, 1979.

Bell, Jackie, Personal Interview (by Karen DeGannes and John E. Hunter), Miami, June 29, 1979.

Black, Maude, Personal Interview (by Arva Moore Parks), Miami, September 5, 1971.

Brooks, Maude, Personal Interview (by Dan Elswick), Miami, October, 1978.

Carter, Harold, Personal Interview (by Mary-Jane Tucker), Miami, August 3, 1979.

Catlow, Patty, Personal Interview (by Dan Elswick and John E. Hunter), Miami, March, 1979.

Caves, Bunny, Personal Interview (by Mary-Jane Tucker), Homestead, May 12, 1980.

De Garmo, Kenneth, Personal Interview (by Margot Ammidown and Ivan A. Rodriguez), Miami, January 27, 1982.

Fields, Dorothy, Personal Interview (by Margot Ammidown and Nancy Hoffman), Miami, July 24, 1979.

Fields, Dorothy, Personal Interview (by Margot Ammidown), Miami, May 6, 1981.

Finkhouse, Gene, Personal Interview (by Margot Ammidown and John E. Hunter), Miami, November, 1979.

Galvin, Nancy, Personal Interview (by Mary-Jane Tucker), Miami, September 11, 1978.

Germain, Frances Almer Tyler, Personal Interview (by Mary-Jane Tucker), Miami, December 5, 1979.

Hobbs, James C., Personal Interview (by Merna Patterson and Mary-Jane Tucker), Miami, August 20, 1980.

Kalfayan, Reverend Father Guregh, Personal Interview (by Herbert Kupferman), Miami, November, 1978.

Kent, Olga, Personal Interview (by Margot Ammidown and John E. Hunter), Miami, March, 1979.

Kilborn, Charles, Personal Interview (by Merna Patterson and Doris Emerson), Coral Gables, April 23, 1980.

Lemon City Pioneers 5-53, Historical Tape Recordings of Four Prominent Pioneers: Jerome Sands, Dr. John DuPuis, Senator Hudson, Mrs. Debbie Moran.

Martin, Sylvia, Personal Interview (by Merna Patterson and Mary-Jane Tucker), South Miami, August 20, 1980.

Mazon, Lillian, Louise Davis, and Kate Dean (daughters of E.W.F. Stirrup), Personal Interview (by Harvey and Mary Napier), Miami, May 29, 1973.

McCrimmon, C.T., Jr., Personal Interview (by Pauline Ramos), Miami, January 29, 1980.

Murphy, C.S., Personal Interview (by Shirley Murphy), Miami Springs, May 29, 1980.

Parks, Arva Moore, Personal Interview (by Mary-Jane Tucker), Miami, April 29, 1980.

Perry, Roy, Personal Interview (by Margot Ammidown and John E. Hunter), Miami, March, 1979.

Rogers, Cheryl, Personal Interview (by Paul S. George), North Miami, August 7, 1980.

Sheats, Leroy, Personal Interview (by Lisa DeParle), Homestead, June 12, 1980.

Smith, Margaret, Personal Interview (by Mary-Jane Tucker), Miami, November, 1979.

Stone, Ben, Personal Interview (by Nancy Hoffman), Miami, June, 1978.

Suber, Mary Thom, Personal Interview (by Mary-Jane Tucker and Lenna Taylor), Homestead, June 6, 1980.

Weiss, Rose (Jessie), Interview Transcript, Historical Association of Southern Florida, Miami, 1969.

Zachery, David, Personal Interview (by Margot Ammidown), Miami, July, 1979.

GOVERNMENT DOCUMENTS:

Coral Gables, Florida. Coral Gables City Hall, City Commission Minutes, 1914-1925.

Coral Gables, Florida. Coral Gables City Hall, Building Permits, beginning 1922.

Dade County, Florida (Miami). County Land Division, Plat Books.

Dade County, Florida (Miami). County Recorder's Office, Abstract Books.

Dade County, Florida (Miami). County Recorder's Office, Deed Books.

Dade County, Florida. Probate Office, Estate Proceedings, Mary Brickell File No. 1645.

Homestead, Florida. Homestead City Hall, Tax Rolls, beginning 1908.

Miami, Florida. Building and Zoning Department, Building Permits, 1923 to present.

Miami, Florida. Building and Zoning Department, Building Plans on Microfilm.

Miami, Florida. Building and Zoning Department, Plumbing Permits, 1919 to present.

Miami, Florida. Miami City Hall, City Commission, Minutes, 1896-1925.

Miami, Florida. Finance Department, Tax Rolls, 1899 to 1925.

Miami, Florida. Risk Management Department, Office Files.

Miami Beach, Florida. Archives and Records Management, Real Estate and Property Tax Rolls, 1915-1925.

Miami Beach, Florida. Archives and Records Management, Water Collection Ledgers, 1923-1925.

Miami Beach, Florida. Code Enforcement, Construction Division, Building Permits, 1921 to present.

Miami Beach, Florida. United States Army Corps of Engineers, Real Estate Records.

U.S. Congress, House. "Report of the Court of Claims," H.R. 175, 35th Congress, First Session, 1858.

U.S. Congress, Senate. "Third Interim Report of the Special Committee to Investigate Organized Crime in Interstate Commerce," 81st Congress, Report No. 307, April, 1951.

U.S. Congress, Senate. "Everglades of Florida," Senate Document 89, 62nd Congress, 1st Session, 1911.

U.S. Department of Commerce. Seventh Census of the United States, Dade County, Florida, 1850.

U.S. Department of the Interior. National Register of Historic Places Nomination Form, The Barnacle, prepared by Woodrow Wilkins, 1972.

U.S. Department of the Interior. National Register of Historic Places Nomination Form, Cape Florida Lighthouse, prepared by Randy F. Nimnicht, 1971.

U.S. Department of the Interior. National Register of Historic Places Nomination Form, Halissee Hall, prepared by Mary K. Evans, 1973.

U.S. Department of the Interior. National Register of Historic Places Nomination Form, The Pagoda, prepared by Mary K. Evans, 1973.

U.S. Department of the Interior. National Register of Historic Places Nomination Form, Plymouth Church, prepared by Mary K. Evans, 1973.

MAPS:

Biscayne Engineering Company. "Plat of Coconut Grove Park," Miami, Florida, 1910-1916.

Bonawit, Oby. "Homesteaders in the Miami Area," Miami, Florida, Historical Association of Southern Florida, 1978.

East Coast Railway, Land Department. "Township 50 to 54 S., Ranges 40 to 42 E., Dade County, Florida," Historical Association of Southern Florida, September, 1901.

East Coast Railway, Land Department. "Township 54 to 58 S., Ranges 30 to 42 E., Dade County, Florida," Historical Association of Southern Florida, December, 1903.

Frances, L. "Your Dream Home in Beautiful Miami Springs—Comprehensive Bird's Eye View," Miami Springs, Florida.

Hopkins, G.M. **Plat Book of Greater Miami, Florida and Suburbs,** Philadelphia, 1925, 1936.

Miami Motor Club. "Location Map of a Portion of Dade County, Florida," Historical Association of Southern Florida, December, 1919.

Perrine Land Grant Company, "Town of Perrine," Dade County Survey Office, 1911.

Sanborn Map Company. Insurance Maps of Miami, Dade County, Florida, New York: Sanborn Map Company, 1899-1921.

Squires, Karl. "Map of Metropolitan District—Miami, Florida." Historical Association of Southern Florida, 1922.

DIRECTORIES:

Parrish, Allan Reid.**Official Directory of Miami, Florida and Nearby Towns in Dade County,** 1904 (reprinted, published by the Historical Association of Southern Florida), 1974.

Polk, R.L. **R.L. Polk and Company's Miami City Directory,** Jacksonville, Florida: R.L. Polk and Company, 1911-1936.

INDEX

PHOTO INDEX